The Scent *of* Eucalyptus

The Scent of Eucalyptus

A Missionary Childhood in Ethiopia

DANIEL COLEMAN

GOOSE LANE

Edited by Laurel Boone.
Colour cover photographs © Wendy Coleman;
b&w cover photograph © Murray Coleman.
Photos on pages 236 and 238 courtesy of the Titcombe family.
All other photos courtesy of the Coleman family.
Cover and interior design by Julie Scriver.
Printed in Canada by Transcontinental.
10 9 8 7 6 5 4 3 2 1

National Library of Canada Cataloguing in Publication

Coleman, Daniel, 1961-
The scent of eucalyptus:
a missionary childhood in Ethiopia / Daniel Coleman.

Includes bibliographical references.
ISBN 0-86492-374-0

1. Coleman, Daniel, 1961- — Childhood and youth. 2. Children of missionaries — Ethiopia — Biography. 3. Missions — Ethiopia. I. Title.

BV3562.C64A3 2003 266'.02371063'092 C2003-904129-8

Published with the financial support of the Canada Council for the Arts, the Government of Canada through the Book Publishing Industry Development Program, and the New Brunswick Culture and Sports Secretariat.

Goose Lane Editions
469 King Street
Fredericton, New Brunswick
CANADA E3B 1E5
www.gooselane.com

Contents

ETHIOPIA
BETWEEN 1945 AND 1991

AFRICA

MASSAWA
ASMARA

ERITREA

MEKELE
ASSAB

LAKE
TANA GONDAR
LALIBELA
BAHIR DAR

BLUE NILE

DIRE DAWA
JIJIGA
HARAR

★ ADDIS ABABA
OBI WOLISO

JIMMA

SODDO SHESHEMANE

RIFT VALLEY LAKES

NEGELE

Reality *in* My Eyes

Dad noses the Toyota into the throng of long-horned cattle. All around us their hooves click on the pavement of Bolé Road. Their ears flick at hovering flies as they ramble along, oblivious of Dad's beeps and the herdsmen's shouts. We are in a sea of brown, tan, and black hides; the humps on shoulders quiver and the ribs accordion at the pump of each animal's leg. Dad and Mom have borrowed the car from the mission to meet Wendy and me at the airport in Addis Ababa. I find my hand rubbing the unreality in my eyes. It's fourteen years since I left Ethiopia, the country of my birth, but the familiarity of this scene makes me feel as if the place has been put on pause while I have been away, and we're taking up the scene exactly where we left off all those years ago. Surely this same flood of cattle herded by these short-panted men were grumbling along this same part of Bolé Road when I travelled to the airport for the last time in April 1979. That exact man in the grey cotton suit, carrying the black umbrella, stepped up on the landing of that roadside shop to avoid these cattle, and this same woman with her baby wrapped in a white *nettella* shawl crowded behind the Daihatsu truck clearing a path to our left through the herd.

The car inches through the swaying rumps toward the side of the street. The road retains the defining elements of a curb and a central boulevard, despite the contest between blue-and-white taxis, pedestrians, cattle, straw-laden donkeys, and vagrant dogs that riddle its surface.

"Got a headache," Dad says. "I'll just stop in here for a cappuccino."

He's suffered from sinus headache for decades, ever since the 1970s, the tough years after the revolution, when he worked in the mission's administrative offices and dealt each day with hostile government

ministries and restive workers. No medication seems to help, though caffeine at the start of a headache can sometimes ward it off.

Once the herd has rumbled past, Mom, Dad, Wendy, and I open the car doors and walk up the stone steps into the roadside bakery and coffee shop. We scrape chrome-legged chairs up to a small table and wait for the woman behind the counter to steam the milk for our order. The radio spits Amharic into the screech of the espresso machine. I'm in my early thirties. I haven't been in Ethiopia for fourteen years, but the familiarity of the coffee shop and the disorientation of jet lag make me feel that nothing's changed at all, that my intervening life in Canada has been a dream. I look across the table at Wendy, who's taking in these images for the first time. I know her arched eyebrows, short blonde hair, and green eyes better than any other face in the world. Her presence here reassures me that the life I've lived since I left Ethiopia is no dream. I have indeed grown up and moved away. I've gone to university in Regina and graduate school in Edmonton. We've been married more than ten years. Nonetheless, this coffee shop and the street outside are so palpably real that they cast a haze over my Canadian life.

The woman brings our order on an enamel tray — three cappuccinos and a glass of mineral water for Mom — and places a coffee spoon on the saucer beside each cup. She is beautiful in the classically Ethiopian way — pencil-thin eyebrows curved over almond-shaped eyes, a narrow straight nose between high cheekbones, skin the colour of the cappuccino in our cups, delicate fingers, and fine-boned hands. The rich breath of espresso displaces the diesel and cattle hide stench of the street. "Thank God for the Italian invasion," we used to joke. "Thank God for lasagna and cappuccino!" Ethiopia was never colonized by a European power during the nineteenth-century scramble for Africa. It wasn't until Mussolini's invasion between 1935 and 1941 that anything like a significant number of Europeans came to Ethiopia to live. The result is that if there's a European influence in the country, it's Italian. The skeleton of the country's major road system was laid down by Italian military engineers, and you can drive into a dusty village that barely has running water and order a latte. I lick the foam off my spoon, the delicious product of cross-country pollination — *cafe-latte, café-au-lait*, coffee-with-milk. Coffee came first to Europe and later to South America from Kaffa province in southwestern Ethiopia. Then it took Italians to

think of steaming the milk and to bring the adapted drink back to its home. Now Dad fends off sinus headaches with the cultural blend.

"We thought we'd spend two or three days around mission HQ in Addis," Mom says as she fingers her water glass on the table. She's loved coffee all her life but lately is finding that it bothers her stomach. She raises her voice over the chatter of the radio behind the counter. "That'll give you time to get over jet lag, and we can look around town a bit. We can go out to Bingham, and, if you like, the old Good Shepherd School property, too. Negussie's in the Poly Clinic up on the Asmara Road, and I know Ato Lakew wants to see you." Her once-brown hair is now mostly grey, but her eyes still have their perky light and her nose still looks too small for the weight of her glasses. Liver spots and freckles on the backs of her hands and forearms tell of her many years in the African sun. Her fingernails are as carefully groomed to a rounded point as they were when I was a boy. She sips her water and says, "We can head down to Woliso and Obi on Thursday and then on to Hosa'ina from there. Dad and I have meetings with church elders and some of our graduating Bible School students in Hosa'ina. We can drive across to Sheshemane and Lake Langano after that."

Like the street scene, her casual mention of people and places from my past throws me off balance. Bingham Academy is the boarding school where I started grade one in 1967. After completing ninth grade at Bingham, I took tenth grade at Good Shepherd School before it was appropriated by the government for a veterans' hospital. Negussie and Ato Lakew are long-time figures in the landscape of our family's friends. Obi mission station is the site of my pre-school years, and we lived at the leprosarium and farm in Sheshemane when I was in grades seven and eight. None of these are dreams — they all exist. They are real. I will see them again in the next couple of weeks.

We climb back in the car, and I stare out at the strange familiarity of the passing streets. It's 1993, and I am on the return journey I have never wished to make. I was glad to leave Ethiopia at the end of high school and never return. Not that I hated my childhood, just that it got complicated by the usual suspects: politics, race, and religion — especially politics. Life had been fairly peaceful until 1974, when junior army officers overthrew their superiors and deposed King Haile Selassie and his government. The revolution changed everything. Missionaries had

been welcome under Haile Selassie, but the Marxist-Leninist junta of Lieutenant-Colonel Mengistu Haile Mariam proclaimed religion the opiate of the people. Mengistu's government begrudgingly allowed missionaries to remain only because the battlefronts in Eritrea and Somalia left his government few resources to run the schools and hospitals without outside help.

One of the virtues of Ethiopia's never having been colonized is that there's no colonial cringe, no special obeisance due to erstwhile white governors. Before the revolution, whiteness had been a strange surprise not related to an old system of power. The pink skin and straight blonde hair I had as a boy drew shouts on the street of *"ferenjie!"* — foreigner — from children and adults alike. My siblings — Sharon, John, Marianne — and I had simply been albino monkeys for the pointing, gesticulating people that inevitably circled the car and peered through the windows when Mom or Dad left us there during an errand to a bakery or a hardware shop. Even our Obi neighbours' warm hospitality had been tinged with curiosity about the flimsiness of our hair and the freckles on our faces. We had always been different, but not until the revolutionary government came to power were we designated as the enemy. Suddenly, we became Imperialists who had come to exploit the poor. Our whiteness became political in a way it hadn't been before. We became dangerous to our friends, including Negussie and Ato Lakew. We had to be watched and to watch ourselves carefully. A false move, a careless statement could get our visas revoked or cause trouble for any Ethiopian associated with us.

I was a teenager during the mid-to-late seventies, and the constant self-surveillance weighed heavily upon me. As a result, when I finished high school and left for Canada, the thought of return never crossed my mind. When Canadians asked me where I came from, I often opted for the short version. "Wheatley, Ontario," I would say. It was my dad's hometown. I spent my first year in Canada there with my aunt when I was eighteen. "You probably never heard of it — only a few thousand people, southeast of Windsor." The blandness of the short version discouraged further questions. It allowed me to fit in. In Canada, pink skin and flimsy hair were no problem. They caused no comment, made you nobody's enemy. I lived one year in Wheatley with my aunt and ten more in Regina, where I met and married Wendy and attended

university. Through all those years, I never felt the slightest desire to see Ethiopia again. But then I moved to Edmonton in 1990 to start a PhD in Canadian literature, and I began reading books by immigrants — Michael Ondaatje, Ven Begamudré, Daphne Marlatt, Rohinton Mistry, Kristjana Gunnars, Austin Clarke. Their descriptions of a life divided, not just between present and past, but between here and there struck a deep chord. They set me thinking about the simultaneity of divided realities.

I know that you can never truly return. Despite whatever you may feel, the places of your past do not stay still while you are living your new life now. They, too, are in the present, leaving the skins of the past to crumble under each passing sun. The past is gone. This doesn't mean, however, that you can avoid its effects. "Childhood is the time of setting the stage," Kristjana Gunnars writes in *The Prowler*. "Later in life you come onto that stage and find it is very difficult to change the props." You can never return to the past, but you also never leave it completely behind you. So I have returned to see these cattle and these blue-and-white taxis, to smell the mix of diesel and hide, to share these sensations with Wendy, who has never been here before, and to try with her to understand — if not change — the props that set the stage for my present Canadian life.

The return trip had to be now. A window opened when the coalition of Tigrayan and Eritrean forces known as the *Yehadig* finally overwhelmed Mengistu Haile Mariam's tattered army a year and half ago. With the collapse of the Soviet Union, Mengistu lost any further supplements to the eleven billion dollars' worth of military equipment that for almost twenty years had fuelled the Ethiopian side in Eritrea's war of secession. Now, with Mengistu in exile in Zimbabwe and a new government in power, Westerners can get visas more easily, and, too, the end of the war means travel within the country is safer these days. Not that getting around in Ethiopia would have been easy if we hadn't known somebody here. The long years of fighting have destroyed what little tourist industry there used to be, and it would have been difficult to rent a car or to book hotels without someone in Addis to make these arrangements for us. Mom and Dad are a year or two from retiring after more than forty years in Ethiopia. If we wished to make the trip at all, we had to come now.

The car rolls between heavy iron gates into the mission's headquarters and curves past the BD to the parking spots where four or five cars nuzzle the tall stone wall. SIM HQ. We used to joke about missionaries' penchant for initials. SIM once stood for the Sudan Interior Mission, when *ferenjies* thought that everything south of the Sahara was "Sudan." Now it stands for Serving in Mission, because this interdenominational society of Protestant missionaries has expanded from its beginnings in Nigeria, Ethiopia, and Niger to include operations in Bolivia, Chile, Bangladesh, and India. HQ echoes the colonial-military ethos that shaped so many of the nineteenth- and early twentieth-century ideas of the missionary enterprise. The BD or Business Department was like HQ's commissariat; Mom and Dad spent most of the 1950s here, filling orders of groceries and building supplies for missionaries at their down-country stations.

As I lift our suitcases and garment bags from the trunk of the car and set them on the asphalt, I can't help but gaze around at this place that was our family's home several times. The two-storey, L-shaped main building houses the chapel, dining hall, kitchen, and parlour/meeting room area, as well as the bedrooms and apartments for visiting and Addis-based missionaries. It seems much less grand now than it did when I was a child. The galvanized iron roof's corrugated surface is pocked with rust and dents, and the fake-brick asphalt sheeting that covers the clay-and-wattle walls looks brittle and tired. The wine-coloured bougainvillea, however, still leaps in crisp, square columns up the stone pillars from the ground floor veranda to the second-floor balcony, regal as ever, the English ivy grows as thick and lush as I remember it around the entrance to the dining room, and the amoeba-shaped bits of lawn between the tarmac pathways and the tiled veranda look so carefully clipped I know that old Ato Debray, the gardener, must have run his hand mower over them within the last few hours.

HQ. Sharon, John, and I had all been born here, three and a half years apart. The older two were born conventionally in a hospital, but I was born "down a-blow." Behind the main building, the HQ compound

descends to Ato Debray's garden and beyond that to two stone houses, one of which was ours at the time. Sharon famously said, when she was only four, that we lived down a-blow. When I came along in 1961, Mom had been ready to deliver me at Princess Tsa'hai Hospital the very day of her own birthday, March 8, but there were no beds available in the maternity ward, and the doctor gave her an injection to delay the contractions. Dad brought her back home to wait out the effects of the injection. They waited too long, and in the middle of the next morning, Dad had to run for Mrs. Brant, a nurse and midwife, who arrived in time to tell Mom she was having her baby right here, right now.

So I am a child of SIM HQ, but I didn't cut my teeth here. A few months after I was born, our family took a freighter from Djibouti up the Red Sea and through the Suez Canal on our way to Canada for a year's furlough to visit family and friends. When we returned in 1962, Dad and Mom received their first down-country assignment to the mission station at Obi, near the town of Woliso, 110 kilometres southwest of Addis. My earliest memories, and my younger sister, Marianne's, too, are therefore not from HQ but from the grassy pastures and farm fields at Obi. HQ featured as a significant place later in my childhood, however, not just because it was a regular stop every time my family came to the city, but also because we lived here several times during my youth. Dad was reassigned to Administration after ten years in Obi, so we lived here at HQ for a short while before he was asked to serve as station manager on the leprosy hospital and farm complex four hours' drive south of Addis at Sheshemane. We lived at Sheshemane between 1973 and 1975, and then we moved back to Addis. The political troubles of the mid-to-late 1970s meant that many mission projects were discontinued, and during the period of adjustment, we relocated several times between the apartments at HQ, the stone houses down a-blow, and other mission properties in Addis to make room for other families who were also being reassigned.

I heft our luggage up the steep stairs behind the dining hall to one of the guest rooms and then walk down the dim upstairs hallway to the washroom to scrub off fifty hours of travel. Airplanes make this kind of trip possible — make it possible to travel half way around the globe, visit places I have known as a child here in Ethiopia, and even to add on a Kenyan safari, all in six short weeks. Despite the advantages of

This Coleman family photo was taken in Leamington,
Ontario, when we were on furlough in 1966.

flying, I still envy my parents the leisurely mode of travel they undertook before planes became cheaper than ships. Up until the 1960s, they made the trip by boat, and Mom and Dad talk fondly of the weeks at sea, when they could catch up on sleep and on correspondence with family and friends. "We used to arrive chipper and ready to meet everybody," Dad has said, when I've asked him about those early voyages. "Now we get there groggy and jet-lagged."

"Didn't you get seasick?"

"Never did. We had a rough crossing once. I guess it was on that last boat trip, when you were just a baby. Sharon and John were little tykes, and Marianne hadn't been born yet. I remember dishes falling off the counters in the kitchen. We had to get the crew to bolt down your crib so it didn't skid back and forth across the cabin floor. But none of us got sick."

Now I run water into the sink in the HQ washroom and breathe the childhood scent of the clay-and-wattle walls around me. Despite the layer of paint, they smell of clean earth — not exactly dank or musty, but cool, with a hint of moisture, as if they retain a memory of the wet brown feet of the workmen who tramped straw into mud until it was the right consistency for plaster. The Amharic word for the mixture is *chicka*, and the donkeys that stagger up Addis's streets laden with haystacks of fine straw called *chidd* are the city's suppliers of construction-grade plaster. All the houses we lived in — from Obi to HQ to Sheshemane, and most of the dorms at Bingham Academy — smelled of this clean earth. I stare bleary-eyed out the bathroom's second-floor window over the choppy sea of galvanized roofs below. In every possible geometry, colour of corrosion, and angle, these corrugated planes of metal pitch in a maelstrom of lean-tos, dwellings, and roadside stands. I remember that the land on this side of HQ was some kind of city property, and squatters regularly pitched their shanties on it. From time to time, city police would come with a bulldozer and scrape the land flat. Overnight, however, the place would be pimpled again with shacks. Now it looks as if the city has given up, for the rust on these roofs shows venerable age.

None of these dwellings was here, however, when HQ was first built in the late 1940s and early 1950s, during the massive growth of the mission that followed World War II. This was an exhilarating time in the SIM. All Protestant missionaries had been expelled from the country

by the Catholics-only policy of the Italian invaders in the 1930s. With the end of hostilities and the return of Haile Selassie in 1942, however, the missionaries were invited to come back and help his government establish clinics, hospitals, and schools. During this period, my parents came to Ethiopia. They met for the first time right here at HQ in 1952, when Mom was working as a secretary and bookkeeper in the office and Dad was put to work in the BD. Whereas Mom had lived for a year in Ethiopia before she decided to join the mission, Dad had wanted to be a missionary ever since his childhood days in Wheatley Baptist Church. Grandma Coleman had regularly billeted travelling missionaries, and the stories these visitors told over the dinner table grew into the boy's dream of life. He set his course by the light of that dream. When he finished high school, the slight young man with the curly brown hair and aquiline nose went to Alberta for Bible training and, upon gradua-tion, applied to join SIM in Toronto. True to form, his story of joining the mission follows the classic vocational path of hearing God's call as a child and then deliberately preparing, step by step, to pursue that call; my father is a man who values established protocols for the way they ensure an orderly life and respectful relations between people.

Mom sometimes quips that Dad entered the mission by the front door while she entered by the back. For her, coming to Ethiopia was an adventure before it became a calling. Only nineteen, she arrived in 1949 as the personal secretary of an SIM missionary from her Lutheran church community in Dickson, Alberta. Dr. Robert Thompson had been seconded by the mission to Haile Selassie's re-established government to standardize the secondary school system throughout the country, and "Doc" told her that when he was putting together his crew, he had seen her face in a dream. His dream matched hers. Here was a chance for exotic travel, all expenses paid, with someone she and her parents knew, and if things didn't work out, she could always go back home. How could she say no? She travelled with him and his family to Addis, and she worked as Doc Thompson's secretary for a year before she joined the mission by the back door — which is to say that she was interviewed and accepted into the missionary society right here in Ethiopia, rather than taking the usual route: application, Bible training, candidacy in-terviews and examinations, and fundraising in Canada before travelling to Africa.

"I had a real riot," she likes to say, "before I met your dad."

She means it literally. For her first assignment as a missionary, she was asked to join a group of teachers who were being posted to Medhane Alem Secondary School in the city of Harar. The easternmost major city in the Amhara-dominated highlands, Harar marks the meeting point between vastly different cultural groups. Here the land plunges to the Somali-populated Ogaden desert that runs east through Somalia to the Gulf of Aden. In 1950, the city's administrative elite were Amhara Orthodox Christians, while many of its denizens were Somali and Oromo Muslims. During her second year there, a boy from a prominent Muslim family decided to convert to the *ferenjie* teachers' Christian faith. Not understanding the differences between the Orthodox and the Protestant versions of Christianity, he went to the local Orthodox priests to be baptized. His naïveté touched the city's ancient but still raw nerve. The Muslims raged against the Amhara Orthodox for poaching upon their youth, and the Orthodox denied any such thing. It was the work, they argued, of the *ferenjies* at the school. As a result, angry townsfolk — Orthodox and Muslim alike — sent a barrage of stones through the windows of the teacherage, and the Minister of Education was forced to remove the missionaries from the school.

I run more hot water into the sink and begin to lather my face with shaving foam. Its musky smell overwhelms for a moment the clean earth of the *chicku* walls. I wipe the steam off the mirror above the sink with a washcloth and lift my razor to my cheek. They were kids really when they first came to Ethiopia — Dad was twenty-six and, at the time of the riot, Mom only twenty-one. Much too young to realize all the nuances of the cultural intervention in which they were engaged. I pull the razor along my jaw, watching its clean, smooth path, until it nicks the top of an old scar to the left of my chin. The monkey bite I received from Tota, our pet vervet, when I was twelve. All these years later, the signs of the past live so intimately in the present. It's easy to question my parents' youth and naïveté, easy from the distance of 1993 to wish they had been better prepared to handle the cultural complexity they encountered. These questions, however, formed in hindsight, need to be considered in the context of the radical choices they had made. Over a decade before the Civil Rights Movement, in a time when most white Canadians saw nothing wrong with residential

schools for Native children or with the policy of excluding Asian and African immigrants, my young parents forsook families and stable incomes to live and work among Ethiopians in Africa. In a way, they were people way ahead of their time, and, as is so often the case with such people, hindsight wishes they had been better prepared.

I plunge my razor into the half-full sink and rinse the foam from its double blades. The foam breaks apart, and the pieces, some of them pink from the blood on my chin, float like miniature icebergs on the water, their slow drift mesmerizing my tired eyes. Suddenly I am startled by the fierce, tinny sound of the muezzin's call to prayer that echoes off the shantytown roofs outside the bathroom window. We kids used to wonder how the imam got all the way to the top of the skinny minaret of the mosque until Dad pointed out the loudspeakers high up on the tower. Five times a day, beginning before dawn, the speakers crackle into life, calling Addis's faithful — mostly Yemenese merchants and down-country Oromos — to prayer. There are only a few mosques in Addis, compared to the many ornate and heavily trafficked Orthodox churches, but even here, at the heart of Ethiopian Orthodoxy, the religious mix is intricate and dense.

The conflagration of religious politics had removed Mom from Harar and placed her here at HQ when Dad arrived in 1952. Such conflicts are a constant feature throughout the mission's history. Right from the start, when Haile Selassie had welcomed the first SIM missionaries in 1928, he had needed to maintain a fine balance between the modernization and the religious dissent they brought. On the one hand, missionaries built medical and educational facilities that the Selassie government couldn't afford, while on the other, their evangelical Protestantism introduced a competitor to the nation's ancient Orthodox Church. The dexterous young king played gracious host to all and gave his heart to none. He pleased the Orthodox hierarchy by encouraging independence from the Egyptian Coptic Church in Alexandria and by confirming its status as the national church. He also welcomed the missionaries and tried to reduce internecine conflict by sending them south to non-Amhara regions, where Ethiopian Orthodoxy was more of a cultural patina than a deeply held belief. The Amhara government had gained power over the Oromo, Walaitta, and Somali peoples of southern Ethiopia only during the late nineteenth century. Amhara

Dad and Mom's Bible class at HQ, 1950s.

occupation meant that many of these southern groups had learned to wear bronze crosses around their necks, but they used them to ward off or appease ancestral spirits more than to help them pray to Jesus or Mary.

When an American physician named Thomas Lambie led the first party of eight Protestant missionaries, sixty-six mules, twenty donkeys, nine horses, twenty-five head-carriers, and twenty-two mule drivers south from Addis to the town of Soddo in the Walaitta-speaking region of south-central Ethiopia, he encountered Amharic-speaking governors who had been primed to receive him warmly by the higher-ups in Addis. He also met Amharic-speaking Orthodox priests who bitterly resented his threat to their religious monopoly, as well as local Walaitta-speakers who were more intrigued by the tools and medicines of the pink *ferenjies* than they were with doctrinal disputes between Protestant, Catholic, and Orthodox Christians. For the Walaitta people, these religious differences had been introduced by their Amhara

colonizers. What did they care about the differences between Rome and Constantinople, let alone Alexandria or Geneva? Why should they care which was the heresy, the monophysite doctrine of Christ's single Godhood or the doctrine of His two-fold nature, fully human and fully divine? What difference did it make whether you prayed to Jesus or to Mary when you were actually beholden to the ancestral spirits?

Meanwhile, Lambie's party built a small hospital and began to preach the good news that a person didn't need a priest or a witch doctor to mediate between divine and human worlds. Instead, the Bible was an open book for all who wished to enter into a personal relationship with God. One did not have to be born into the Church or into the Amhara tribe, baptized as an infant, or confirmed as part of any single denomination. SIM was an interdenominational Protestant mission; its members came from a variety of churches — Baptist, Methodist, Presbyterian, Evangelical Anglican, Mennonite, and others. To them, the brand didn't matter as much as the experience. You were a Christian, not because of the label you wore, but because you had made an individual decision to accept Jesus into your life and to be "born again" — that is, to have Him enter your life and transform your primary commitments and goals. Central to the missionaries' purpose was the effort to make the Bible accessible to the local people. Amharic Bibles existed, but very few Walaitta people spoke Ethiopia's official language fluently, and those who did were largely in the back pocket of the Amhara-Orthodox regime. The missionaries thus launched a two-pronged campaign: first to teach local people to read and write in Amharic, and second to translate parts of the Bible into Walaitta so the people could read it in their own language.

They didn't have much chance to realize either of these goals, for the Italians invaded in 1935 and had pushed south to Soddo by 1937. Determined to make the country Catholic, Mussolini's soldiers evicted SIM missionaries and Orthodox priests alike. The priests fled north to their homelands in the high, rugged mountains of Gondar and Wollo. The governors had already fled into the bush weeks before, where they were reported to have joined the fleeing remnants of Haile Selassie's army. The SIM workers left Ethiopia sadly, feeling that their few converts, just over a hundred of them, had very little chance of keeping their new faith alive without the missionaries' support. Six years later, after the

Italians had been pushed out by Allied troops, the first SIM missionaries returned to Ethiopia. They learned, much to their surprise, that during their absence the number of believers in Walaitta had mushroomed to ten thousand people, worshipping in a completely indigenous church.

This remarkable social and spiritual movement during the missionaries' absence has become central to SIM's understanding of its continuing presence in Ethiopia and of its relationship with the indigenous denomination that grew out of this movement, the KHC — the Kalleh Hiwot (Word of Life) Church. The missionaries flooded into the country after the war and swelled the mission's ranks into the hundreds. They worked in partnership with the KHC by supplying Bible School teachers, providing services for the printing and distribution of Christian literature, and establishing schools, clinics, and hospitals throughout the country. Once again, as with Lambie's original party, this provision of practical services helped to legitimize the presence of *ferenjies* and their evangelical faith in the country. As Dad often put it, we were there to support the local church, not to run everything ourselves. Then he would chuckle and quote the Norwegian missionary who said, "Vee didn't come to *do* the vork. Vee came to *overlook* it!"

I'm wiping the last of the shaving cream from my face when I catch sight of a flock of pigeons outside as they wheel down out of the cloudy sky and settle, amidst much clapping of wings and skittering of claws, on the metal rooftops below. Even in the dull light, flashes of iridescent green and purple leap from their rose-grey necks. A couple of males strut among the females. Their heads thrust back and forth, and they hum the pigeon's contained version of a turkey gobble — *whoodel-whoodeloo, whoodel whoodeloo*.

They make me think of John's pigeons. Shortly after we moved back to HQ from Obi in 1972, my brother persuaded Dad to help him build a huge three-by-three-metre cage of wooden uprights and chicken wire for his pet pigeons. Hour by hour, we would watch the birds establish and re-establish their intricate hierarchies, from king and queen to the lowliest female, who always gave way at perch or grain. We put hands full of gravel in the cage and watched them load their corn-grinding crops. We traced the bowing, aggressive circles the lead male danced around the female of the moment. We gaped at the confusing, flapping violence of pigeon sex. One morning, we woke to find someone had

slipped over the high stone wall from the shantytown, cut a hole in the chicken wire, and made off with as many of John's birds as could be caught in the dark. One or two of the pigeons had escaped, and they now paced uncertainly back and forth on top of the cage, while John wired the hole closed. They turned their heads sideways and arched their necks to get a better look as he opened the door to the cage and put grain in the tray to entice them back inside. Over the next week, all but three of the birds came back. "Homing instinct," John said. "Whoever stole them didn't cage them long enough, so they still think this is home."

I watch the pigeons strut and quarrel on the rooftops below the window, and I realize that it was a kind of homing instinct that brought the missionaries back after World War II. With the astonishing spread of the KHC precisely during the time of their absence, it was no longer possible to assume without question that missionaries were necessary to the growth of the church. I read *Born at Midnight*, Dr. Peter Cotterell's history of the partnership between KHC and SIM, in preparation for making this trip back to Ethiopia, and I was struck at how the question of missionaries haunted the pages of his book. At one point, Cotterell quotes Clarence Duff, one of the original 1928 missionaries, who said, "'the presence of the missionaries had been a positive hindrance once the first converts had been made' . . . and so the mission's expulsion turned out, in fact, to be a major contribution to the growth of the church." So why didn't the missionaries stay out, once they saw how well the new church could do on its own? Why couldn't they let the indigenous church be indigenous?

I'd say because of a kind of spiritual homing instinct. The missionaries simply couldn't keep themselves away — the spiritual sustenance was richer here than it was in their European or North American homelands. They had helped to light a vital flame in Ethiopia that outshone anything they had experienced in *status quo* Christianity back home. Who would prefer the pallid existence of Christianity in North America, where churches grow more from migration between congregations than from widespread social change, to the dynamism of the KHC, where yearly baptisms number in the hundreds and sometimes thousands? Who could blame the returning missionaries for wanting to warm their hands by such a fire, to hear the believers' stories of triumph over the hippo-hide whips and prison sentences of the Italians? As they listened

to their Ethiopian friends' stories, they began to see reasons why they should return to sustain the miracle that had taken place.

For one thing, only a few members of the new church could read, and the widespread illiteracy had introduced some strange ideas that extended from weighty matters of doctrine to trivial matters of domestic life. The first delegation of Walaitta church elders, for example, had a great shock when they came to the capital city to visit the Davisons, the first SIM missionaries to return to Addis in 1942. The down-country visitors rose in collective alarm when the family's terrier bounded into the living room at the heels of the Davisons' boy. It wasn't that they were afraid of the little dog. They had taken literally St. Paul's injunction, "Beware of dogs" and believed that Christians should not keep dogs. The new believers made other reading errors, too. They outlawed goats from their herds because they had read in Matthew 25:32-33 that in the last days the sheep would be separated from the goats. The Italian attempt to suppress their newfound faith seemed very much like the last days to them, and the Walaitta believers wanted to do everything they could to prepare for God's return. So, along with dogs, they got rid of goats. They called Communion "eating the secret" and held the ceremony before dawn behind closed shutters so no unbaptized person could witness it. The returned missionaries had to guide the church leaders to key Biblical passages and explain that the Lord's Supper should actually be a public event, that references to "sheep," "goats," and "dogs" were to be understood figuratively.

Mr. Davison reported in 1945 that "the need for Bible instruction amongst pastors is appalling," not just because so few could read but also because those who did read had to translate from the Amharic Bible to the local Walaitta language. Although the church in southern Ethiopia had spread like mountain fire during the missionaries' absence — not just throughout Walaitta, but also into neighbouring Kambatta and Sidamo regions — they saw a clear need to return and change the wildfire of enthusiasm into the steady glow of tried and true doctrine. They returned to Ethiopia in great numbers in the 1950s, 1960s, and early 1970s, and they helped the KHC establish seminaries, Bible Schools, and hundreds of primary and secondary schools throughout the country.

Footsteps approach in the hallway outside the bathroom door. "You still in here?" Wendy says, poking her head inside. "Your mom just

stopped by. She's wondering if you want to head over to Bingham right away after lunch." I rinse out the sink, repack my toiletries bag, and walk with her down the hall to our room.

The drive across the city from HQ to Bingham passes through the area of the city known as the markatto, which we used to say was the world's largest outdoor market, though I don't know if it still is. The blue-and-white taxis beep and swerve around cyclists, *chidd*-stacked donkeys, and vagrant dogs. A teenaged boy drives a sheep like a wheelbarrow — its two back legs clutched like handles in his fists and its front legs playing the part of the wheel. In the open windows of butcher shops, flies buzz around quarters of beef whose blood runs down the street into an open ditch. A belch of black diesel exhaust plumes from the back of an ancient Fiat truck loaded with eucalyptus poles. The dense compost of so much life gives me that dizzy feeling again. I hadn't realized how deeply these images are sown within me.

Not that everything's exactly the same, for the city looks more decrepit than it did to my youthful eyes. The years of warfare leading up to the 1991 surrender have beggared everything. Shop fronts and public buildings look run down and decayed, boulevards that used to hold flowers and shrubs are now hard-packed dirt or mud, and the power poles bristle with dozens of haphazardly connected wires, as though people have shinnied up and spliced in their own lines. As if it isn't hard enough to avoid running over chickens making a break for freedom or coolie men bent under heavy grain sacks and heedless of cars, Dad has to dodge potholes. "By the time you get to Bingham, you'll have your PhD," we used to say — Pot Hole Dodger — but the craters and canyons in these streets are of a magnitude I have never seen before. Dad says that a couple of days ago, he saw a truck tip over on its side when it dropped a wheel into a rain-covered hole.

If HQ and the city streets are familiar, even in their dilapidation, Bingham is so exactly the same that I doubt my senses. At least the other places show signs of having aged. Bingham itself seems to have been frozen in place since I was last here. In fact, now that I think of it, it

The main building at Bingham Academy.

seemed to have been frozen all the years I lived here, too — right from the moment I entered grade one in 1967 until 1976, the year I finished grade nine, the school's top grade back then. You still enter by the same creaking gates, swung back by the elderly *zubunya* or watchman whose job it is to listen for cars at the entry to the two-hectare compound. The paved driveway still curves up and past the front porch of the main building, which bears the sign "Bingham Academy" just under its roof-line. Roland Bingham, a Toronto man, founded the Sudan Interior Mission, along with Walter Gowans and Thomas Kent, with their pioneer journeys into Nigeria in the late nineteenth century. Kent and Gowans died of malaria, and our schoolhouse leagues were named after these two martyrs, while the school itself carries the name of the survivor. Whereas missionaries of Mr. Bingham's generation tended to leave their children in their homelands to be educated, missionaries of my parents' generation had established this boarding school here in Addis Ababa so that their children could remain close by. If you take

note of the way MKs — missionary kids — are cared for, you can distinguish between distinct eras of missionary belief. In the colonial era, when missionary pioneers modeled themselves on explorers such as David Livingstone, MKs were pretty much dispensable. They stayed with friends or relatives or foster parents in Britain, the States, or Canada while their parents soldiered off into remote regions of the world with the gospel. Then came the post-war era, when missionaries like my parents didn't believe the call to be a missionary required a choice between the gospel and their children. They wanted to have them nearby, at least, if not with them, and missionary societies like SIM responded by establishing boarding schools in the countries where the parents worked. SIM built Bingham Academy in Ethiopia and Kent Academy in Nigeria during the 1940s and has since opened boarding schools in Liberia and Bolivia, too. More recently, from the 1980s and 1990s onwards, many missionary parents choose to home-school their children, so many MKs nowadays stay in the family setting and don't even go to boarding school at all.

Sharon, John, Marianne, and I are of that middle generation who went to boarding school, and so if I were asked to identify where I grew up, I'd have to say Bingham. It wasn't exactly home, but it was where I lived my childhood. Bingham was the constant when my family moved from Obi to Addis, then from Addis to Sheshemane, then back to Addis again. At Bingham I lived, played, and studied with friends. Here the comforts of routine were maintained, especially during the chaotic years at the start of the revolution, before we knew who exactly was in power, and the army and militant student groups exchanged gunfire in the streets. Bingham was where I learned to read, where I first met and played with other white kids my own age. It was where I broke my arm and had to wear a cast, and where I first held a girl's hand. It was where I became Danny Coleman. John says that in its early days, the school had been run after the severe fashion of a military academy, with inspections for shiny shoes and cleanliness of hands and faces, and with rules forbidding parents from visiting their children for the first six weeks until the kids — and the parents — had "toughened up." A big change occurred, though, when a principal named Roy Wallace and a school manager named Rawlin Reimer arrived in the 1960s. These two and their wives did a lot, John says, to create a family atmosphere.

This gentler ethos was in place by the time I arrived. I have very little memory of severity here and retain instead many images of the story times, outings, long hours of play in the eucalyptus woods, and after-school sports and drama clubs that made our days alive. Some MKs sustained deep wounds from having to leave their families and live in the dormitories, but I never knew any different. Sharon and John had gone to Bingham in grade one, and I just assumed it was the way the world worked. When you were six, you left your family and went away to school.

As we climb out of the car and I take in the long-familiar sights, I rub again at my eyes. Here is the polished wood floor of the main building's front porch, where, one Halloween night, six grade nine boys lifted Mr. Pitman's tiny Fiat 600 up the two steps from the tarmac to the porch. How brilliant, we ten-year-olds thought, to put a car on the porch! How would our shop teacher ever get it down?

The porch railings, the stone retaining walls that slant up from the driveway to the flower beds above, and the soccer field beyond fit my memory so exactly that, once again, I doubt my Canadian life. I take Wendy's hand to assure myself that I have indeed gone away, that I have lived a real life in the intervening years. That this woman I met and married is physically here. That there are two realities, one in Canada and one here, and they are not mutually exclusive. They run in parallel, though far apart.

We step through the front doors into the main building, where Mrs. Fahnestock greets us. "I've got things on the go in the kitchen," she says, after giving me a welcome-back hug. "But give me a holler if you need me." We've come during summer holidays, so the place is empty of children, but otherwise the building seems completely unchanged. It still houses the big kitchen, the dining hall, and the eight large dormitory rooms — four for boys and four for girls — each of which used to hold bunk beds and dresser drawers for twenty or so children. It also contains apartments for the dorm parents who supervised our tooth-brushings and lights-out times, in addition to a dividable lounge and library area that had one piano on each side for music practice. On Friday film nights, the divider would be pulled back and the whole student body of about a hundred and seventy kids would watch documentaries on Yellowstone National Park or Laurel and Hardy shorts. Some of the

dormitory rooms were transformed into workrooms or storage spaces in the 1980s, when the number of missionaries outside Addis had dropped so low that Bingham stopped taking boarding students. Mom says there's talk of perhaps reopening some of these dorms, now that the government has changed and missionaries might be able to work down country again. Wendy, my parents, and I step into the workroom where my bunk bed stood when I was in grade three. The walls exude the cool scent of clean earth, the cedar floors still gleam with floor wax, and the windows open onto the stone-paved patio outside.

I remember lying in my bunk beside the open window, the moonlight falling across my bedspread, and the sounds of the night watchman hawking phlegm into the coals in the wood-fired water heater outdoors.

"*Zubunya! Zubunya!*" we shout out the window.

Silence. Then a cough and another sizzle of spit in the coals.

"*Zubunya!*"

"Eh?" he finally growls.

"*Zimbel!*" we order, barely suppressing our glee. "Shut up!"

He'll never know which of us shouted the saucy orders in the dark, so we know there's little chance that Mr. Zable, our dorm parent, will scold us for failing to respect the Ethiopian staff who tend the gardens, wash our laundry, cook our food, and guard the compound at night.

The main building stands on a slope, and on the downhill side its basement has two separate entrances that give ground-level access to a laundry area and a maintenance workshop. The parking lot's red volcanic cinders separate the main building from the two-storey "new dorm," still so-called even though it had been built before I came here in the first grade. The ground floor used to be devoted to staff apartments and the school infirmary, while two long ramps led up to the second floor, which consisted of a dorm parents' apartment between two wings of children's rooms. These rooms, much smaller than those in the main building, used to house bunk beds for six or eight children. I lived in several of these rooms at various stages of my schooling: grades one, two, four, five, seven, eight, and nine. The concrete block walls and tiled floors meant hard surfaces in the new dorm, compared to the *chicka* of the other buildings on the school grounds. It was difficult to resist the temptation, when I was seven, to race up one of the ramps,

clattering a stick along the rungs of the iron railing and filling the whole building with a harsh, metallic song. I had to sprint straight into my room and toss the stick out the window into the woods behind the building to avoid a serious tongue lashing from Mrs. Mead, the infirmary nurse downstairs. I now stand beside Wendy, give the railing an experimental knock with my knuckles, and savour the thrum that travels into the heart of the building. This painted iron stayed right here in this exact place after I left high school and went to work in the fish store in Wheatley, while I went to university in Regina and met Wendy, and when the two of us moved to Edmonton for graduate school. All that time, this metal railing remained precisely here, begging each brave child to jangle the dorm with its strident song.

And so it goes: the barn-like gymnasium with its concrete floor and wall-less canopy of eucalyptus poles and galvanized iron; the woodpile behind it; the laundry lines that sway out like loose harp strings from the back wall of the school vans' parking garage; the playground farther down the slope with its merry-go-round and monkey bars and the playhouse we designed and built in Mr. Pitman's shop class; the concrete-block classroom duplex behind the small bungalow that houses the administrative office; and uphill from them, the two-storey *chicka* classroom building; the triangular, cut-stone fish pond that made a central gathering place in front of the library. All seems unaltered over the past fourteen years. Dad, Mom, Wendy, and I step into the library. I loved this place, its windows that bathed the tables, chairs, and bookshelves in broad streams of golden light. The library was a retreat from the noise and commotion of wall-to-wall kids. I used to love boys-against-girls prisoners' base on the soccer field, acorn fights in the eucalyptus woods, and squabbling with my friends over which of us would play the role of highway superintendent over the elaborate system of Dinky Toy roads we had carved into the red earth behind the new dorm. But I needed solitude, too, and Mrs. Ricker, the librarian, had hidden reading chairs among the book stacks where a student could watch dust motes whirl in the sunlight that spread across the page in his lap. All these years later, the place retains the precise aromas of solitude — old paper, binding glue, the vinyl of new encyclopedia spines, and floor wax.

We walk out of the library and follow the cut-stone path around to

the left and downhill under the tall eucalyptus trees towards the Rickers' house. The scent of these trees is the vapour of childhood. To my young nostrils, their sharp, crisp menthol was as cool and comforting as Vicks VapoRub or Colgate toothpaste. Even on a hot, dusty day you could rub a eucalyptus leaf between your fingers and hold it to your nose to evoke a movie image of a cold mountain stream. I'd seen our Oromo neighbours at Obi place a roll of eucalyptus leaves in a nostril to clear blocked sinuses, but when I gave it a try the smell was so strong I feared burnt brain cells. The eucalyptus here at Bingham provided much of the equipment for our childhood games — branches for forts, acorns for ammunition, sticks for bows and arrows, and leaves for dollar bills.

Bahir-zaff is its Amharic name, and it means "overseas tree," for eucalyptus was imported from Australia in the nineteenth century to solve the country's shortage of firewood. "It was a flaming success," Mr. Ricker quipped in our social studies class. "Eucalyptus contains a natural oil that makes it perfect for kitchen fires. It burns fast and hot." Thus, *bahir-zaff* kept the country cooking. However, it was too successful, really. The trees absorbed the nutrients from the soil so greedily that they depleted it for anything else. Too quickly, indigenous species gave way to the aggressive newcomer. Its aggression suited us Bingham kids perfectly — the lack of undergrowth left us plenty of room to carve our Dinky Toy cities in the exposed red dirt and to run freely in its scented shade.

Amid all the moving our family did in the 1970s, we lived one year as a family among these trees at Bingham. 1976-1977 was my only year in Ethiopia when I didn't live in a dorm. Downhill from the library and to the right of the tennis court behind it stands the turquoise bungalow that we called the Rickers' house because the librarian and the math teacher lived there with their family for many years. When large numbers of missionaries left the country during the late 1970s, Bingham's enrollment fell off dramatically, and the Rickers took a posting to Rift Valley Academy, a school for MKs in nearby Kenya. We moved into the Rickers' house around the time I completed grade nine at Bingham and entered grade ten at Good Shepherd, a grades one-to-twelve school across the city that was administered by a collective of missionary groups.

The year in the Rickers' house completed the unravelling of my Ethiopian life that had begun with Dad's transfer from Obi to Addis in 1972. Obi is our family's idyll. Having lived and worked a whole decade in Ethiopia before they moved to Obi, my parents were by then fluent in the Amharic language, and they had a fair understanding of Ethiopian etiquette, too. As a result, they were readily able to communicate with Amharic-speaking neighbours at Obi and even to branch out into learning the local blend of Amharic and Oromifa. After ten long years in Addis, where they had looked after the needs of other missionaries — kept their accounts, bought their supplies, looked after shipments to remote down-country stations — Obi finally gave them the chance to engage in front-line missionary work themselves. They gladly devoted their energies to getting to know neighbours, establishing elementary and Bible schools, and attending monthly *mahabir* meetings of the local KHC. When I look back upon my childhood, Bingham is where I grew up, but Obi is the closest I can come to home. This is where all four of us children spent our formative years. Marianne was born two and a half years after we moved there. She and I are too young to remember Mom and Dad's earlier life in the BD at HQ. By the time our family was transferred back to Addis, Sharon had already been at college in Canada for a year, and John followed her before we moved to Sheshemane a year and a half later.

After ten stable years at Obi, then, our family began its nomadic phase. With Sharon and John gone, the remaining four of us moved and moved. Not just Obi to HQ to Sheshemane and back to Addis, but also, in Addis, to different dwellings for short periods of anywhere from several months up to a couple of years. Down a-blow for a time at HQ, then the printing press compound in the Akaki district on the edge of the city for ten months, then back to one of the apartments at HQ, before moving to the Rickers' here at Bingham. We seemed to be moving in circles, like leaves in the rising political storm.

The revolution was already two years past by the time we moved here to the Rickers', but the battle for political power was still being fought in the streets. Although it was widely known that Lieutenant-Colonel Mengistu Haile Mariam had engineered the execution of Haile Selassie's sixty cabinet ministers on November 23, 1974, he had still not muscled aside Brigadier General Teferi Bente as Chairman of the

Provisional Military Administrative Council. The PMAC had suspended the constitution and declared a state of emergency, but these measures had not managed to snuff out the radical university students who had formed the EPRP, the Ethiopian People's Revolutionary Party, which opposed the army's attempt to consolidate its hold on power.

There are scenes from this struggle that I wish I had never seen. About twenty SIM kids, like me, had completed all the grades at Bingham and needed to go across town to Good Shep to finish high school, so the new dorm at Bingham was redubbed a hostel, and these twenty inhabited it much as they had done when they were Bingham students, with the exception that they rode across town in a small Borsani bus to go to class. Yared Lakew, the son of Ato Lakew, who worked at HQ and was a long-time friend of my parents, was given the job of driver. Because my family lived right here on the Bingham campus, I lived at home for the first time, and I rode to school with the kids on the hostel bus. In an effort to squelch the EPRP, the government had declared a sundown curfew, enforced with a shoot-on-sight policy, so Yared made sure we were home long before the sun sank low over the city's rooftops. After he dropped us back at Bingham, he had to hop in his VW Beetle and hustle home to get there before dark.

The EPRP, for its part, intensified resistance. Its members formed commando cells that defied the sundown curfew and painted anti-government slogans on stone walls, raided army depots for weapons, and carried out assassinations of military leaders, their family members, and student collaborators. The army responded with what it called the *Kai Shebbir*, the Red Terror. The nights in the Rickers' house in 1976 and 1977 crackled with gunfire that echoed off the metal roofs of the surrounding Kwolfe neighbourhood. Questions from single-action rifles were answered by the annihilating roar of machine guns. The silences between these exchanges weighed heavily in the stomach, like an undigested ball of raw dough. I knew what I would see from the bus windows in the morning. I had seen it before. We would round a corner, and there on the roadside would lie what looked like a pile of crumpled laundry. The half-painted slogan on the wall above told of how the jeep's headlights had caught the young EPRP member seconds before the spray of bullets shattered the storefront glass and smeared the concrete with a brown-red stain of blood. In the morning's bracing air, people

wrapped in their heavy *shemma* shawls would pick their way through the broken glass, their eyes averted. They were afraid to look, lest the corpse belong to someone they knew. The military police would knock on relatives' doors and demand payment for the bullets wasted on scouring out enemies of the state.

One day, Yared Lakew came to our classroom doors the minute school was out at Good Shep and herded us all to the bus. There had been an incident, he said, and we should get home as quickly as we could. Five minutes later, he guided the Borsani around a curve a kilometre or two from school, and he pointed into the woods to the left of the road where the charred remains of a Peugeot sent up wisps of smoke. He'd just missed seeing what happened, he said, on his way to get us. The car had still been burning when he asked the group of bystanders what had taken place. Apparently, two young men dressed in fatigues had escaped from the nearby army camp with the back seat full of ammunition. They'd been pursued by two military jeeps. At this corner, they'd careened off the road, leapt from the car and rolled and ran and rolled again in an effort to escape through the trees. The first few rounds from the jeep had turned the Peugeot into a shooting inferno, and the next few left the two men twisted at the eucalyptus roots. The bodies were gone now, but the car remained as a warning. Yared told the story in a tense, staccato voice, and he hit the horn with exasperation as *chidd*-bearing donkeys wandered into the middle of the street. He jerked the wheel of the bus to avoid them and decided to take the back route past the Coffee Board warehouses to see if he could get us home more quickly that way.

We'd hardly driven five hundred metres down the Coffee Board road when someone yelled from the back of the bus, "Yared! Stop! He's going to shoot!"

I had seen the armed man running beside us on the shoulder of the gravel road, but I was so astonished when he dropped to one knee and aimed his rifle at the bus that I hadn't been able to find my tongue.

Yared jammed on the brakes and the bus skidded to a halt. Acrid dust from the tires floated in our windows and clouded the gesticulating man.

"*Ah-coom! Ah-coom!*" he shouted. "Stop the bus! Everybody out!" He fumbled with the bolt of his weapon.

We had been stopped at checkpoints before, but never like this —

never by a single official, with no road barrier and no other *kebele* militia around. Part of the new government's effort to control the population had been to establish *kebeles*, or associations of armed civilians who functioned as local patrols. Everybody in each neighbourhood had to register at the *kebele* office and be prepared thereafter to show their registration papers on demand. The qualification to join this militia seemed to be zeal for the new regime rather than any kind of training in public management or the use of arms. You could never tell what would happen when you encountered *kebele* people. Often their enthusiasm seemed to derive more from the guns in their hands than from love for nation or neighbour.

The man leapt up and trotted across the gravel, his rifle gripped in both hands across his chest — apparently his movie image of commando style. As he ran, spit flew from his lips and the furrows on his forehead snapped up and down as he screamed at Yared for not stopping upon command.

"*Yekirta,*" Yared said. "I didn't see you. I'm sorry."

With jerks of the rifle muzzle, the man lined us up. Then he threw his rifle strap over his shoulder and began to paw through our school bags. "Have to check everybody and everything," he said in Amharic. He clearly assumed that Yared would be the only one who understood. "From these children of *ferenjie* pigs to some of our own army boys. You hear two tried to steal weapons for the EPRP today? Our own soldiers! There are enemies everywhere. Can't trust anyone." The girl whose bag he was searching — I don't remember whether it was Mary Dye or Ruth Cumbers — bit her lip to keep it still. A tear ran unchecked down her cheek, but she made no sound, even when he shoved the bag roughly into her hands. Panic watered my eyes, too, as he gripped her shoulder and pushed her back into line at the side of the bus. We listened to the buzzing in our ears as the *kebele* man rummaged his way down the line of kids.

"*Arah-bahk-ih,* Comrade," said Yared in a gentle voice. "These are just schoolchildren. They don't have anything but papers and books."

The man finished digging through David Iwan's bag at the end of the line and thrust him against the side of the bus.

"Enemies of the people!" The man flashed his eyes down the row of

us. "Left hands of the landlords who raped this country for years! Don't you be deceived."

He stomped back to the head of the line and clambered up the bus steps. We stood in the warm afternoon sunlight and tasted the iron of road dust on our tongues while the man rattled down the aisle inside. It was all a big and dangerous show. He had the gun. The revolution had empowered the common man. *Ferenjies* would have to submit, like everyone else, to the liberated masses. He was the new Ethiopia we read about in the government-controlled *Ethiopian Herald*. Western Imperialists had propped up the feudal regime of Haile Selassie and his retinue of bloodsucking landlords for years. Now it was time for the common people to take control and push the high and mighty aside. The man blustered back out of the bus and gestured with his rifle for us to file back in. "And next time," he snapped at Yared, "when a *kebele* official tells you to halt — stop immediately!"

I remember lying on my bed that night right here in the Rickers' house with the volume cranked up in my headphones, trying to fight the jangling in my stomach. My eyes fixed upon the brown spots Mom and Dad had let me paint on the yellow walls of my room. I had wanted to make leopard print, but the smudges of brown I had produced looked more like the aftermath of a mud fight than the pelt of a dangerous animal. My books, pencils, and papers were scattered across the sheet of particle board, laid across two tall stereo speakers, that served as my desk. I lay back on the pillow and threw an arm across my forehead to shade my eyes from the glare of the ceiling light. As soon as I closed my eyes the puckered forehead and spitting lips of the *kebele* man took over once again. Even the heavy metal wallop of *Detroit Rock City*, my favourite Kiss album, could not wrestle down the trembling.

I knew I was afraid — but of what? Partly of what might have happened today on the bus, partly of my own mixture of rage and fear. Mainly of the confusion, not just on the street but also within me. I knew the revolution hadn't all been bad. I had heard Dad say that land redistribution had been way overdue — that rural Oromo or Walaitta farmers shouldn't have had to give half their crops to rich Amhara landlords in Addis. In addition, some of Haile Selassie's cabinet ministers

had kept Swiss bank accounts into which substantial portions of the country's treasury had disappeared. So change had been necessary.

But why did we *ferenjies* have to be its enemies? And how would I avoid learning to hate Ethiopians if they hated me? I knew that not all Ethiopians hated us. Yared had been there with us today, quietly urging the *kebele* man to reason. There were all the people — Ha'da Saifu and Negussie and Mulugeta and Zenebech at Obi, Ato Debray and Yared and his dad Ato Lakew at HQ, Ato Warhana and Ato Anisi at Sheshemane — who had been good friends to me and my family. In fact, before I came to boarding school at Bingham, I hadn't lived near enough to any white families to have any friends but the local Oromo kids — Mulugeta, Zenebech, Negussie. None of them had hated me. It was the revolution that had barbed a formerly paltry fence between us and them and, I realized with a jolt, made us a liability to the people we loved. It hadn't occurred to me until I lay on my bed that night in the Rickers' house that the person most in danger at the side of the bus that afternoon had been Yared, not any of us missionary kids. Pink skin and foreign visas made us immune to the local struggle for power. Yared had no such immunity, and his very job placed him on the wrong side of the line.

"Why are we still here?" I asked my parents a night or two later. "This place is crazy and dangerous. Lots of other missionaries are leaving, why can't we?"

We were sitting in the living room after supper. Dad lay on the gold brocade couch with the pink rubber hot water bottle wrapped in a tea towel and laid across his forehead. One of his sinus headaches. Mom sat by the pole lamp in the matching armchair, knitting, her lips pursed in concentration as she hooked yarn over and under. Over and under, over and under. Click, click. It was rainy season, and the hot-dust smell of the electric heater vied with the scent of damp eucalyptus from the trees that towered over the house.

I asked this question because we'd had another incident. Earlier that day, Mek'des, the woman who worked in our kitchen, told Mom she

wouldn't be in to work for the next week. With a face that had aged decades overnight and a head shaved bald as a sign of mourning, Mek'des said she needed to arrange funerals for her husband, sister, and brother-in-law. Over the weekend, armed men in military fatigues had burst down the door of her home, and, before the dazed household could understand what was happening, they had grabbed her three family members and hustled them out the door and down the street. She never saw them alive again. The armed men vanished, and there was no way to know who they were. Anybody could be wearing army fatigues. When she went to her regional *kebele* station to seek help, she was immediately photographed and interrogated for two hours in case her family might have had dealings with the EPRP. It wasn't until the next day that the three bodies were found tumbled into a roadside ditch. Each had been shot in the back of the head.

That night I asked my parents why we couldn't go home.

"That's a tough question, dear," Mom said. She looked up from her needles to the spot on the rug where Marianne was curled up with Pupsi, our miniature black poodle. The dog lay on his back, his four limp feet raised, while Marianne rubbed his tummy with a distracted hand. "But it's important to stay, because we can't leave our Ethiopian friends without support."

Marianne's fingers combed through Pupsi's curly hair. The orange coils in the heater ticked and buzzed. Mom's needles clicked.

Under the hot water bottle, Dad cleared his throat. "We know this is hard on you kids, that it's difficult not to be afraid. But we need to remember that God is in control, and nothing can happen that He doesn't allow." The tea towel muffled his voice. "And how can we tell KHC people that God will protect them if we can't endure these troubles ourselves?"

So we stayed. Or at least we intended to stay — and Mom, Dad, and Marianne did stay — though in my case the intention didn't work out. At the end of that school year, the government appropriated Good Shepherd School, explaining that the campus was needed for a rehabilitation centre for war vets. Without a school to attend in Ethiopia, therefore, I went to live with family friends in Calgary, where I took grade eleven. During that year Mom and Dad put my name in for a spot at Rift Valley Academy — the mission school in Kenya where the

Rickers had gone — for my final year of high school. Marianne went to Rift Valley, too, as did a number of the kids I had grown up with at Bingham — Tim Bascom, Bev Radach, Ruth Cumbers, Mary Dye. Some of these friends' parents had been reassigned by the mission to neighbouring countries, but those of us whose families remained in Ethiopia came home for Christmas and Easter holidays. In fact, my last departure from Addis occurred when I returned to RVA after Easter break in 1979. I matched my family's house hopping with school hopping, spending each year of high school in a different institution. All this moving and uncertainty shook my roots free of the soil in which they had been planted.

Except Bingham, I now think, as I stand with my parents and Wendy on the cut-stone sidewalk beside the Rickers' house and look uphill towards the library. Despite all the uprooting, vestiges of this red dirt, these eucalyptus woods, the dormitory rooms, and the library sunlight from my early years here at Bingham have lodged, not just in memory, but deeper down than that — somewhere in the marrow and structure of my bones.

We walk back up the stone sidewalk from the Rickers' house past the library and towards the soccer field on the other side of the two-storey classroom building. As we round the corner, we're stopped by a shout — "Dan-ih-el!"

I turn towards the sound of my name and am amazed to see the gardener — the very same man who had tended the marigolds, snapdragons, and zinnias that graced the Bingham grounds when I was a boy.

"Dan-ih-el! Dan-ih-el Col-eh-man!" he pronounces my name Amharic style. "*In-kwan bedahina metu!* Welcome! How wonderful that you have come back safely!" He grasps my pink hand with his two callused ones, leans first over one and then the other of my shoulders, and kisses the air by each of my ears, twice on each side. "You've grown up! *Indeminde-note?* How are you? Praise be to God!" He giggles a high laugh of glee. "Dan-ih-el! How have you come to be here? I can't believe it's you!"

I give myself to his embrace, overwhelmed with embarrassment and delight. We terrorized this man daily, little boys who could not resist mucking up the beauty of his gardens. He once chased Timmy Bascom

and me with a stick after he found the six calla lilies we had decapi-
tated and dropped on the asphalt walk in front of the classroom
building. We had been watching the silver filigree of a spider's web
stretched across one of the windows of our third-grade classroom,
hoping to see the spider emerge. We began to argue about which had the
more lethal bite, a spider or a bee. I insisted that a bee was the more
vicious insect because it could sting. Timmy voted for the spider.

"And it's not even an insect," he added. "It's an arachnid!"

"Is not!"

"Is so. I read it in the *World Book* in the library!"

There was no point in arguing with the library. "Well, whatever. But
I still think a bee would win in a fight."

As I spoke, a honeybee settled into the open trumpet of a white calla
lily in the garden that bordered the sidewalk.

"Look at this!" I said, and I pinched the flower's mouth closed with
a quick grab, as if it were the mouth of a paper bag. I broke the flower
from its stem and gave the package a vigorous shake. Timmy looked
over my shoulder as I stepped to the window and dumped the addled
bee into the spider's web.

The bee buzzed powerfully in the web, flailing at the sticky filaments.
Sure enough, the spider poked part of its head out of the crack in the
window frame, but the bee's wings were too strong for the lacy threads.
It broke a hole in the web and hurtled angrily up into the sky above us.

Five callas later, we found a stronger-looking web on a window
ledge of the grades five and six classroom. Timmy dumped the bee out
of the bell of the flower, only to find that he'd squished it between the
white plastic of the petal and the thick orange prod of its spadix. The
dying bee convulsed in the web, and a huge grey spider emerged from
the whorl of its hiding place. It was just approaching the bee when an
angry voice shouted, *"T'abat! Min ainet lidjoach!"*

We wheeled around to see the gardener down by the grade-three
classroom. He waved the limp white rag of our first calla in one hand
and one of the bamboo canes he used to stake up hollyhocks in the other.

"Bare-assed baboons! Don't you have fathers?" He shouted as he
started towards us with the cane raised high.

We sprinted to the opposite end of the building, leapt down the
steps to the lower level, sprayed driveway gravel from our flying feet by

the parking garages, and ducked under the clothes lines on our way to the safety of the dorm. We never did find out which had the more vicious bite — a spider or a bee.

Now, over twenty years later, the same man grips my palm in both of his as he smacks his lips over each of my shoulders in turn. "Dan-ih-el! Dan-ih-el! *In-kwan bedahina metu! Igzabier yemesgen!* God be praised!"

I realize to my mortification that I don't know his name! He had been the Gardener. Someone who chased little boys out of his flower beds with Amharic insults and raised sticks. He was one of the fixtures of the place, and I never learned his name. Nonetheless, out of the hundreds of children who passed through this school, out of the many boys who trampled his petunias and dug soccer balls out of his roses, he remembers mine.

This aspect of the return trip continues to shame me repeatedly in the weeks to come. Despite all the tension — the *kebele* officials, the guns at night, and the officially encouraged suspicion of *ferenjies* — despite the very real danger we posed to those with whom we lived and worked, what overwhelms me now is the warmth of people who knew me when I lived here as a boy. Whether seeing Ato Lakew at HQ or Ha'da Saifu, the woman who worked in our kitchen at Obi and who now works in the HQ laundry down a-blow; whether going to visit Negussie, our childhood friend, who awaits treatment for typhoid fever in the Poly Clinic or having dinner at the home of Ato Kaydamo, the senior pastor at the main Kalleh Hiwot Church in Addis — I am repeatedly overcome by the sheer delight of these friends who celebrate my parents' good fortune at having an adult child come home. Their glad welcome flies in the face of the fears I developed during the dangerous years of the revolution. I learned to distance myself from Ethiopia, a distance I widened when I went to live in Canada and pushed my past into the back of my mind, only to find upon my reluctant return now, all these years later, that these kind people — many of whose names, like that of the gardener at Bingham, I have forgotten — embrace me like a long-lost member of an extended family. The joy of their greetings makes me doubt the fear I remember, and I find myself rubbing and rubbing at the reality in my eyes.

A Curriculum *in* Clothes

I put on my favourite blue shirt this morning and, as usual, found my fingers fumbling with the buttons. Oh yes, I realized, this is the shirt Hazel, my mother-in-law, bought me because she thought it's just my colour of blue. And it is. I get regular compliments when I wear it. It brings out the blue in my eyes. But she found it in Ladies' Wear. Well, it *is* the right colour, so who cares what section of the Bay she bought it in? Regardless, I was fumbling with the buttons.

Who sat around, I wondered, in the backroom of what clothing design shop deciding that women's belts and buttons should do up *this* way, and men's *that*? And how did my fingers come to believe these silent rules of gender, that *that* is a more natural way to do it than *this*? It made me think of the leotards. Blue leotards.

This is a preschool memory from our years at Obi. Dad had not yet traded in the Jeep for the VW Beetle, so that makes me about three and a half. The family is headed to Addis from Obi. An early morning trip — on the road at dawn, mist in the chilly air. I am sitting on the cold vinyl of the Jeep's back bench, and I am utterly mortified. To make sure I'll be warm enough, my mother has put me in tights — we called them leotards — before pulling on my pants. Leotards! I have seen my older sister Sharon wearing leotards, but boys *do not* wear leotards. Boys wear socks, Stanfields boxer shorts, short or long pants, rubber boots, Alligator-brand runners, or even shiny black leather shoes on Sundays. But boys do not wear leotards. They are tight and clingy in a completely un-boyish, un-me-ish kind of way. They are not free and they are not loose. They clasp me under my pants, gripping me in a self-image I do not like and do not want.

In the light of the kerosene lamp before dawn that morning, Mom

had squatted beside me to help me with my shoes. I could smell the Lux soap with which she had scrubbed her face. Her permed brown curls tickled my cheek as she knotted a lace. "Nobody will see," she had said, and she jabbed my shirttail into the waistband of my corduroys. "They'll look just like socks. Your pants cover the rest. They'll keep you warm. Stop fussing."

Her words gave me no peace. It wasn't a matter of appearance; it was a state of being. I was *in leotards*. I was going to meet other children that day in the big city, children I didn't know, and there would be this hidden defect, this private debilitation, just when I needed to feel my strongest, my most confident. I would be negotiating the toys, the games, the sandbox, and the leader-follower stuff in leotards. This was impossible. Unthinkable.

The vinyl backs of the driver and passenger seats formed a stiff wall between me and the front of the Jeep. I had spoken my mind and it had done no good. I was banished to the wide, stiff shelf of the backbench. This was happening to me much too often in those days. There, within sight, was the camaraderie of the front, where my new baby sister Marianne rested in my mother's lap while the warm wash of conversation ebbed and flowed between driver and passenger. When I had been in the front, the adult talk had made a comforting white noise behind roadside excitements such as the guts of a mangled goat spread like hotdog fixings down the asphalt or donkeys piled so high with *chidd* they were walking haystacks. Now, in my fury, I didn't bother to rub the foggy windows with my palm and look out at the speeding scenes. Instead, I sat and stared hatred at the backs of my parents' seats. I was in the back, I was in exile, and I was in leotards.

Did Mom relent as the day grew warmer and relieve me of the navy blue tights? Was I exposed before the other kids as a sham, an oddity, an embarrassment? I don't remember. But I do remember the indignation. Someone else's idea of heat and cold, someone else's idea of how to keep warm, someone else's idea of the appropriate thing had heated my face with shame and frosted my heart with rebellion.

I am curious about where that shame and rebellion came from. We had lived on the mission station at Obi all my conscious life. We were far away from any fashion guides that would tell me what clothes were restricted to boys or girls. Sometimes missionary families came to visit,

and I would meet other non-Ethiopian children my age. Other times, such as on this particular day, we made day trips to Addis, where Mom and Dad bought supplies and groceries. There at HQ, I would come in contact with a few other missionaries' children. These were my only glimpses into the world of Western dress, and they were brief. My world consisted pretty much of my own family and the circle of neighbour Oromo friends — Mulugeta, Zenebech, and Zenebech's sister, Fantaye — who inhabited the cluster of thatch-roofed houses at the edge of the mission station at Obi. Furthermore, Sharon and John were boarding at Bingham Academy in Addis most of the time, so this subtracted the regular influence of my older siblings. What did I know of television? What did I know about the boys' clothing section of a Sears catalogue? Absolutely nothing. So where did I learn with such certainty that Leotards Were Not For Me?

Years later, when I retold the story about the leotards and my vexation, my mother, now retired and living in Alberta, introduced elements of the story I had not remembered. She could not be exactly sure, she said, but that early trip to Addis when Marianne was just a week or two old was likely the time she had to take Dad to the hospital in the city. He had started to run an alarming fever four or five days before, and the mission nurse at Obi was away. No remedy Mom tried had any effect. Finally one early morning, after reading the frightful numbers on the thermometer, Mom decided to load Dad onto a cot in the back of the Jeep and take him to Emergency at Princess Tsa'hai Hospital in Addis. She was frightened. She had just come home from the maternity ward in the hospital herself, she had a week-old baby and a three-year-old boy — besides the older two at school — and her husband was deathly ill. I doubt that she had much time to explain to me why the leotards were necessary. I doubt that she had time during the rest of that anxious day to set my mind at ease about either my father or my clothes.

So the trauma of the leotards is all I retained. The atmosphere of that day's distress must have linked itself so tightly to those navy tights that it displaced entirely any images of a pale little boy fussing nervously on the Jeep's back wheel housing, while his father lay shivering and sweating on the cot. It must have been a confusing day. Mom would have been too preoccupied to offer assurances, Dad was incapacitated,

and the new baby had dislodged me from the front seat. As a result, I could not find my place. None of these anxieties were concrete enough to anchor a memory, and, because the fever did pass and Dad did come home well again, I had no later images to remind me Dad had been sick. If my mother is right in connecting the leotards with the time she rushed my father to the hospital, then my lesson that clothing is gendered was imprinted by fear for the stability of my family. The whole ordeal got glued to the leotards, to which my panic stuck: Boys Do Not Wear Leotards.

That same year I had a knitted vest as vivid as the yellow breasts of the black-headed weaver birds whose nests bent bamboo stalks down by the Obi creek. The weaver birds' yellow singled them out from the mouse birds' brown and sparrows' grey, just as the vest set me off from the faded clothing of Mulugeta, Zenebech, and little Fantaye. Actually, many features besides the sweater vest distinguished me from my playmates. At three years old, I had freckled, pinkish skin, blue eyes, straw-straight hair, black rubber boots, and — best of all — a wooden wagon with bright red wheels. The wagon, along with the other toys my parents had brought from Canada, made me more than interesting to my Oromo friends. It made me de facto leader of games, the supplier of ideas, equipment, and gear.

I did not know life could be any different. I could not remember living anywhere else but Obi. My parents had moved here to the rural pastureland at Obi mission station when I was less than a year old. Woliso, a town of a few thousand people, hummed its market life five kilometres away. Farmers' compounds of round, thatch-roofed houses clustered in family groupings across the Obi region, as they did across much of the cool plateau of Showa province. I had plenty of playmates in the neighbouring compounds, but none of us knew anything about life in a city, let alone another country. Though my family went to Addis from time to time, the city was a distant thought, a place where Sharon and John went to boarding school. My world remained secure within the pasture fences of Obi station.

Sharon, me, and John, sitting
in the red-wheeled wagon.

Mulugeta, me,
Marianne, and
a boy whose
name I cannot
recall, and
Zenebech.

Zenebech and me.

Mulugeta and me.

I did not know of a place where other children besides me had rubber boots and wagons and lemon-coloured vests. I did not think it odd that Negussie Kumbi's stepmother, who lived down towards the creek, stroked my hair and exclaimed how limp it was. I patiently bore her speculation that my freckles must be the scars of terrible infantile smallpox. How glad my parents must be, she murmured, that I had survived. My singularity seemed natural to me. I did not find it troubling, because to me it was no trouble. I liked my friend Mulugeta, and he liked me. We played and quarrelled in Oromifa mixed with Amharic. When I came in for supper, I related my adventures in three languages: the local mixture of Oromifa and Amharic for Ha'da Saifu, the woman who worked in our home, and a combination of English and Amharic for my mother. These facts of life were as naturally mine as the brilliant yellow sweater vest and the red-wheeled wagon. I was different from my playmates, special, and I liked my difference.

One rinsed afternoon during rainy season, Mulugeta careened around the wet yard in the wagon, Zenebech and I trotted behind, pushing. I had slumped beside the record player indoors since Sharon and John had gone away the week before at the start of another school year. Mom had grown weary of changing the record on the battery-operated phonograph and thinking of ways to entertain me, so when the rain let up after lunch, she gladly sent me out to look for Mulugeta and Zenebech. Mulugeta was two years older than me and several centimetres taller. His head was shaved smooth but for a tuft of nappy hair just above his forehead. "Easy to keep clean," his mother said. "And the tuft is so his guardian angel can grab him quickly in moments of danger." Zenebech was the same age as me, but smaller, and her angel could grab any part of her full head of hair. Sometimes her mother put it in cornrows, but today it was loose about her slim neck. Bent together like a mule team, the girl and I splashed through shallow puddles in the short-cropped grass. The rims of my black rubber boots slapped my calves, plocka-plocka, giving each step an after beat. Zenebech's quick brown feet ran smooth and silent. Together we sang bright laughter when Mulugeta ran the red wheels right through a green patty from one of Gashé Fergassa's cattle. Shit and mud and water flew from the wheels while the boy in the wagon swung the steering tongue from side to side, cutting figure eights and three-sixties.

Gashé Fergassa taught in the mission school, and Dad was glad to let him pasture his few cows on the mission station grass, for it saved the expense of hiring someone to mow it with a scythe. A picture in our family photo album showed how tall the grass had been when we first arrived at Obi. In the photo, John, Sharon, and I sat in the wooden wagon and the grass towered one whole metre over our heads. You couldn't even see the rooftops of the station houses in the background. Now, in the very same place, the cows had clipped the grass short and green, and it sped under our feet as Zenebech and I splashed through puddles on the soccer field by the clinic.

And then it happened. The jubilant driver flung the handle far to the left, and I lost my grip on the back of the wagon. Down I went into the mud. I rose unhurt in body but in distress of many kinds. I had neither skinned a knee nor twisted an ankle. I had not sniffed water up my nose or bumped my head on the speeding wagon. I hadn't been hurt anywhere, but I began to cry. First, there was the cold, damp surprise on my skin. Then, there were the giggles that squeaked between the fingers Mulugeta and Zenebech clamped over their mouths. Worst of all, the rust of Obi's red earth doused the bright yellow flame of my one-of-a-kind vest.

My rage found only salty, hot tears. Mulugeta could spatter his clothes with mud; it made no difference. They were a nondescript beige already from his mother's weekly washings down at the Jarsa River, whose waters carried the same red silt that stained the puddles on the soccer field. Zenebech's clothes matched his exactly. She could dip her skirt in the mud and no one could tell which part had been dipped and which had not. My friends' clothes blended with the soil in a way mine never had and never would. My yellow vest, however, changed shockingly and instantly at the briefest touch of earth. This vest was my distinction; it was my self-legitimating badge of leadership. And it had betrayed me entirely. The very property of its distinction — its clear and brilliant colour — was dangerously vulnerable to the simplest brush with earth. With one minor turn, muck and water had bleared my glorious vestments to a limp and sorrowful sack.

The day I asked my mother about the leotards, I also mentioned the fallen vest, to see if her memory would shed some light on this, my second earliest memory. We wondered together why it stuck so firmly in

my mind. What was it about the muddy vest that heated my memory's glue gun? Did she lecture me when I came in sodden from the yard? Did Ha'da Saifu give me a tongue lashing about the extra work? After all, it took the two of them a full day to do the laundry — heat the metal tub of water on the back of the wood stove, fill the hand-agitated washing machine, dump in the sweet-scented Omo laundry soap, crank the clothing piece by piece through the wringer, and finally hang them out to dry. It required a second day for Ha'da Saifu to iron the clean clothes in the backyard with the charcoal-heated iron. Was I afraid they would be angry at my dirty clothes?

"I doubt it," Mom said, chuckling. "You were always such a fussy kid. You hated getting dirty or making any mess. You always wanted everything just so. It seemed ages before I had to wash or mend any of your clothes — for a boy, you were much too clean!"

My smudged yellow vest, then, must have offended my own sense of order and propriety. When it was clean, it had functioned as a sign of my place in the world. It showed that I was white and rich and not Ethiopian. When it lost its brightness, though, I couldn't find my accustomed place.

Mom and Dad tried to raise their children with an ethic of equality. They never instructed us in a strict separation between us and Ethiopians — or between boys and girls, for that matter. They worked as readily with Miss Ott and Miss Scotty, the German nurse and American teacher, as they did with Gashé Fergassa and Ha'da Saifu, the Oromo teacher and Amhara housekeeper. Our mother taught the same kinds of Bible School courses our father did. When Dad was transferred to Administration later on in Addis, Mom became accountant for the mission's more-than-million-dollar budget in Ethiopia. So our parents modeled no clear divisions in the gendering of their work lives or in their relations with Ethiopians. They warned us against assuming any superiority to our Oromo friends. They were careful never to teach us that our foreignness made us better than our neighbours. Equality was a value they prized. Nonetheless, the secret discriminations of the leotards and the vest composed a curriculum of their own, and I learned the distinctions and divisions they implied anyway.

At the age of six, I followed in my sister's and brother's footsteps to Bingham Academy in Addis. The Bingham grounds had much to offer a boy my age — even more than the pasture fields at Obi. Two hectares of eucalyptus trees cried out for games of capture-the-flag and the building of forts. There was a gymnasium, too, and a playground and a soccer field. But best of all, behind the backstop on the sports field there was something called a bag swing. I didn't know why it was called a bag swing; there was nothing baggy about it. It was made of an inverted T-bar that dangled at the bottom of a Y-shaped chain whose two top ends were secured twelve metres up in two vast eucalyptus trees. To a first-grader like me, the bag swing looked like an instrument of death. John told me that several kids were known to have broken arms or legs falling off this dangerous, fascinating thing. I could see why. A six-metre-high ramp of eucalyptus poles had been built to increase the height of the takeoff. Really crazy junior high boys such as Weenie Iwan were known to have dragged the swing all the way to the top of this ramp, leapt on the seat formed by the upside-down T, and sailed out, spinning and bucking, to the height of the tree-tops of the *bahir-zaff* forest that sloped away below the swing. I gazed in terrified admiration as fourth-grade boys John's age proved their courage by going all the way up to the halfway point of the ramp before jumping on the killer swing. John assured me that you didn't *have* to go on the bag swing to be a student at Bingham.

The school had originally been built outside the city, but with urban expansion Kwolfe district now sprawled on all sides. A two-metre fence was built around the perimeter, as much to keep little kids from wandering off into the unpaved streets and alleys as to keep out petty thieves. What had been farm fields and bits of woodland around the school were subdivided and hacked into muddy yards that sprouted shacks, concrete-block houses, and galvanized iron fences. Bingham had become a green park marooned in an increasingly squalid shantytown.

The school was only a hundred and ten kilometres from home, but it might as well have been a whole continent away from the pastures

and fields of Obi. Here I found myself among hundreds of kids with skin as pink as my own, most of them had hair as straight and fine as mine, and they dressed in a rainbow of colours. If I had been demoted when my yellow vest was soiled at Obi, I was washed into complete anonymity at Bingham. Everybody had a wagon at home. Everybody had leather Sunday shoes and black rubber boots. Everybody had a grandma or a grandpa Back Home, though Back Home didn't always mean Canada. For some of my classmates, it meant Australia, for some the States, and for others England. It would take several years before I knew what each of these names meant. For now, I gathered snippets from older students' conversations to sketch out a ground for my own place in the world: "Canada's bigger than any of your countries," I would say. "It's bigger than England and Australia and the States." I varied this assertion with another: "Did you know that Canada beat the States in a war?"

Being Canadian also meant that my underwear was different from the underwear of the other boys in my dorm. The tag in the waistband of my cotton boxer shorts proclaimed they were "Stanfields — Made in Canada," whereas the other boys all wore briefs, either "Fruit of the Loom — Made in USA" or skimpy, brightly coloured "Pelicans — Made in Taiwan." Though I defended my boxers loudly, I secretly knew briefs would be less bulky under my pants.

At Bingham, clothes required more work than they had at home. Back at Obi, I had simply put on whatever my mother had laid out for me to wear that day — even on the days when she took strange ideas like leotards into her head. Now, my daily attire involved a complex process which I had known about but in which I had never truly participated. Each room in the new dormitory held three double-decker bunk beds, a tall wooden wardrobe, and a set of dresser drawers. When my five roommates and I got up for Verse Group, the hour of Bible verse memorization held each school day at seven a.m., I had to open the dresser drawers allotted me and decide which socks, boxer shorts, trousers, and shirt to wear. I needed to apply the lessons I learned as a preschooler so I wouldn't make the mistake of wearing a shirt that made me look like a girl or pants that might pass as something an Ethiopian would wear. Before I left the room, I had to make sure my discarded clothes were all neatly folded into my drawers so our room

could pass inspection. Wrinkled clothes on the floor or on our bunk beds meant Mr. Johnson would keep us back from the breakfast lineup after Verse Group, and my roommates would be mad at me for the delay.

Clothes now meant labour. Folding. Putting away. Choosing. Laying out. They also meant laundry duty. When my clothes were dirty, I made sure the Danny Coleman nametags Mom had painstakingly sewn on each article of clothing were securely attached to each sock, shirt, or pair of boxers. Then I put them into the cloth laundry bag that hung on the back of the door in our room. A regular rotation determined which of us boys took this bag down to the school's central laundry once a week. The boy would then go on the assigned day to pick up the clean clothes.

Although laundry duty meant an incursion on precious playtime, I secretly liked going to the laundry. The Ethiopian women who worked there reminded me of Zenebech's and Mulugeta's mothers down at the Jarsa River at Obi. The thump and splash of sodden clothes falling into water echoed antiphonally with the same kind of gossip and laughter I remembered. I would lug the bag of dirty clothes down the new dorm's ramp, across the cinder parking lot, and under the clotheslines to the main building. I would pass through the basement entry into the laundry area and make my way around the chain link fence that kept little kids away from the water tubs to the open patch of concrete where these women sorted colours from whites. I liked to stay and help them sort because the laundry ladies would cluck over me and pat my straw-straight hair with their soap-scented hands. They would bend over the piles of clothing, their hair tied up in brightly coloured scarves, and make fun of my skinny, pink arms. How lucky for my parents, they would say, that I had survived infantile smallpox. I liked their voluble mothering so much that I volunteered to switch chores with my roommates — sweeping or dusting — for laundry duty so I could go there more often. Each time I went, I knew these ladies would spatter me again with the Showan mixture of Oromifa and Amharic that I was beginning to forget in this place where my friends came from different regions and could not know the Obi dialect. Their attention reminded me of the distinction I had enjoyed at home.

One day, as I watched the women sort flannel shirts, blue jeans, and underwear into piles, I realized that they made their living from my

clothes. They came every day to our school and washed MKs' clothing all day long, and this gave them money to buy clothing, food, and schoolbooks for their own children. I had seen Ha'da Saifu pegging up my pants and my mother's sheets on the clothesline at Obi, but I had not realized this was her job. I had thought she was simply a part of the Coleman household. She had always been there, telling me to wash-wash when it was time for dinner or swinging the iron in the backyard until the coals inside glowed as red as my cheeks when I closed my mouth around a flashlight.

I remembered my mother telling about the time Ha'da Saifu had run out to the clothesline in the first spits of a rainstorm, dumped all the wet laundry into our best lace tablecloth, joined the four corners together, slung the sagging load over her shoulder, and staggered toward the house.

"She said the old thing was all full of holes anyway," cried my laughing mother, while she dabbed her eyes with a hanky.

Like Ha'da Saifu, therefore, the women in the laundry at Bingham gained their living from my clothes. My spotless shirts were the radiance of their work. Every day they ironed the crisp collars and razor-edged creases that set me and my schoolmates apart from the shapeless garments worn by the Ethiopian kids outside the school grounds — that set us apart even from their own children, who sometimes met them after work at the school gate. The mud on my play clothes related directly to the fortunes of these women's families. My clothes were not just a meeting point, but also a dividing line between them and me. I was from rich, pink people, who paid poor, brown people to clean our clothing. I felt lucky to be on my side of the line.

The new khaki jacket my mother brought me on Field Day-Halloween, when I was in grade four reinforced how lucky I was. But it also made me aware of a new inner division I hadn't really noticed before. On the one hand, the jacket was brand new and showed I was precious in her eyes; on the other hand, it made me embarrassed to be seen by my schoolmates as a Mommy's boy, still dressed by his mother. With this

The new jacket.

jacket, I came to a new understanding of the complex work she put into my clothing, and at the same time I learned to guard a distance between us.

Field Day-Halloween weekend mixed a costume parade with a track and field meet, bobbing for apples with high jumping, and a haunted house with a hundred-metre dash. This weekend confused all the rules. You had to stay inside the chalk lines for the three-legged race, but there appeared to be no limits to what you could dream up for the Halloween parade. Mr. Ricker, his beard orange as a carrot, pranced around the costume parade in a wig and a grass skirt short enough to narrow the nostrils of more than one parent. The next morning, sombre as a Calvinist, he wielded the starting pistols and trophies at the track.

During the Field Day-Halloween carnival, regular school patterns gave way in the presence of parents. Some parents took their children out to dinner and brought them back to the dorm long after lights out. Other parents, eager to sit with their own children at table, unknowingly displaced bewildered students from their assigned seats in the dining hall. My schoolmates suddenly evinced a loyalty to parents I had never before seen. I myself felt divided between authorities and allegiances. How could I tell my parents I had to be in bed in the dorm by eight o'clock? What would my dorm parent, Mrs. Johnson, say if my real parents kept me out past curfew? How could I explain to my roommates that our pledges of friendship must be temporarily suspended because my parents demanded my company? The presence of parents divided me between the comforts of family and the camaraderie of the dorm, between glad childhood and embarrassed youth. I wanted to be with my parents, but I didn't want to appear too needy.

I felt both glad and embarrassed on this particular Field Day as I perambulated the sports field with my parents. I wanted the entire world to see the new jacket they had brought me, but I did not want to look too grateful lest my friends think me a sissy. How could I display my pleasure without looking like a wimp? The new jacket featured a durable outer shell of tightly woven, twilled khaki and a soft inner liner of light cotton that felt cool on my bare arms. A brass zipper ran straight down the front from the tabbed collar to the wide hem at my waist. Up, warm; down, air. The jacket shell featured top-sewn seams — two horizontals at my collarbone pieced the yoke to the bodice, and two

verticals fell from armpit to hip. Slash-style pockets at my sides awaited marbles or acorns or balls of chocolate icing rolled off the cake in the dining hall. This jacket was a beauty, and it was brand, spanking new. It was not a hand-me-down from John. My mother had bought it years before with only me in mind.

Her foresight was a thing of wonder to me then. Indeed, it still is now. How had she known, four years before, when the family was last in Canada and I was still a preschooler, what size and style of jacket I would like all this time later? I knew of only four possible sources of clothing. The first was hand-me-downs. The second was the local *markatto* where *ch'at*-chewing Yemenese merchants sold dry goods from Taiwan and India. The third was the *missionarie barrelle*. And the fourth was my mother's prophetic shopping trips when the family went on furlough to Canada once every five years. This last source was easily the best. The first was boring because hand-me-downs brought nothing new into our family's collective wardrobe, and they also suggested that we were too poor to afford new clothes. The second didn't supply the distinction from Ethiopian clothing my yellow vest had taught me to expect. The third, the *missionarie barrelle,* embroiled me in a paradox of embarrassments unique to missionary culture.

The *missionarie barrelle* was our family's frenchified euphemism for the used-teabag charity that church groups in Canada reserved for missionaries. These groups would save their second-hand clothing and stow it away in seaworthy steel barrels. When they had gathered a full shipment of used articles, they would send the barrels off to missionaries in Africa or Asia. During the gathering period, when clothes were still being collected, sorted, and folded, the half-filled barrels crowded a locked room in the basement of their church. The costs of shipment could be bypassed, however, when the missionaries came back home on furlough. Then our family would be led kindly but firmly downstairs, where we would wait by the door while the key scratched in the lock.

From a practical point of view, the *missionarie barrelle* was a gold mine. Perfectly good clothes, unobjectionable but for the speedy obsolescence of fashion, were folded neatly into the mothball-laced barrels. There were sturdy plaid shirts and denim overalls for boys, pleated wool skirts and bobby socks for girls. Yet, in Canada, I hated the *missionarie barrelle*. I feared we would emerge from the basement in

trousers or dresses the children upstairs in Sunday School might have worn last year or maybe even last week. How could I know what messages this polo-necked shirt or those corduroy pants were sending? How could I know if I was being introduced to some boy while wearing his old jacket from last winter? And who was I when wearing the jacket he had chosen to express himself?

In Ethiopia, however, these same clothes worked differently. Like any other school, Bingham had strict fashion codes among the students, but the lack of television and up-to-date catalogues meant a delay in fashion time, so second-hand clothes weren't necessarily out of style at school yet. Furthermore, how could my friends Mulugeta or Zenebech at Obi know if my yellow vest was hand-me-down, *barrelle,* or store-bought? And how could Timmy or Philip at Bingham know if I had got my Canadian overalls in a Hudson's Bay store or from the *barrelle*? They couldn't know. In fact, in comparison to Mulugeta or Zenebech or to the laundrywomen's children at the school gate, even the used clothes from the *missionarie barrelle* made me look rich.

Nonetheless, the suspicion of hand-me-downs at school meant my new jacket must be distinguished from the shadow of the *barrelle*. It was not easy, though, to make this clear. I knew it was brand-new, but how could my friends know unless I told them directly? How could I tell them directly without appearing proud or, worse yet, having to go to Mommy for proof?

For, truth be known, my jacket had, indeed, come out of a barrel — not the *missionarie barrelle*, but a barrel nonetheless. Four years before, when I was half my present size, my mother had somehow divined not only how big I would be but also what colour and style I would like. For four years, unknown to me, this khaki jacket had been folded away in one of my family's own packing barrels, up in the attic of our house at Obi, where it waited for me to grow into its shape — for my arms to reach the right length, my shoulders to spread to the right width.

"I never got much help, really," my mother says, when I ask her now about those prophetic shopping trips. "No one I knew back home had to buy for their children four years down the road. And truly, in the end, the *barrelle* didn't help much either. There was no point in shipping a bale of clothes all the way across the Atlantic if you kids wouldn't wear them." She therefore tried to observe our present likes

and dislikes, estimate for each of us the distance between mortification and delight, and dress our future bodies in her mind's eye.

To accomplish this delicate operation, my mother had to derive prescience from my early prejudices. She had to note carefully my reactions to dirty vests and tight leotards, to boxer shorts and flannel shirts. Then she had to chart a cautious course through the minefield of my evolving tastes. Though the khaki jacket was not as bright as my yellow vest, the cut and style distinguished this garment from any locally bought item Mulugeta or Zenebech would ever wear. There was nothing of the clingy effeminacy of the leotards in the jacket's loose, boyish look. I could race around in it and not be hampered; I could splash it with mud and send it to the laundry and it would come back clean. Best of all, it was brand-brand new. When push came to shove in the dormitory about new and used clothing, my dignity would have at least this leg to stand on. In this jacket, my mother had read the signs of my precocious tastes, taken a sighting down my growing years, and hit my discriminating bull's eye. I was proud of her marksmanship. I was at school, however, where it was death to be known as a Mommy's boy. I couldn't really let on how much the jacket meant to me. More than this, there was something troubling about being known so intimately, even by my own mother, for I was engaged in the complicated business of trying to craft a self that would float on the school-survival ethic of manly independence. She knew my past, and so she represented a continuity that threatened the new me that I was trying to make.

I did my best, therefore, to capitalize on the confusion of the Field Day-Halloween rules and turn the tour of the sports field into a costume parade. My earlier articles of clothing had carried plenty of significations of their own. They had flagged the kilometres of my journey to this moment. Perhaps now this jacket, too, would speak loudly on its own. It would demonstrate my authenticity as a boy, a *ferenjie* from Canada, a prized child in a family of means. It would do all this without my saying a single word.

Not My Home

This world is not my home, I'm just a-passin' through,
My treasures are laid up somewhere beyond the blue.
The angels beckon me from heaven's open door,
And I can't feel at home in this world anymore.

Our voices, thin and high, bright as birds, rose in the late afternoon air in the chapel at Bingham. Outside, the row of young pines bent whispering in the breeze. Beyond them, the patch of tall eucalyptus between the chapel and the new dorm rattled their spearhead leaves. We sat on the varnished wooden benches in orderly rows arranged according to grade — the grade ones wriggled in the front row while lanky grade nines disguised the presence of chewing gum in their mouths at the back. What I remember most are the songs and the ten-cent pieces. We were handed a copper coin on the way into Loyal Ambassadors for Christ, the Sunday afternoon chapel service, and were expected to put it in the offering when it was taken up later in the program. The drop and roll of ten-cent pieces from the grade one bench peppered the songs and choral readings of LAC. We were up and down from our seats chasing our wayward coins. If you rubbed the coin hard with your thumb, you could make a shiny new profile of Emperor Haile Selassie emerge from the dirty copper before you put it in the collection plate. If you sucked on the coin for a minute first, the grime loosened more easily, and you could make Miss Macdonald turn green if you let her see you do it.

Miss Macdonald had a class, eyi-eyi-yo,
And in that class she had some kids, eyi-eyi-yo.
With a nose-picker here and a bed-wetter there,

> *Here a picker, there a wetter,*
> *Everywhere a picker-wetter.*
> *Miss Macdonald had a class, eyi-eyi-yo!*

This song could get you thrown out of LAC, but if you whispered "eyi-eyi-yo" quietly, you could ripple the grade one bench with giggles.

"This world is not my home," warbled Timmy Maret beside me on the bench. Timmy flicked his long red hair out of his eyes and rubbed spit across the Emperor's receding copper hairline while he sang. The old Negro spiritual was one of our favorites. What did we know about African slaves in the American South? What did we know of the clapping and swaying gospel choirs in African America? Nothing. As far as we were concerned, this was our chorus, a song that explained to us why we were here, and why we lived here so lightly.

Just like Abraham in the Bible, our parents had heard the call of God to leave kith and kin and go to a land God would show them. The story was simple. Once you had heard God's call and been saved, you realized that this world was not your home and you were just a-passin' through on your way to heaven. Your real home was never here, always Somewhere Else. This realization changed your whole life. You gave up the ways of the world and committed yourself to the ways of God. When my mother left Canada at nineteen for Ethiopia and my father was in his early twenties, they gave up the care of their own parents for the care of God. They had become charged with the responsibility to witness to others, to help them realize the spiritual choices they needed to make.

"I am the door into God's sheepfold," Jesus had said. And we carolled:

> *One door and only one, and yet the sides are two,*
> *Inside and outside, on which side are you?*
> *One door and only one, and yet the sides are two.*
> *I'm on the right side, on which side are you?*

Witnessing was tricky. You had to screw up your courage to confront people with choices they didn't want to face.

Our missionary parents had organized weekend crusades at their down-country mission stations. We knew the requirements: first, an

Two men standing in front of thatched houses in the Obi region.

inspiring guest speaker; second, simultaneous translation from the guest speaker's tongue to Oromifa or Amharic; third, a *dass* of eucalyptus poles bound together into scaffolding and spread with branches for shade; and finally, a pasture area for the people's hobbled horses and mules. When these arrangements had been made, you were ready for action. The actual services had several other essential components: preaching through translators, singing in the five-note Ethiopian scale, taking up an offering, and praying out loud.

Therefore, armed with conviction and a clear procedure, Dougie Stinson and I hosted crusades in the boys' dorm. Dougie had hair as blonde and short as my brush cut, and he had even more freckles than me. He had gentle eyes and a ready smile, so we became fast friends right from the start. His parents were stationed way down country at Burji, so he shared my know-how about organizing crusades. Some of

the city boys had never been to one, and they envied our superior knowledge. For, not only did we know about crusades, but also, having been raised on remote stations, we had learned Amharic and Oromifa from our playmates and knew the intimate urgencies of translation. Dougie and I called our listeners from board games and Marvel Comics and Dinky Toys and GI Joes; we called them in their blue jeans and bathrobes and T-shirts and overalls. After our audience had seated themselves under the *dass* of bedsheets stretched between the bunk beds in our dorm room, we began the solemnities. We warped an old-time hymn by singing it in the five-note Ethiopian scale:

> *There were ninety and nine that safely lay*
> *In the shelter of the fold,*
> *But one lost lamb was far away,*
> *Far out on the hills and cold.*
> *Away on the mountains, wild and deep,*
> *Away from the Shepherd's love and care,*
> *Away from the Shepherd's love and care.*

A wastebasket passed from hand to hand, and imaginary bills of great denomination were placed ostentatiously in the collection. Timmy Bascom, whose parents worked at the Leimo hospital, had seen down-country crusades too, so he knew that if you didn't have lots of money you could bring a goat or an umbrella or a used jacket as an offering. He went to his dresser drawer, lifted out a clean white T-shirt, and laid it at Dougie's feet. Then, with a dignity beyond my years, I stepped behind the pulpit of dresser drawers and began to speak in a tongue never heard by human ear. Dougie translated into an impassioned dialect of Amhar-English. My sermon leaned heavily on the words *ha-ti'at* and *Yesus Cristos*, and the boys responded with the appropriate exclamations of *Amen* and *Igzabier Yemesgen*. For the benefit of the city-bred boys who didn't know Amharic, Dougie would translate the "thanks-be-to-Gods" and "original sins" so the poor lost anglophone lambs would feel included.

Many boys were struck by conviction and got saved at our crusades. Then we commissioned them through gospel words from a song we'd learned in school:

I will make you fishers of men,
Fishers of men, fishers of men.
I will make you fishers of men,
If you follow Me.

The songs we sang taught us to understand all kinds of figurative language. When Miss Macdonald had taught us "Fishers of Men," she had also taught us actions that went along with it. We had stood in the afternoon light that slanted across our wooden desks in the primary classroom, and, though we tried to cast our imaginary lines farther and reel them in faster than each other, we knew the chorus was not about real fishing. It was about witnessing, about hooking people and bringing them to God.

Now that Dougie and I had fished the boys from their sins, they in turn would fish others.

We had accomplished our objective, so we could proceed finally to the closing prayer. This element required the translator to borrow from the liturgical model of Mrs.-Johnson-before-bed-time. Every evening after story time, our dorm parents would lead the grade one to four boys in a nighttime prayer. During her husband's comforting, monotonous prayer, Mrs. Johnson would keep a sharp lookout through her horn-rimmed glasses, and she would snap her fingers sharply at anyone fooling around. Her vigilance reminded us of the close watch we needed to keep over our own fidgeting, wayward selves, as we'd been taught in another LAC song:

Oh, be careful, little hands, what you do!
Oh, be careful, little hands, what you do!
For the Father up-a-bove is looking-down-in-love,
So be careful, little hands, what you do.

With Mrs. Johnson's fierce-fingered model before us, I flattened my pulpit voice into profound prayer, while Dougie Stinson snapped away at the briefest flicker of a new convert's eyelid.

So it was that many were saved in the grade one to four boys' dorm. Eventually our captive audience was free to return to their Dinky Toys

and library books. Dougie and I, meanwhile, savoured this demonstration of our righteousness. We had discharged our obligation to witness. We had shown ourselves worthy inheritors of our parents' missionary calling. We knew from their conversations that you couldn't be a missionary if you believed all doors led into God's sheepfold. You needed to be sure of the One True Door, and you needed to be clear about which side you were on. When we were old enough, we knew we would go to Bible School to learn what we believed. After three or four years of learning, we would emerge, filled up with beliefs and ready to carry them to the ends of the earth. This was the life path taken by our parents, and we expected to follow it ourselves when we grew up. We chorused:

> *Far, far away, in heathen darkness dwelling,*
> *Millions of souls forever may be lost.*
> *Who, who will go, salvation's story telling,*
> *Looking to Jesus, counting not the cost?*

We knew the answer. Our parents would go — our parents *had gone* from their Canadian or Australian or American homes to Ethiopia, salvation's story telling. They told the story in hospitals, mission schools, leprosariums, and orphanages. They preached it under thatched roofs in the countryside and tin roofs in the cities. They preached it in *dasses* and in the open air. And we were the offspring of their adventure.

Even before I was old enough to read the words in the hymnal, I mimicked the vowels and consonant-clusters while the older kids sang the LAC theme song every Sunday afternoon. The kids old enough to read sang,

> *I am a stranger here within a foreign land.*
> *My home is far away, upon a golden strand.*
> *Ambassador to be of realms beyond the sea,*
> *I'm here on business for my King,*

while I sang something like this:

> *I am a strain-er here withinna foar-in laan*
> *I ho is far away ah-pawna old-en straan*

Am ass a door teebee of relmsby on da sea
I'm here on biss-niss or I'm King.

Eventually, we sang the hymn enough times for me to pick out the words. Knowing the words, however, didn't clear up the matter of their figurative meanings. I knew the "golden strand" meant Somewhere Else like heaven, but I also thought it might mean Somewhere Else like Canada, which was the mythic home my parents talked about. Canada was a rich place with lots of gold. I had been there once when I was a preschooler and our family had gone on furlough. I could remember Grandpa Adamson's black Chevrolet whispering down a highway as smooth as glass.

Our chapel hymns celebrated the impossibility of home and the permanence of pilgrimage. We were not like the thorny *garar*, or acacia trees, rooted deep in the red Ethiopian clay. We were like the *bahir-zaff*, imported from Australia. There were no *garar* trees on the Bingham school grounds. The forest that covered much of the two-hectare campus was almost all *bahir-zaff*, except for the line of cedars along the fence by the water tower and the pines by the chapel. We built forts out of the fragrant green boughs of the eucalyptus and made ammunition out of their light acorns for our after school wars. A big strip of bark would make a shield behind which you could safely pelt the other team when they tried to steal your home flag. The hardy *bahir-zaff* replenished themselves easily. You could transplant the Australian seedlings, let them grow a few years, and then chop them down every other dry season, and they would still send out new green shoots, even here on the other side of the world. We were like the *bahir-zaff*. We had been transplanted for improvement's sake. Our roots went deeper than those of the few diplomats and embassy people who sent their children to Bingham. These embassy kids would attend Bingham for a year or two and then their parents would be transferred, and we never saw them again. Even though we stayed in the country only as long as our parents' work permits were renewed, we knew that we were here long-term.

I knew, too, that we were singing about God the figurative King, not a real king like Emperor Haile Selassie, Lion of Judah and King of Kings. Yet this knowledge didn't stop me wondering if Ethiopia was a foreign land. But how could it be a foreign land when it was the only

land I knew with any certainty? I knew I was a foreigner in Ethiopia. It was not my land, but I knew no other. So which land was the one "Far, far away, in heathen darkness dwelling"? Maybe it depended on where you stood when you sang the song.

How were we students to understand ourselves? Sent away to boarding school at the age of six, I saw my mother and father for a weekend once every month or six weeks. Some children, whose parents could only get to Addis by plane, had to wait for Christmas, Easter, and summer holidays to be with their families. There were some kids who felt abandoned by their parents at Bingham, and I certainly hated to go back after weekends or holidays at home in Obi. I think I speak honestly, however, when I say that, although I missed my parents, I loved school. The dorm was twenty friends at a permanent pyjama party. These friends became as much like family members as my older brother and sister, who had gone to Bingham before me and were there to help me adjust to life away from home.

Bingham offered plenty of diversions — besides periodic crusades in the boys' dorm. The library had rows and rows of books that were washed every afternoon with warm sunshine from the big west windows. Upstairs, a whole room full of *National Geographic* magazines offered pictures of sharks and naked people and volcanoes. The wide, green soccer pitch urged us to whinny and gallop like the Black Stallion and his wild mares.

Our teachers during the younger grades were the Protestant equivalent of nuns — single women who had devoted themselves to God's work and who gave us a strict but kindly education. Though Miss Macdonald, Miss Wolman, and Miss Willey didn't wear wimples or veils, they did share an unofficial uniform very similar to that worn by nuns today. They all had short hair, wore horn-rimmed glasses, and dressed in white or cream-coloured blouses with pleated skirts. They wore flat, sensible shoes, and they shared an apartment above the grades one and two classrooms down the hill from the soccer field. We understood that this

was their very private domain, and so we never dared to ascend the stairs even to peek in at what must surely be a sumptuous abode. These women were the sources of all our knowledge, and we expected that their splendid intelligence must accompany a perfect sophistication. Miss Wolman's grass was proof of the elegance of their tastes. To the left and right of the sidewalk leading into the classrooms and protected by low, perfectly scissored boxwood hedges, she nurtured two six-metre squares of mesmerizing, short, blue-coloured grass. I had never seen a golf green so had no way to imagine where she had found this impossible thing. We knew that any kid tempted by the unmatched colour and density of this grass to place the tiniest bit of a toe on it was sure to get the strap for desecrating Miss Wolman's cherished lawn.

Of the three primary teachers, I had Miss Willey longest, for she taught me both grades three and four. She had salt-and-pepper coloured hair that curled around her ears and at the top of her collar. She presided over our learning with a ready smile and a quick, alto voice. Her classroom was a calm, quiet place where you were expected to work hard, but there was also time for fun. Each morning, you had to make sure you got to the blackboard early enough, not only to write your answers to the multiplication and division problems that she had listed on strips of Bristol board, but also to flip the chart over and correct yourself before the bell rang. If you got there too late, you would have to waste precious recess time standing at the board while your friends played prisoner's base on the soccer field. This danger aside, there were exciting contests in Miss Willey's class. A bar graph near her desk recorded in different-coloured columns the number of pages each student had read. At the end of the week, the student with the tallest column got a candy bar. Philip Jackson usually won. However, I won once by planning a blitzkrieg upon the blue set of *Our American Heritage* hardcovers on the shelf at the back of the room. If you finished your arithmetic or spelling lesson before the others in the class, Miss Willey would let you sit quietly at your wooden desk and read. For a whole week, I stole every minute I could to rush through the engrossing volumes on Abe Lincoln, Kit Carson, Davy Crockett, or Daniel Boone. Timmy Bascom gave me the idea when he won the week before with the same set of books.

The dorm, too, offered homelike comforts. In fact, Mrs. Johnson had told us we should think of it as home-away-from-home, and she

tried hard to make it so. There was solace in story time just before lights out, when she gathered bathrobed and pyjama'd boys on her living room carpet and read Laura Ingalls Wilder's "Little House" books aloud. While Laura's Pa bowed his fiddle, we sang:

> *Oh give me a home*
> *Where the buffalo roam,*
> *Where the deer and the antelope play,*
> *Where seldom is heard a discouraging word,*
> *For what can the antelope say?*

That last line should have been, "And the skies are not cloudy all day," so when we chortled our replacement of the song's last line, Mrs. Johnson frowned and said, "Some boys are just a bit giddy." She didn't click her fingers, though. Clicking was reserved for prayer.

Wilder's stories of homemaking in a land we could only imagine riveted our ears to Mrs. Johnson's voice. We listened raptly to step-by-step directions on how to make sugar donuts or calico curtains. What did we know about the best way to saw ice blocks from a frozen lake? What did we know of keeping sleigh horses' noses defrosted on frigid Dakota nights? Nothing. But these stories were our stories, acquainting us with the world far, far away which our parents called "home."

After story hour we went to the bathroom to brush our teeth and wash up. Every event had its own entertainments. In the bathroom you could see how far you could stand from the sink and still hit the bowl when you spit out your rinse water. You could play the same game when you peed at the urinal. Then, you could slick back your hair with a wet comb and pretend to be Mr. Mead, who ran the workshop and whose hair was always glossy despite the grease and sawdust of his job. Or you could smuggle partial tubes of Colgate toothpaste and enjoy the peppermint taste at your leisure the next day in your fort of *bahir-zaff* branches. In the fort, you could get dizzy on the menthol smell of green eucalyptus, a scent as pungent as the English-made jars of Vicks VapoRub that Mrs. Mead, the school nurse, kept on a shelf in the infirmary. There was always something interesting to do at Bingham — so many things to do that, sometimes, visits from Mom and Dad felt like an intrusion.

A weekend visit home to Obi, however, would quickly dismantle my indifference. I would develop sudden headaches when we had to drive back to Addis and school. I could even turn on a mild temperature when Mother put a thermometer under my tongue. Such scenes watered my parents' eyes when they waved goodbye and drove out of the school gates. They hated to live apart from their children, but what else could they do and still follow the call God had placed on their lives? They had given up their own parents for God, and now they had to give up their children too. Bingham was the best solution, my parents reasoned, not only because it gave us a good education but also because it was run by our own mission. This allowed my mother to serve several terms on the school board and to have some influence on our lives at school. Our parents loved my siblings and me and wanted to be with us, but God's work came first:

> *Seek ye first the Kingdom of God*
> *And His righteousness,*
> *And all these things*
> *Shall be added unto you.*
> *Allelu, alleluia.*

We sang the words, and I knew what they meant. God came first, family second. We children were loved, but we stood in line behind God.

The song, however, was subtler than this obvious meaning. It celebrated a contradiction. If you put God first, the song said, then everything else you desired would be added as well. The tricky part was that you had to keep the order straight. You couldn't pretend to put God first just to get all the things you really wanted. That would be cheating. You had to put God first, period. We knew the story of how God told Abraham to take his son, Isaac, to a mountaintop and offer him as a sacrifice. It was a test. Not until Abraham actually raised the knife, glinting in the sunlight, could God be sure that Abraham loved Him first. When God was sure, He rewarded Abraham with flocks and herds and a whole nation of descendents through his son Isaac, who, of course, was spared the knife.

"You get the whole Jewish nation from putting God first," I told

Timmy Bascom one night while we were brushing our teeth in the bathroom. "And the Arabs come from putting your own way first. Abraham and Sarah got tired of waiting for God's promise. So instead of waiting for Isaac, they set it up so Abraham could have a baby with Hagar. But she was just a servant and wasn't married to Abraham, so even though Ishmael was older, Isaac got his father's blessing. That's why the Jews and Arabs are always fighting."

"Is not," said Timmy. "You're mixing it up with the story of Jacob and Esau, when Jacob stole his older brother's blessing." He stepped back two steps, bulged each cheek in turn with rinse water, and then spewed a stream at the sink. His square jaw rounded into a smile when most of it hit the target. "See that?" he exulted. When he laughed, his small round ears lifted slightly with his dark eyebrows, while the black cap of his hair seemed to slide back on his head.

"Is so," I retorted. "It happened with Isaac and Ishmael, too. It all depends on putting God first."

The chorus taught us a paradox: when God's work came first, family would come first, too — in a different way. God would see to it. I understood, as did the embassy kids, who didn't stay in the dorm because their parents lived and worked in Addis. Even though they lived at home, they knew their mother's or father's day at the office had to come first. Thus, they didn't complain about being raised by nannies and housemaids and chauffeurs. They had to negotiate their parents' commitments, just as we did. We did not know childhood could be any different, for the missionary story was the air we breathed. We needed that air to sing our songs. And these songs carried compensations for us children, too. If heaven was our real home and we were merely passin' through this earth, so too our real father was God. This father was a King, Creator of the Universe, Potentate of Time, and we were soldiers in his victorious army. The hymn "Onward Christian Soldiers" was our grade one class's favourite LAC song. The martial rhythm inspired parades down the dormitory hall, regiments of roommates who shouldered brooms and mops and shouted the words:

> *Onward Christian soldiers, marching as to war,*
> *With the cross of Jesus going on before.*
> *Christ the royal master leads against the foe*

Forward into battle, see His banners go.
Onward Christian soldiers, marching as to war
With the cross of Jesus going on before.

Marching was the closest we ever got to dancing. It made our hearts race. Our arms and legs entered the music in time with our roommates' arms and legs, and the music welled up in our bodies till it burst out our lips with all the force of our lungs. We drummed on plastic pails and waste-baskets until Mrs. Mead banged on the ceiling of the infirmary below. We heard none of her protests. Parade! Parade! We were soldiers on parade!

We were as full of glory and purpose as the parades I had seen at the village school near Obi. The orderly lines and the straight-straight backs had made the Oromo students more than children. They had looked ready and strong, as though they had made a firm resolve and were on their way to secure it. The tri-coloured flag of Ethiopia — green for growth, yellow for gold, and red for blood — rippled powerfully from the top of a long *bahir-zaff* pole. The Emperor's insignia of the Lion of Judah, with his standard clutched proudly in one paw and jutting over his powerful shoulder, shimmered and danced in the middle band of yellow-gold.

Etyopia, hoy!
Dess ye-bellish
Be-Amlakish hile be-Negusish
Tebaberowal inah arbignochish . . .

The national anthem soared from the marching lips, a proud prayer of accomplishment and praise. I knew some of the Amharic words. I knew the first three lines meant "O Ethiopia,/ Sing out your joy/ In the power of your God and King," but I didn't know until I was an adult what *Tebaberowal* (united together) and *arbignochish* (your patriot-ancestors) meant. What did I know of the Oromo resentments against the Amhara landowners who came at harvest time from Addis to collect their half of the tenants' crops? What did I know of the secret indignation building toward the overthrow of Haile Selassie in 1974? Nothing at all. His Majesty's noble hairline was permanently etched on the copper

A parade at the village school near the Obi mission station.
Ato Asfaw, with the baby at his feet, is the teacher, and Ato Amara,
standing by the flagpole, owned the land where the school
was located and acted as the school director.

coins. His reign was as necessary as money. He was *garar*, as permanent as Ethiopia itself. The song made a family of all Ethiopians forever.

To my preschool eyes, the Oromo marchers were uniformly Ethiopian, and I couldn't join in the parade because I was Canadian. They had brown skin; I had pink. My preschool playmates, Zenebech and Mulugeta, would learn Amharic at their school, while my school would teach me English. My young heart had thrilled with the grandeur of the parade as well as the sight of Ato Asfaw, one of the teachers, thrashing with a green *bahir-zaff* switch the bare legs of a student whose feet could not find the beat of the march.

The songs at Bingham confirmed what I had already known. Our marches were different from theirs. "*Etyopia, Hoy!*" was a song to which I could never belong. Our hymns, like theirs, urged us to be happy under the power of God and King, but our God and our King were different from theirs. Our God was real and our King, figurative. Their King was real (I had seen him walk down a red carpet) but their God, questionable. They couldn't have the same God we did because we sang "One Door and Only One." As a result, we couldn't be united together, nor did we share the same patriot-ancestors. We were not *garar*; we were *bahir-zaff*. We were not endemic, but an improving strain. So I couldn't be part of the Obi parade; it was out of the question. And every Sunday in LAC, with an awareness that grew by tiny increments, I stood with the others at the grade-one bench and sang:

> *I am a stain-er here withinna foar-in laan.*
> *My home is far away uh-pawna gold-en straan.*
> *Am ass a door teebee of relmsby on da sea,*
> *I here on biss-niss for my King.*

Ferenjie Nature

I'm glad now that I never did in fact get around to setting the first trap. John had shown me back when we lived at Obi how to set a box trap for wild birds. It was very simple. You got a heavy wooden box and placed it open-side down on the grass. Then you tied a long piece of string to a stick, which you placed under one end of the box to prop it up. Next, you spread a handful of grain or breadcrumbs under the propped-up box to attract birds. Finally, you unwound the string so you could sit back a ways and keep a lookout. When a bird ventured under the open jaw of the tilted-up box, you tugged on the string so the stick pulled out from under the box, which dropped over the bird. The tricky part, John had told me, was getting the bird out from under the box, because you had to lift the box enough to get your hand around your quarry but not enough for the bird to see the crack of daylight and flee for the open sky. John had schooled me to patience in the business of trapping birds. It worked best, he told me, if you put the handful of bread crumbs under the box for several days running before you actually sat with the string in your hand and looked for the chance to give it a pull.

John's instructions on box traps came back to me after he and Sharon had gone to finish high school in Alberta, and the remaining four in our family had moved to Sheshemane. So many exotic birds flitted between the loquat and avocado trees at Sheshemane that I developed the fantasy of building my own aviary. I would build a huge birdcage, I dreamed, out of chicken wire and wooden studs, much like the pigeon cage John and Dad had built when we lived at HQ in Addis, but instead of filling it full of boring old, poop-dropping pigeons, I'd fill mine with the

brightly painted birds that flickered among the sweet-scented gardens and orchards around the missionaries' houses at Sheshemane. There were sparrow-sized, black-and-white pintailed whydahs, whose sixty-centimetre black tail feathers floated behind them when they flew like streamers on a boy's kite. Paradise flycatchers had dark blue, crested heads, rusty red shoulders and breasts, and two startling white tail feathers that matched the whydah's in length. Then there were the tiny fire finches, which looked as if they'd gone crazy in a puddle of red barn paint, and their cousins the cordon bleus, which looked like court jesters with their sky-blue breasts and ruby-red cheeks.

I never analyzed why I wanted to capture these bits of bright feathers and put them in my private aviary. Was it that I wanted intimacy with their otherness? Or maybe a sense of borrowed brilliance? Did I think they would add colour or mystery or vitality to my everyday life? Perhaps I thought my status would rise among the children of the missionaries who served as doctors, horticulturalists, and maintenance men in the leprosy hospital and rehabilitation farm at Sheshemane. Maybe I thought a cage of exotic birds would command the respect of older boys such as Eddie McClenny or Mark Rogers or Danny Creighton. But why did I need to capture these wild birds to accomplish these goals? Why wasn't it good enough simply to have them swooping and chattering around our yard? Why didn't I think developing extensive knowledge about the names and habits of these birds would be enough to distinguish myself among the neighbourhood of missionary boys? What is the source of the zookeeper's impulse — to bring wild creatures into our control, our way of life? I did not ask these questions, but I also never got around to setting the traps.

Maybe I didn't because of Owl. This non-name, "Owl," makes me wonder if our family's inability to assign creative names to our pets may have been a sign of our unconscious discomfort with the whole process of domestication. As with our later pets — Bambi the miniature antelope, Tota (the Amharic word for "monkey"), and Pupsi our poodle — Owl's species became its name. We did bring the owl, the dik-dik antelope, and the vervet monkey into our household and out of their native worlds, but despite our best efforts to make them welcome, they resisted our attempts to incorporate them into our lives, and the non-names remain as signs of the distance they managed to keep. The only one who

John, our mother, with Owl perched on her finger, and me.

did fit seamlessly into our home was Pupsi, but he was different from the others — he was American.

I still have a black and white photograph of my brother, my mother, Owl, and me taken by Dad at Obi somewhere around 1968. A stubby, ten-centimetre burrowing owl grips Mom's forefinger. John's ten or eleven, and I'm seven. We grimace directly at the camera, while Mom turns a quizzical gaze upon the bird on her finger.

The snapshot is overexposed. Bullets of sunshine ricochet crazily from the white shirts John and I wear as we stand in front of the white wall of the *icka-bait*, the shed in which our family's shovels, rakes, donkey feed, and kerosene are stored. The dreadful rays over the

photographer's shoulder have knotted my eyebrows and mouth into a violent frown. My shirt suffers from characteristic over-tuck, the creased white cotton jammed askew into my tight waistband. John squints, too, but his hands lounge in his pants pockets — philosophic in the face of solar assault. His white shirt slides smoothly into the band of his pleated pants. The round shadow of his head bites a half-moon out of the flowered shoulder of Mom's cotton dress.

Amazingly, the nocturnal hawk, which can detect the slightest rustlings of a night insect, trains two unblinking eyes upon the blazing cameraman. The owl is fierce symmetry. Two ear tufts stand erect at the corners of its skull; a pair of black semi-circles frames its face in dark parentheses. A white X joins the opposite ends of these parentheses and crosses exactly above its hooked beak. Each eye fills one of the lateral triangles formed by the X, so everything converges at the beak. The only dissymmetry occurs in its wings. Apparently, Owl had been settling its balance when the camera shutter fell, for one wing leans, partly open, against Mom's bent wrist. With pinions extended, this wing is twice the length of its stubby torso.

We had bought the pygmy predator from neighbourhood children, who would knock on our back door from time to time and display a creature they had stunned with a stone while watching herds in the field. They would come with a dik-dik or a baby baboon or a hornbill on the off chance that the pink *ferenjies* might pay a *simuni* coin or even a whole *birr* for the bit of dazed wildness. Sharon, John, Marianne, and I wanted every stunned and blinking animal. Something in us longed to feed and nurture them all. We wanted to purchase their lives. Mom, however, wouldn't allow us to keep the ones that looked too badly wounded. She feared our grief at their dying as much as she desired to discourage the stone-throwers' entrepreneurial poaching. This time, though, she gave in. The owl did not seem damaged, and, despite its talon of a beak, it appeared too small to cause any serious harm.

The night bird was an aloof pet and not the kind you stroked or cuddled. Through the day, this member of the order *Strigiformes* gripped the curtain rod above the living room window. It stood so stiffly that it did not look asleep, but we had no other name for its daylong stillness. It emitted no sounds, did not seem to have any voice at all. In fact, it offered only two proofs that it was alive. It ingested the bits of ground

beef Mom gave it, and, after Dad turned off the kerosene pressure-lamps at night, we heard its feathers whistle softly through the air in our rooms. We dreamed under warm blankets while sibilant wings searched our exhalations for small prey.

Owl had a third vital sign. After a couple of nights, Mom noticed dry chalk streaks on the living room curtains. These signs of vitality in the owl bowel spelled a change of quarters. Our little predator could stay in the house with us in the daytime, Mom announced, but it must go in the old rabbit cage outside at night. This small, forty-five-centimetre square box of a cage had been vacated two months before when Dad had not seen our bunny cropping grass in the yard and had backed over him with the car. The empty cage seemed a good place for Owl. The nocturnal airborne missions had been vaguely troubling, but the daytime curtain streaks called for categorical action. Owl-bowel went outside.

Horror struck after only two nights. After we had finished breakfast cleanup on the morning of the third day, John and I rushed outside to visit our banished friend. We could not comprehend what we found on the floor of the wire-mesh cage. Feathers and bones. A tiny skull with a hooked beak midway between the eye sockets. Two sets of skinless claws, peeled like tiny bananas right down to the hollow white bones. There was not a sign anywhere of recent life — not a single proof. We gazed upon the disassembled parts of a museum exhibit.

It remained for our neighbour friend Negussie to give us a name for what we saw. "*Goondan*," he said, squatting with us before the cage. "It's the work of Ant."

Our family had gained plenty of experience with these centimetre-long black ants over our years at Obi. They were often called army ants because they marched in tightly packed columns of such great numbers that they wore two-centimetre-wide dust paths down through the grass. They filed through the countryside and pillaged every edible thing along their way. If one of us kids stepped unknowingly into their trail, we were soon yelping as they cut bloody pieces from our skin. Whenever Mom heard one of us scream out in the yard, it didn't matter who was looking — she would have our pants around our ankles in a second to pick away the ants pinched so fiercely into our skin that their legs wriggled uselessly in mid-air.

Ants had their own mythology. Their omnivorous urge was a timeless,

natural law. Negussie told us about the unwatched neighbour baby at Obi whose mouth and nose were so thickly overwhelmed by *goondan* hordes that she suffocated. John traded this story for the one Dad had told us about the missionary nurse in the outback who had once used the pincers of army ants for sutures.

"She squeezed the lips of the patient's wound together with one hand like this," John said, pinching index finger to thumb. "And then, with the other, she held an army ant like this by the thorax and brought it close to the seam until it took a bite. Then she broke its head off of its body and picked up another ant. After she had done this several times, the closed wound was sewn shut with a row of black bead stitches!"

Not to be left out, I told about the night Sharon dreamed her hair had caught fire. She could still smell the smoke in her nostrils when she woke to find that a division of ants had streamed across her pillow and begun to build a garrison in her hair. All three of us knew a Christian had to be careful not to leave a Bible open on the floor or a *goondan* battalion would capture a page and carry it off to Babylon.

Dad fought them with the most powerful weapon he knew — DDT. "You kids keep away from here," he would bark as he crouched at the foundation of our house, where he sprinkled a moat of white powder. They were indomitable, however, always finding another way, surviving his chemical warfare, returning with an insurgency of their own. We would find them seething around the chicken bones in the kitchen garbage one morning, and then, having stripped the bones clean, they would disappear as mysteriously as they had arrived. Now they had got Owl, carried off its molecules to their secret underground cells.

Negussie seemed untroubled by Owl's demise. "*Goondan* is like that," he told us. "He appears, eats all he sees, and disappears. It is his nature." Negussie's eyebrows arched high on his forehead and gave the impression of a permanent smile.

This explanation seemed to satisfy John, but not me.

"It's because we put it in the cage," I muttered. "If Owl was in its burrow and *goondan* attacked it, it could fly to a high branch and pick them off."

"You're such a *ferenjie*!" Negussie teased. "Always, always responsible for everything!"

"It's not our fault," John reasoned. "We didn't know."

But I *did* feel responsible. And I didn't think ignorance excused us. Because we didn't know how things worked in the nighttime world of owls and ants, we had hobbled Owl, and his enemies had picked it to dry bones while we'd been breathing softly in our beds.

"You know what?" I said to John and Negussie. "It never once said 'Who'!"

Negussie looked mystified.

"That's what we think owl says in English," John explained. "The owl's call is like the question, 'Who?'"

Maybe I never built the aviary at Sheshemane because Owl had made me wary of cages. It could also be that the lesson on independence I learned from Bambi put me off the idea. Like Owl, Bambi had been another silent miniature that we tried, unsuccessfully, to incorporate into our household. We hadn't named her, either, as she came, already named, from the home of Mr. Raja Thomas. The Indian schoolteacher taught in the government high school, first in Woliso town, and later in Indabirr, eighty kilometres to the southeast. Mr. Thomas and his family took occasional furloughs back home, like we did, to visit relatives and friends. So we took care of Bambi at Obi for the two or three months they were in India.

I am startled when I look up "dik-dik" in my dictionary. The Amharic word for the animal, *madaqua*, is also the Latin name for this genus of tiny East African antelope. Was the Amharic domesticated into Latin? Or was the Latin word crossbred into Amharic during the Italian occupation in the 1930s? Names migrate in surprising directions: an Indian family with a Christian surname and living in Ethiopia called their Latinate *madaqua* "Bambi," and by so doing they introduced me to Walt Disney long before I ever saw the movie.

Our Bambi had enormous long lashes that circled large, round eyes as dark and lustrous as her nose. Black and copper hairs shot through her short brown coat. Her slim legs tapered to neat black hooves, while two seven-centimetre horns crowned her chiselled brow. Bambi called for much more petting than Owl did. Compared to Owl-bowel's chalk

streaks, Bambi's droppings were cute. Her delicate, edible-looking raisins nestled discreetly in the grass of our backyard.

Forty centimetres at the shoulder and twenty more at the tips of her little horns, Bambi could not convince us that she was full-grown. To us, her name and size made her infantile, just as, later on, we regarded Pupsi always as a puppy even when he was middle-aged. Having grown from infancy in the Thomases' house, Bambi didn't hold herself apart like Owl. She didn't resist our need to pet and stroke. She preferred leftover tea to water and diverted us greatly with her taste for peanut butter. The sticky substance made her work her black tongue around her mouth in a most un-Bambi-like manner. At night she stayed in the *icka-bait*, but during the day she foraged clover near the menthol-scented *bahir-zaff* trees in the backyard. Our need to circle her slenderness in our soft, pink arms overwhelmed us so often that she hardly needed her tether rope.

One day, while Marianne, John, and I lavished her with adoration, we noticed a neighbourhood dog eyeing our delicate friend. John threw a stone at the shaggy yellow beast, and it shied back a few paces. There, hyena-like, it lurked just out of stone's throw. At that moment, Sharon called us in for lunch.

Not now! How could we leave now? What would happen to Bambi?

"Mom says get in here right now," she replied with all the authority of the eldest child.

We got in there right now, heavy with gripes as we washed copper-brown hair from our hands at the sink.

Lunch was a tense affair, with Marianne, John, and me devoting all our attention to the window that opened onto the yard. What was happening out there? What kind of mother called the watchers from their posts just when a guard was most urgently needed?

Suddenly, high-pitched yelps filled our ears, and, half a second later, the yellow dog galloped around the corner and into view. Two fifteen-centimetre streaks of bright blood shone upon its matted chest. The whole family scrambled for the back door, only to find Bambi calmly cropping clover near the stand of eucalyptus. A wispy cravat of snapped tether fluttered gaily from her throat, and her horns glistened liquid scarlet.

Here was no Owl hobbled by our cage. She had broken free and

defended herself. This time, when Sharon called us back in for dessert, we trooped in without a grumble.

Something changed in me that day. The *madaqua's* decisive act of self-defence chased away not only the dog but also her infantile name. Like an insect breaking from an outgrown carapace, she discarded the cuteness we had settled on her. Her round eyes took on a darker intelligence, and her black hooves looked sharper than before. We spent less time now clutching her in our arms and pressing our faces into the warm, musky smell on the side of her neck. Instead, we sat on the back steps watching her ears flick at flies, and we listened for her antelope alarm of one sharp foot-stamp at the approach of a neighbourhood dog. The dik-dik had outgrown our solicitude. She had shown that, for all our anxious responsibility, she had little need of us. The result was that we, in turn, felt less need of her. Thus, when the Thomases returned from India and we took her back to their house, we parted from her with grave hearts and dry eyes. None of us felt quite right about keeping her any longer. We knew she could take care of herself.

If Owl and Bambi had discouraged my aviary-building impulses, Tota, the monkey we kept for a couple of months at Sheshemane, put them finally to rest. Back when we lived at Obi, our friend Negussie had found the infant vervet monkey clinging fast to the breast of an adult female some shepherd boys had killed in a maize field. Wary of the frightened baby's teeth, he had pried its four leather hands loose and gently bundled the agile limbs into a cloth shawl so that only its white-fringed, black face showed. Then he had taken the struggling package home. He raised Tota on table scraps at his father's home in Obi, and when he moved to Addis to apply for teacher's college, he took the full-grown monkey to live with him at his sister's house in the city. This is where I first saw Tota.

By this time, we were living at Sheshemane. John and Sharon were both in Canada, and Marianne and I were the only kids at home. Dad had taken me along on a day trip to Addis, and, while we were in the

city, the two of us had stopped in to visit Negussie, his sister Almaz, and her children. While Dad and Negussie talked, I shifted from foot to foot in the flagstone courtyard and watched Negussie's monkey. I had heard Negussie describe Tota but had never seen the constantly moving animal before. Its grey-brown body blurred the air from eavestrough to porch railing to overturned wheelbarrow and back to eavestrough, and its tether chain streamed behind. Its hands never missed a grip, but if they ever should, its tail was insurance. I watched the monkey, while Negussie's three-year-old nephew watched me, two wet fingers in his silent mouth.

The images in my head of the Swiss Family Robinson made me beg Negussie to let me have Tota. I was thirteen years old and aware, but not fully aware, of the power my begging would have. I knew that Negussie owed much to the ministry of missionaries. He had been cured from childhood TB of the spine, he had been given the chance to attend elementary school, and he had been converted to the Christian faith. His whole new life — physical, vocational, spiritual — had come to him through the work of the missionaries at Obi mission station. When I asked Negussie to let me have Tota, therefore, I was tapping gratitude and obligation that I knew about but could not fathom. Nor was I fully aware of the implications of my request. I had not thought, for example, that he would need to explain to his shy nephew that Tota was going away with his pink friends from Obi. I did not consider that the nephew might miss his playmate. Or perhaps I did not care. Perhaps I had grown to expect the deference accorded to the *ferenjies* who had saved Negussie from a bedridden life.

Then again, maybe Negussie's nephew was glad to see the little bugger go. Maybe for his family, too, the monkey had been an impossible pet. For Tota could bite faster than an eyeblink. All the dexterity that filled me with awe when Tota sailed from roof to porch to wheelbarrow could turn without warning into a rage of fear and sharp teeth. The monkey bit me in the calf when we were taking him to the car. He bit me again on the other leg when we were getting him out of the car after the four-hour drive to Sheshemane. There is a little welt on my jaw that I occasionally nick with the razor even now when I shave — made by Tota's sharp incisors. He bit Bobby Bowers four times. He sunk

his teeth into Colin Creighton's thigh. Tota was too high-strung for the neighbourhood of missionary children at Sheshemane. And we kids were too curious to keep our distance. We could never predict when one of our sudden movements, a startling voice, a thoughtless gesture, might set Tota off again.

Because the eighty-centimetre-tall creature had arms and legs and a face that worked like a human's, and because he could stand erect and take things in his hands or sit with his legs crossed at the ankles, he pulled on our hearts like infants do. We wanted to love the creature. We wanted to dress him in doll pyjamas and push him around in a pram. His mannerisms were close enough to our own to look familiar, but his shorthaired body and leather features were different enough to make his every action a human parody. We laughed till our lungs ached at the way he scratched behind his neck like a puzzled old man. We thought it cute that he raised a glass of water quizzically to his lips with two hands, exactly like a toddler who has just been weaned. His dexterity was truly amazing. Not just in leaping and climbing, but in eating, too. Tota loved to eat grasshoppers. "Crunchy on the outside and soft in the middle," Mom quipped, when I told her we needed a Mason jar to collect insects. Tota could accept the open jar from my hand, grab a grasshopper, put the insect into his mouth, reach back into the jar for the next and the next, one at a time, until he had eaten ten grasshoppers before any one of them could spring free. The vervet's hand streaked the air between jar and mouth. How he put the ten grasshoppers in his tiny cheek pockets I never did learn.

For all Tota's ability to entertain, however, his nervous nature made him impossible to keep. The number of bitten kids finally forced Mom and Dad to realize the inevitable. Tota would have to go. By this time, Negussie had been accepted into teacher's college in Asmara, way up in the northern province of Eritrea, and there was no chance of giving Tota back. Dad therefore reluctantly carried the chain with its dangling monkey to the back seat of the car and drove out to a stand of fig trees down near the creek. Wary of Tota's sharp teeth, Dad gently removed the leather collar from the animal's neck and watched him scamper into the trees. We had noticed that monkeys never lived in *bahir-zaff* woods — something about the sharp scent, perhaps, or the lack of fruit

for them to eat. If you saw them anywhere, it would be near fig trees. So Dad went down to the creek, hoping the figs would recall Tota to his natural way of life.

I was relieved when we finally set Tota free because, by this time, my fear of the monkey had overwhelmed my fascination. I felt lingering guilt, though, over Negussie's monkey. First of all, I had taken him from Negussie and his family, who may have had better ways of living with him, for all I knew. Since Ethiopians didn't keep pets in the humanizing way Westerners do, I suspect that in Negussie's household the monkey had been more a curiosity than a pet. I doubt he had been expected to negotiate the kind of cuddling and fondling we pink kids lavished upon him. Our assumed responsibility, our need to love and nurture, seemed itself to be the problem; the trouble was with us, in our own *ferenjie* nature.

Secondly, I knew that, even though Dad had taken him to the fig trees, letting Tota go into the woods was no solution. The monkey's life was filled with human beings and his belly accustomed to table scraps. Now that he had been trained away from a wild creature's fear of people, the damage was done. We had never taken him into our house — his agility and wildness had ruled out that possibility right from the start — and he had passed the nights out in the *icka-bait,* as Bambi had done at Obi. He was far from domesticated, but nonetheless he had learned a hybrid life and was now neither fully wild nor fully tame. I knew Tota would last only a day or two before some farmer killed him with a stone for boldly entering a cookhouse in search of food. We lacked the nerve to put the animal down ourselves, and we couldn't take him back to Negussie's sister in Addis, so we just let him go into the woods. By letting him go, we released him to his likely death.

The troubles we had with trying to make pets of Owl, Bambi, and Tota make it all the more striking that Pupsi, of all our pets, was trouble-free. Once again, he was a miniature whose description became his name. When Pupsi first came to us, he was a ball of black wool the size of my hand. He would crawl up inside my sleeve and fall asleep in the cocoon

at the elbow. Pitiful and helpless, he would cry at night for his mother. We put a ticking clock in his bed along with a hot-water bottle to comfort him. His little claws would snag in the long hairs of our carpet, and he would stand in the middle of the living room and cry until someone came to his rescue. When we picked him up, he would lick our noses. His breath smelt slightly of sour milk. Whereas Owl, Bambi, and Tota had tolerated, more than enjoyed, our attention, Pupsi ate it up. He whimpered when we went away and exploded with delight when we came home. *This* was a satisfying pet.

You would think his perfection would inspire us to come up with a creative name, but once again we fell back upon the habit of description. He was a puppy, and his name made sure he would stay that way.

Pupsi was American. We'd acquired him the year after we moved back to Addis from Sheshemane. At our mission's English language church, which was attended mainly by missionaries, diplomats' families, and the members of foreign NGOs, Marianne made friends with a girl named Nancy Benz, whose father worked in the U.S. embassy. Nancy had brought her poodle from the States, and it had given birth to a litter. She was looking for homes for the puppies. Thus transpired the smoothest animal adoption my family ever managed. He sat on your lap in the living room and slept at the foot of your bed at night. He soon learned to go outside to pee, so we didn't have to worry about him outside at night in a cage or in the *icka-bait*. He came and went with us through the back door like any other friend.

This *ferenjie* dog was as natural in our house as he was strange in Ethiopia. Mek'des, the widow who worked in our kitchen, had never been able to figure out what manner of beast he was. His hair curled like a sheep's, but he walked on clickety claws. And he barked. We had told her he was a kind of dog, but he was like no dog she knew. He was too small, for one thing, and he wagged a stub rather than a tail. He lived inside our house and did not venture outside our compound into the alleys where local dogs roamed. For all his black wool and strangeness, Mek'des concluded, he apparently posed no harm, because Mr. and Mrs. Coleman let the children roll and tussle with him day and night.

The only thing that made perfect sense to her about this animal was his name. Pupsi's hair was fizzy, just like the American carbonated cola.

Therefore, despite all our efforts to get Mek'des to say "uh" for the first vowel of his name, she insisted on a short, flat "eh." To her, he would always be "Pepsi." Even a non-English speaker could do better at choosing an American name than we could.

Of the apartments and houses we lived in for brief periods in Addis, the Rickers' house down the hill on the Bingham compound was Pupsi's favourite. A long hallway with a polished cedar floor passed the study, the bathroom, and two bedrooms before it reached Mom and Dad's bedroom. Pupsi understood that this hall was made for him. One of us kids would lift him with one hand under his chest and the other under his belly, give him three demented rocking-horse swings, and on the fourth send him skidding down the hall on his smooth paws. He would slide right onto the braided rag rug in Mom and Dad's room, scramble to get his clickety claws under him, and speed back up the hallway to our outstretched arms. When he wanted to play this game, he would start it himself by racing full speed along the length of the hall, pouncing on the rug, sliding on it into the side of the dresser, struggling back onto his feet, and speeding back to the living room. We laughed to the edge of bladder control while we watched him clickety-click.

Mek'des would smile at his hallway antics, but you could see that she still wasn't sure about him. Ethiopians didn't keep pets. They had animals — donkeys to carry firewood and water, oxen for ploughing, cows for milk, and hens for eggs — but they kept them only for practical jobs. The dogs that frequented their compounds were useful as night-time guards, but they weren't coddled or fed inside their houses. Their mongrels foraged abroad for their suppers. When Ethiopians approached a compound gate, they would prod these ever-present curs away with the point of an umbrella or a walking stick. You never knew if these hang-abouts had rabies, so it was best, Dad told me, to do as the early Walaitta elders did and beware of dogs.

In fact, the only Ethiopian I knew of who kept pets in the house like we did was none other than Haile Selassie himself. Once, when I was eight or nine, I had seen his airplane land at the Addis Ababa airport, and when the short and dignified emperor stepped from the fuselage and descended the red-carpeted gangway, a Chihuahua had popped out of the plane and bounced pertly down the steps at his heels. I had given

a startled laugh when I saw it. From where I had stood on the crowded observation deck, the dog had looked like a yellow rat with tall, bat-like ears and a curly tail. It had been marvellously out of place amongst the decorated generals and cabinet ministers who lined each side of the royal path. I wondered if one of them might accidentally squish it when he stepped forward and bowed to the passing king. For these dignitaries, though, it was as if the tiny dog didn't exist. They had stood at stiff attention and bowed with tight, sober faces, and I could see that nobody was likely to reach down to scratch the saucy creature behind one of its pointed ears.

I liked the emperor's interest in pets. It made him seem not quite so stiff as those sweating generals and cabinet ministers at the airport. He kept other animals as well. Mom and Dad had taken us kids to see the cages near the palace where His Majesty's lions paced back and forth behind the iron bars. They paced and paced so much that I could see paths worn into the concrete floors of their pens. If we went at feeding time, we would see the lions wrench strips of meat from the bones that had been placed in their cages by the keeper. The fur around the lions' mouths would grow dark with blood and the air would grow rank with its heavy scent. These bones stank — not like the clean, white bones at the bottom of Owl's cage.

It made sense to me that the King of Kings and Lion of Judah should keep these lions, for the lion was the nation's symbol. The muscles rippling the flanks of these big cats had looked just like the powerful limbs of the lion on every wind-blown national flag. I understood, too, that His Majesty's Chihuahua portrayed a different kind of power than the lions did. The lions represented his public power — the glory of Ethiopia — while the tiny dog represented the power of his private whim. He was the emperor, after all, and that meant he could do things not customary for most Ethiopians. He had hundreds of servants to do his bidding, so he didn't need donkeys and cows and chickens to carry his loads or supply his food. He could afford to keep these toy animals just for the fun of it, like we kept Pupsi.

That's why Pupsi was so much more satisfying than Bambi or Owl or Tota — because he seemed to like the fact that we kept him just for the fun of it. He depended on us to supply everything he needed, from food to water to a place to pee. In exchange, he supplied us with love

and entertainment. Marianne and I could rely on his bouncing around our feet when we came home from school. We knew he would make the signs of delight at seeing us that Bambi would never have made. He needed us to put water in his dish, to take him out for his walk, to reward his good behaviour with a treat. Other missionary kids in Addis liked to come over to our house to play because Pupsi was so funny and cute. He made us popular with our friends without the necessity of a box trap, a cage, or the fear of biting. Because he was agreeable to the whole arrangement, he was our family's most successful pet.

Though the arrangement had to change when Mom and Dad were transferred to Canada in the 1980s, times had changed enough in Ethiopia for it to be fairly easy to find Pupsi a comfortable home. For, even though the pet-loving Emperor was long dead, there had arisen a new class of Ethiopians since the 1960s who were accustomed to *ferenjie* ways and would be glad to make a home for our American poodle. I had finished high school and left Ethiopia a year before my parents were transferred by the mission to serve as representatives in Western Canada, so I wasn't there when we gave him away, but I knew exactly where Pupsi went to live. The Mamo Gebre Meskels were old family friends, going back to Mom and Dad's first years in the BD in Addis, when Ato Mamo had become a believer in Dad's evening Bible class. We had visited their house many times over the years, so I knew Pupsi lived in luxury. Ato Mamo had studied in Italy and then returned as the CEO of the Ethiopian Petrol Corporation, before being demoted by the revolutionary government. The family owned an elegant stone bungalow that had a walled yard lined with rose bushes, bougainvillea, and short palms. Pupsi would run free on their emerald lawn.

And so Pupsi found a housedog's life in Addis Ababa and was not forced to survive the alleys like local dogs. When Mom and Dad saw him again on a return trip ten years later, he had a grey muzzle and moved more slowly than before. He had gained weight from the generous table scraps he ate from a dish in the Mamos' kitchen. Mom told me that when they entered the house, he ran on clickety claws down the polished floor of the parquet hallway, slid to a stop at Mom's feet, and popped up on his hind legs to lick her hand.

"It was like old times," Mom said, "because Mrs. Mamo said in English, 'Down, Pepsi!'"

Sex *and* Salvation

"What were you boys doing when I walked by a minute ago?" Mr. Adams asked. The Johnsons were on a year's furlough so the junior boys in the new dorm were under the care of Mr. and Mrs. Adams. Mr. Adams placed a hand on each side of the doorframe and leaned his balding head into Lawrence's and my room. It was time for lights out, when he did his nightly walk down the hallway to make sure we all were settling down to sleep. Lawrence and I hadn't realized he had heard our giggles when he passed by.

"What were you laughing about?"

The hot flush that crossed my face at Mr. Adams's question brought me to my second conversion to Christianity. I had first been "saved" as a preschooler when I asked Jesus into my four-year-old heart to cleanse me from my four-year-old sins. The confusion I felt now under Mr. Adams's searching eye, however, made me realize that even now, in the fourth grade, there was still enough sin in my heart to need washing white as snow.

"You can tell me," Mr. Adams said. He stepped forward and leaned one hip against the chest of drawers where Lawrence and I kept our folded socks, underwear, and T-shirts. He had small ears with just enough of a point on the top to make them look remarkably alert. "What were you doing?"

We had been playing a doctor game. Most of the rooms in the new dorm slept six boys, except for the small one Lawrence and I were assigned that year, which had room for only two. The two of us had just taken our baths and were lying, freshly washed, combed, and tooth-pasted, on Lawrence's bottom bunk in our flannel pyjamas. Lawrence's

fine brown hair had lain wet on his pillow, and I could see the silver glint of his braces when he giggled. I had been sitting on the edge of his bed. I had slipped my hand inside Lawrence's fly where I curiously fondled the hardening flesh and the silky pouch within. Lawrence could not keep the glee from squeaking between his clenched teeth.

This new game was scary and hilarious. I had never touched anyone *there* before, and no one had ever touched me *there*, except Mom or Dad with a soapy washcloth at bath time when I was little. Every school morning I put on my boxer shorts, T-shirt, and socks, and then I covered these with shirt, pants, and shoes. My body was always covered. Even at nights in the dorm, we put terry-cloth bathrobes over our pyjamas when we went in to the Adams's living room for story hour and then to the bathroom to brush our teeth. There were cubicles around the tubs and showers, so the boys didn't see one another naked at bath time. To guard against somebody flicking my bottom with a wet towel, I always made sure the cubicle's curtain was carefully closed.

To touch and be touched intimately by somebody outside my family — and not roughly or as a joke — was unknown to me. The sensation was wonderful. I loved being close to Lawrence, hearing his laughter, sharing his excitement. I liked the smell of his shampooed hair and the smoothness of his clean, tanned skin. I was glad to venture inside Lawrence's clothes, to satisfy my desire to know what it was like in there. I also wanted Lawrence to know what it was like inside of mine. I wouldn't want just anyone to know me inside my clothes. However, Lawrence had been one of my roommates for more than three years, ever since we were in grade one. He was sometimes funny and sometimes sad. He had a narrow face with close-set eyes and a pug nose. I trusted him, and I knew he trusted me. He wasn't the kind who would flick me with his towel.

Our audible delight drew Mr. Adams's attention as he did his nightly rounds. Now, here he was, calling for an account. He had smile lines around his eyes and mouth, but at the moment his face was serious. Had we done something bad? It looked like it. His face was Old Testament sober, like in my Bible storybook where Moses frowned and pointed his finger at his terrified brother Aaron, while the Israelites danced around their golden calf. Behind Moses, smoke boiled on a mountain slope.

"We were just playing," I said. I knew before I started that I didn't

have the right words for this conversation. In the game itself, there had been no words — only sensations and excited laughter.

"Playing what?" Mr. Adams wouldn't be put off.

"With, with the-thing-below-our-bellies." It was out. We were really in for it now. Would he take off his belt and whack us silly?

"It's called a penis. You can call it by its name."

I had not known an adult term for it before. I only knew the little-boy words: wee-wee, pee-pee. Even "wiener" was a new name I'd learned from older boys. None of these words seemed appropriate for this explanation to Mr. Adams.

There was no belt, no lecture, no accusing finger. "The penis," Mr. Adams continued, "is for sex between men and women when you grow up. So it's best not to play that kind of game now, okay? You boys get in bed and have a good sleep. It's time for lights out."

He must have thought we already knew about the penis and sex, for he offered no further explanation. There was no anger or punishment or boiling smoke. I was left with a new word, a large silence, and the troubling sense that I had wandered into something solemn and big. The intimate game Lawrence and I thought we had invented turned out to be already well known to adults. It had a language and rules of its own. I was ashamed of being a child, embarrassed by the authority of an adult who could see consequences I could not yet see. Adults *always* seemed to know better. When would I know better so I could avoid these stupid mistakes?

Mr. Adams's intervention posed another problem, too. It made me doubt the intimacy I had felt with Lawrence. Had Lawrence known about the penis and sex before and not told me? Or was he as ignorant as I? Much of my delight had come from the feeling of merging with Lawrence, of being inside each other's pyjamas. His laughter sprang from my touch; my laughter was born of his. Mr. Adams's question, however, sliced this mutual exchange into discrete parts. It put me back in my own body, inside my own clothes. I was no longer sure if Lawrence had felt exactly what I felt. Had his laughter risen from the same place as my laughter? How could I know? Maybe I had perceived his delight through my own, like looking at a blue sun through an empty jar of Vicks.

In the nights that followed, these doubts grew into fear. I would be

on the verge of falling asleep and my eye would catch the gleam of a white shirt in the closet. Someone was standing there! Someone tall and unmoving stood watching us through the open closet door! Just then the *bahir-zaff* tree outside our window would sigh in the breeze. I could hear the Watcher breathing! My every muscle tensed. But there could be no escape. The Watcher had chosen the perfect hiding place, for the closet was right beside our only exit. He'd grab me in an instant if I made a dash for the door. Every night he made his silent appearance, watching and watching. What was he looking for? Had someone sent him to check on Lawrence and me? Was he waiting for something? I grew red around the eyes from long nights of anxiously watching the Watcher.

I needed peace.

Finally, desperate from a week of troubled nights, I made a plan. I kept my bathrobe under my blankets at lights out, and when the Watcher made his appearance in the closet, I quietly pulled the terry cloth over my pyjamas and found my slippers with my feet. I trembled past the darkened closet door and out into the cold expanse of the hallway. Down the cool tiled floor I padded to the Adams's apartment, where Mr. Adams sat reading in the living room.

"Mr. Adams?" I ventured. "I want to become a Christian."

Did he link my desire for conversion to our earlier conversation? Did he feel the impulse to reassure me, to say, It's okay. What you were doing with Lawrence is a natural part of growing up? If he did, he didn't let on. Instead, he read me the Bible verse I had already memorized in Verse Group: "If we confess our sins, He is faithful and just to forgive us our sins and to cleanse us from all unrighteousness."

"Do you want Jesus to forgive your sins and to live in your heart?" he asked me. His face was serious, like it was the other night in Lawrence's and my room, but it seemed more tender to me now.

"Yes, I do."

"Then let's pray together."

I knew how to do it. I had done it before. My first conversion to Christianity had occurred after Mom and I had read our nightly bedtime Bible story in our house at Obi mission station before I came to school. Some of those Bible stories were scary. Like the picture of Aaron, terrified before Moses' accusing finger and the smoking cloud. Or the story of

David and Goliath on the recording of Bible stories that Mom some-times put on our battery-operated record player. "DO YOU THINK I'M A DOG?" roared the giant on the record. And I would run and find Mom at her desk or in the kitchen and ask her to turn it off.

Getting saved had been the answer to those fears. It dissolved trouble and complexity and left you clean and pure. I had cuddled up close to Mom on the couch. I asked Jesus to come into my heart and save me from my sins. Mom prayed, too, and her voice was warm and serious, so I knew I had done the right thing. I knew that with Jesus in my heart, I would be saved from the big-voiced giants and the boiling cloud of smoke on the mountain.

When Mr. Adams invited me to pray with him to ask Jesus into my heart, therefore, I knew the whole procedure. And I was totally prepared for the joy and peace I encountered that night. My messy heart was now nice and clean, and Jesus could set up house in there. I could go back to the room I shared with Lawrence without any fear. And I did. The Watcher in the white shirt never visited our closet again. I was immensely relieved. I went to bed in the evenings confident of rest and woke in the mornings refreshed and ready for the day. I felt a gentle warmth towards Lawrence, who, unknown to himself, had played a key role in my salvation. This current extended to Mr. Adams, the kids in my class, and the boys in the dorm. There was a clarity within; I had nothing to hide or fear. I had invited Jesus into my heart, and he was making grace in there.

Some weeks later, my parents came to Addis to get groceries and some supplies for the Obi mission school, and I found I had more accounting to do. They came out to Bingham to have supper with us kids before heading home again that evening. After the meal, we sat together on the stone steps in front of the dining hall. Sharon had already graduated from Bingham and was finishing high school in Three Hills, Alberta, so we were five on the steps. Of the four children, Marianne and I looked the most alike. We had the same slight build, Mom's sprinkle of freckles across nose and cheeks, and the same crescent moon shape outlining our chins. In comparison, Sharon in Three Hills had more of Dad's roman nose than the rest of us, while John had almost no freckles, and his ears were lower on his skull than anyone else in the family. John was nodding his carefully combed blond head at

something Mom had asked him about his schedule for memorizing five hundred scripture verses, and Marianne had borrowed Dad's pen and notebook to show us how she had learned to write her three best friends' names in the grade one class. Without warning Dad turned to me and said, "Mr. Adams told us you accepted Jesus as your saviour. Do you want to tell us about it?"

Oh, no! I had not foreseen that this event would get back to Dad and Mom. What would they think of me? I was a two-timer! Getting saved had seemed the right thing to do that night in the dorm, but how could I tell them about it now? Would I have to say the word "penis" in front of my grade-one sister? Would I have to tell them about the Watcher?

"You can be sure that God never abandons you once you have accepted him," Dad said. "The Bible says, 'I will never leave you nor forsake you.' You can be confident of your salvation and don't need to repeat it later on."

I know, I know, I thought. It's just that, well, it's too complicated. It's too embarrassing to try to explain it now. I'm sure that if I tell you the penis part you'll feel just as awkward as I do. And you'll think I'm a scaredy-cat if I tell you about the Watcher.

"I just needed to get right with God," I said piously. "I wanted Jesus to be in my whole heart."

I had been caught off-guard. When would the accounting stop? I had not possessed the vocabulary to account for the doctor game in answer to Mr. Adams's question in the first place, and now I was caught without vocabulary again. How was I supposed to explain my second conversion to Christianity? You only had to be saved once. Everybody knew that. Once you prayed to accept Jesus into your heart, he was in your heart. You didn't need to keep on inviting him in, as if he were deaf. I didn't have the religious terms to describe the crisis and resolution I had just been through. I didn't have the sexual terms to describe it, either. Not just the terms; because our family didn't talk easily about sexual matters, I didn't have the freedom to describe it. So I just clammed up, and I felt the recent clarity and warmth inside me shrink.

My third conversion to Christianity took place when I was fifteen and under conditions similar to my second conversion. I was learning exciting things from Vanessa, a girl who was in the class above me at Good Shepherd School, the high school I attended on the outskirts of Addis. Vanessa had honey-coloured hair that fell to her shoulders. Her brown eyes were shot through with gleams of copper and amber, and her skin was olivey-brown. She said her great-grandmother had been Cherokee. She had perfectly even white teeth, chewed breath-freshening gum, and was the most exotic-looking girl I had ever known. She was an American army kid and knew things beyond the scope of my missionary world. I had never been to a drive-in theatre or a burger stand, didn't have a driver's license, and had never been on a "date." I had had girlfriends before, but at Bingham we had simply spent time together after school or arranged to sit together in the same pew during chapel service. Only rarely, when our chemistry really heated up, had we gone down in the *bahir-zaff* woods to hold hands and maybe even kiss.

Good Shep was a bigger world than Bingham. Whereas Bingham had been run by SIM, Good Shep was run by a group of mission boards, so the students came from a wider variety of religious and cultural backgrounds, and the diversity meant a more liberal atmosphere. Vanessa had been raised in back-seat-of-the-Chevy America, and she grew bored quickly with my courtly ideas of romance.

Between classes, at recesses, and during lunch hours, she would take me by the hand and lead me out behind the buildings near the fence. There we would excitedly exchange the four- and five-page letters we had written one another the night before. We hurriedly stashed these in our notebooks to be savoured in our afternoon classes, and we got right down to the real business of "making out." Her tongue twined around mine. The tip of my tongue traced the smooth surfaces of her teeth. Her breath was warm and moist, her mouth musky. Her hands traveled inside my shirt and sent traceries of fire across my back. My heart hammered in my ears. We were addicted. At nights, after track meets and soccer games; during breaks in our rehearsals for the school operetta; mornings, after chapel; afternoons, before Yared's bus arrived and we took our separate ways — Vanessa and I met behind the classroom buildings to make out.

"Hurt me," she breathed in my ear. Hurt her? How? Why?

I was in over my head. The illicitness, the danger, the mutual vulnerability engrossed me totally. It compelled me toward a feeling of fusion with a person utterly different from me. It struck me as odd that people showed non-verbal love with their mouths. I had known kissing my whole life long. My parents had kissed me throughout my childhood with that closed-lipped smacking kind of kiss that was at once loving and respectful of our bodies' privacies. I was used to enduring the pecks on both cheeks that were part of the routine exchange of greetings in rural Ethiopia. I remember seeing Orthodox Ethiopians bowing and kissing the priest's cross or ring. Vanessa's kind of kissing was completely different. The whole thing of being close-close, face to face, and tasting her lips and accepting her tongue into my own mouth — it built a head of steam I had never experienced before. It felt "deep" somehow — emotional, even spiritual. It required mutual acceptance and openness. I shared my body, my health, my hygiene with her and allowed her into my private places, where nobody had ever ventured before. It was like Lawrence and I in our pyjamas, except this was right inside of me, not just inside my clothes. I grew completely dizzy when Vanessa and I necked behind the buildings. I lost sight of where she began and I left off.

I was also sure that this passion must be wrong. We went out behind the buildings to do it. We didn't want others to catch us. I, at least, did not think I could survive my parents' knowing what Vanessa and I did. I dreaded that I might be called to account. For, once again, I had no words. The possibility of being called to account only added to the dizziness. It fanned the fire under our passion; it became a kind of fuel.

Then, suddenly, it was over.

Our break-up happened too fast for me to understand it. I had told Vanessa about the difficulty of my guilt. What did our necking behind the buildings mean? Why didn't we want others to see us? I had told her that I planned, when I grew up, to be a missionary or a minister. It was the only language I had for the tension I felt between the heavenly calling of the spirit and the earthly delights of the flesh. At first she followed my lead and confessed that God had called her to be a minister's wife. In the following days, however, she seemed less interested in sneaking off behind the classroom buildings at lunch hour.

She began to take great interest in my friend, Ian. Before I knew it, we were finished. She informed me she was no longer my girlfriend.

I was too slow for this. My heart and mind tangled up. I had never let someone get so close to me before. I'd never trusted anyone with so much of my unformulated self, with the pulsing readiness inside my clothes. Now my guide had left me stranded on an unknown road. I needed to get back to familiar ground, to return to reference points that could help me gather myself together again.

The break-up with Vanessa brought about my third conversion. I had entered the spinning wonder of fusion with another person, and I had been shocked when that fleeting moment shattered. Like Mr. Adams's intervention in my games with Lawrence, the break with Vanessa made me doubt my deep feeling that the pleasure I received was identical to the pleasure I had given. My hot breath and knocking heart were jammed back inside my own skin. They were not signs of the magical space we had shared. The sharp separation had been restored: she was over there and I was over here. This division shrank the experience, made it feel small and selfish, not generous, as I had dreamed.

I felt both angry and guilty. Angry that Vanessa could so easily drop an experience that for me had been profound. Guilty that she might have done so because what I thought was deep fusion was really self-absorption. Maybe, I thought, my own passion blocked me from seeing that she wasn't as completely entranced as I had been. I worried once again that I had done wrong. If it wasn't wrong, then why did I feel upset and sad?

This fear motivated my return to God. Instead of the Watcher in the closet, though, this time my terror was given shape by a novel about the End Times called *The Seven Seals*. This book made a futuristic nightmare out of the persecutions predicted in the book of Revelation. As believers' arms and legs were hacked off at public executions in the novel's brutal, anti-Christian, twenty-first-century America, I realized how shallow my faith really was. I knew I could never stay true like the martyrs did in the story. I would deny my faith in Jesus on the spot to save my skin.

In fact, I was pretty sure I already had denied Jesus when I had made out behind the buildings with Vanessa. Didn't Revelation warn about a scarlet woman who would seduce Christians from the true path? To be a Christian meant denying the delights of the flesh, no

matter what others said or did. It meant keeping yourself pure for God. Everyone knew that you had to die to the body so the spirit could live. I closed the final page of *The Seven Seals* late one night and knelt at the edge of my bed, where I begged God to forgive me. I whispered that I was sorry for being sidetracked by Vanessa and for forgetting Him. I asked Jesus to come back into my heart and make me clean again. I was troubled by the vertigo inside me, and I wanted Jesus to bring me peace.

Over the next weeks, I began to read my Bible every evening with all the passion I had previously given to my nightly letters to Vanessa. I cast all my cares upon God, and asked Him to make me a new person who wasn't absorbed by selfish desire. I wanted tranquility in my heart.

It was not to be. The apocalyptic feeling I'd been fed by *The Seven Seals* was powerfully enforced by events in Ethiopian politics. After weeks of carefully avoiding the sight of Vanessa and Ian at school, I was startled one day in the break between French and biology when a pair of hands cupped my eyes and a familiar voice murmured in my ear, "Guess who!"

Vanessa turned me to face her, and her arms circled my neck. Then she pulled me to her. "You were always the one I loved!" she cried into my collar. "I was such an idiot. And now it's too late!"

"What's going on?" I stammered. "What's the matter?"

"We've got forty-eight hours to pack up and leave," Vanessa mumbled, her breath moist against my ear. "All American military and their families. We fly back to the States on Thursday. Mom and Dad brought me to school to get my stuff out of my locker and say good-bye. We're going home to pack."

She lifted her wet face from my neck and crushed her lips against mine. Her fingers ran through the hair on the back of my head, her breasts pushed against my chest. Right there in front of all my class-mates. "You were the one I loved best!" she said. "Write me in Denver." Then she was gone.

So it was over, and yet it wasn't over. I had given her up and rededi-cated myself to God. I had seen my error in letting her distract me from the pure path of the spiritual life. The minute she opened her arms, however, I returned in a flash. I didn't understand myself. How could I get a feeling of peace inside if I kept flipping back and forth between resolutions? Why wouldn't sex leave me alone, so I could get on with

my salvation? I had no chance, however, to observe any other reversals, for now, again, she was gone, this time forever.

I was wrong again. For, despite all odds, I saw Vanessa in Denver only four months later.

When the school year ended, my family went on a three-month furlough to Canada to reconnect with John and Sharon, now both in college, and to visit relatives and friends. Two events influenced the timing of our trip. A conference for Christian families called Basic Youth Conflicts was going to be held in Toronto in early July. Mom and Dad thought the conference might spark good conversations with John and Sharon, who were nineteen and twenty-two and whom we hadn't seen for a couple of years. The second event was the Lonneburg family reunion, organized by Mom's cousins, that was to be held later that month in Colorado Springs. The reunion would give us children a chance to meet many of the uncles, aunts, and cousins who were so distant from our lives in Ethiopia.

Basic Youth Conflicts intensified my struggle between sex and salvation. The conference was held in a huge hockey arena, like those stadiums where Christians were put to the guillotine in *The Seven Seals*. I was as impressed by the immense dome of the roof overhead as by the speaker's ability to hold the attention of the three or four thousand people who occupied the orange plastic seats. We copied notes carefully into the new-smelling, red vinyl binders we had been given at registration, as our leader pointed at the diagrams and outlines on his overhead transparencies.

"A family's father is like a diamond-cutter's hammer." The crisp public address system brought the distant dot of a speaker as close as if he were talking directly to me, or even inside my own head. "The mother is like his chisel. You kids are diamonds in the rough. If you are willing to submit to your parent's instructions, your rough edges will be shaved off, leaving you pure and glowing for Christ. The family is God's workshop. It's a place of protection from bad influences, where the raw material of youth can be stored up and seasoned until it reaches

maturity. And you know those frictions when you kids want to do something and your parents tell you 'no'? Well, that's when those rough edges are getting trimmed off cleanly. Sometimes it doesn't feel so good, but that's just in the short term. It's the long term, the final diamond, that counts."

I copied down the man's crystal voice in my red binder: "Lots of kids rebel against their parents. They reject the discipline their parents give them. They get into situations they don't know how to handle, but they've run away from the protection of their parents' advice. If you're one of these kids, get it right as soon as you can. Go to your parents and confess your rebellion. Tell them you're grateful for their guidance. Tell them you want to put things right — with them and with God."

He set his finger on the problem, I thought. I had been hiding away from my family's workshop when I was out behind the classrooms with Vanessa. If I'd listened more closely to my parents, I wouldn't have got so deeply entangled with her. My fascination with sex was one of those flaws in the stone that needed to be cleanly severed. Then I would emerge a diamond, sparkling and clear.

I recalled again the Bible verse I'd read with Mr. Adams: "If we confess our sins, He is faithful and just to forgive us our sins and to cleanse us from all unrighteousness." I knew that confession was gutless if you just confessed to God in your head. If you made your confession to someone else, though, you would be accountable, and you wouldn't repeat the sin again. That night, after we'd had supper, I told my mother and father I had done wrong at Good Shepherd School. That I had been rebellious and had hidden from them the extent of my relationship with Vanessa. I didn't tell them everything about those days behind the school buildings, but I asked them to forgive me for hiding away. I didn't want to hold secrets from them.

Were they surprised by the applications I took from Basic Youth Conflicts? Did they want to reassure me that this, too, was a natural part of growing up? If they did, they didn't let on. Like Mr. Adams, they took seriously my desire to get it off my chest. They simply thanked me for being honest with them and for wanting to get things right with God. Then we prayed together, me leading and each of them in turn, with voices warm and serious, that God would re-enter my heart and give me peace.

When we finished praying I asked them if, when we went to Colorado Springs, we could get in touch with Vanessa in Denver. I needed to clear my conscience with her, too.

I could see they weren't so sure about this idea. But I told them the Lord had really been speaking to me about the wrongs I had done her, and I felt strongly that I needed to tell her I was sorry. They said we could see about dropping over for a visit with her family when we were at the Lonneburg reunion.

Three weeks later, Vanessa met me at the door with a hug. "Isn't this great?" she said, as she led me downstairs to her basement room. "Who would have thought we'd see one another again!"

I glanced uncertainly at my parents as we descended. They were sitting with her parents by the coffee table, where teacups and a tray of cookies waited.

Vanessa closed the door when we got to her bedroom. "So my brothers won't snoop," she stage-whispered. She turned to where I stood awkwardly on the small carpet by her bed. "Man, have I missed you!" she said as her arms went around my waist. Her lips nuzzled my neck. Her tongue entered my ear. Her breath smelled like peppermint, and it was so close it sounded as if it came from my own lungs. The roots of my hair shivered. She pressed against me until my knees buckled against the edge of her bed.

Vanessa lay on top of me. She pulled her face back from mine and said, "I need to look at you. I can't believe you're really here."

I ran my fingers through her honey-blond hair.

"Vanessa," I said, loving the copper highlights in her brown irises. "I wanted to see you . . ."

"No kidding!" she whispered into my forehead. "I miss the old days we had at Good Shep. It's hard to start all over again, you know, in a new place."

"Yeah, well. I've wanted to see you so we could talk." I loved her body curving into mine. Her weight made me feel the life in my own skin. I was determined, however, to press ahead with my mission. I could never be a sparkling diamond if I didn't have the guts to say what I'd come to say.

"Talking's great, Dan." Her eyes gleamed as she spoke. "But necking's way better, don't you think?"

She rolled under me and slipped her hands under my T-shirt. They traced the ridges of my shoulder blades, my ribs, the soft slope of my waist. I kissed her high cheekbones, each of her closed eyelids, her lips. Her peppermint lip gloss tingled my tongue.

I pulled away and sat up with my back pressed against the wall by the bed.

"I wanted to tell you, um, that I was sorry," I stammered between deep breaths. "I think I treated you badly back at Good Shep."

"No way," she replied. She scooted across the bed and leaned her head against my shoulder. "It was me who treated you badly. Don't you remember? I went off with Ian. I wanted to make you mad."

This wasn't going the way I had planned. I had come here to right the wrongs I had done. She wasn't supposed to remake them into the moves of a lovers' game.

"I mean," I persisted, "that I wasn't really thinking about you. I was just thinking about me."

"Yeah," Vanessa said. "I know. I would have been pissed off, too, if the guy I wanted all to myself went off with somebody else. But it's okay now, Dan. I knew you were mad at me. That's why I came to tell you I loved you before we had to leave. I wanted you to know."

"Well, that's not exactly what I mean. I mean that when we used to go out behind the classrooms, even before we broke up, I was being selfish."

"Me, too. I didn't want anyone else in the world."

Why was this so hard? The language I knew — the confessions and the diamonds and the "getting right with God" — wasn't working. I was losing sight of what it was I'd come to say. How could I tell her the complex thing I didn't fully understand myself? I loved our physical contact, but it made me feel guilty. It was wonderful because it held out the promise of communion, but it was troubling because what I thought was communion kept turning out to be unevenly shared. How could I say I was sorry for my part of that failure without throwing a shadow on her sunny sensuality?

"I just want you to know," I said lamely, "that I really wanted the best for you."

"What a sweetie you are!" She chuckled contentedly. "Always thinking of me. Let me taste your lips again."

Thus, despite my best efforts, I didn't say what I'd come to say. As always, I didn't have the words I needed for sex. Nor for salvation, for that matter. Later, on the drive back to Colorado Springs, Mom asked me how things had gone with Vanessa.

"Pretty good," I said. "I told her I was sorry, and we had a good talk."

What else could I say? I had followed the formula I'd written in my binder at Basic Youth Conflicts. I'd confessed my sins, and Vanessa had forgiven them. That was an important step towards putting things right with God. I knew that Mom and Dad had gone against their own instincts in taking me to see Vanessa in the first place. Nonetheless, they'd done it anyway, giving me the benefit of the doubt. I needed to make them feel it had worked. How else could I show I was thankful?

There remained in me, however, a big, mixed feeling. I couldn't sort out my motives. I knew I had been sincere in wanting to put things right with Vanessa, Mom and Dad, and God. I had wanted to feel clear inside. Not to have secrets, not to be caught between complex layers. I didn't want to be hiding anything from my parents. I didn't want to hide anything from anybody.

In our tent at the Lonneburg reunion that night, I lay in my sleeping bag and tried to pray as I watched the shadows of tree branches cast by the full moon on the canvas roof. They sighed and swayed slowly in the night breeze. "Create in me a clean heart, O God," I recited from Psalm 51, "and renew a right spirit within me." I caught sight of a man's head and shoulders among the weaving shadows. He neither grew larger nor shrank in size. He just rocked slowly among the silhouettes, silent and watching. My Watcher! After the jolt I felt when his outline came into view, however, I felt no fear. I had seen him years before. I knew he wasn't really watching me. He was an illusion made of the magical mix of moonlight and branch.

I thought about my old familiar ghost, the white shirt hanging in the dark closet. I recalled my fear that I had sinned with Lawrence, that I was being watched. I realized how I'd always thought in opposites: clarity over here, confusion over there; peace here, turbulence there; salvation here, sex there.

What struck me, as I lay there in my sleeping bag, watching my old Watcher, was how my opposites came hand-in-hand. My experiences with Lawrence and Vanessa were driven by my desire to know other

people. That was its excitement — and its trouble, because the oneness I longed for was either too brief or an illusion in the first place. Sex was a golden hope that got me running forward, arms outstretched. Then something or someone slammed the gate.

My Watcher swayed among the shadows on the canvas ceiling, and I began to see my own patterns. When sex's bubble burst, I predictably limped back to God with my bruised hope, wanting comfort. If people couldn't satisfy my desire to know and be known, maybe God could. Maybe God could understand me inside my skin. It turned out that sex was my regular reminder of hope and its fragility. That's why it led me from one conversion to the next. The desire to be saved sought out the connectedness of sex, and the trouble of sex made me seek the peace of salvation.

Schwagged, No Kidding

"Get up, Coleman! It's riot drill!" Timmy Maret's red head swam in the air above me next to his upper bunk.

"Stop fooling around, Maret," I mumbled into the warm musk of my pillow. Why couldn't he be quiet just for a little while? Talk, talk, talk.

The siren stabbed the air a second time, however, and destroyed the last possibility of sleep. Two long wails, a pause, followed by a short wail cut off mid-cry. Through the past months, the riot alarm had shrilled regularly at Bingham Academy, but always during classroom hours. This was the first time we had heard it in the dorm before our usual wake-up call. Despite the early hour, however, we knew exactly what to do.

Timmy was down on the floor and pulling on his pants before I'd even swung my feet from under the blankets. Across the shiny-tiled floor of our room, Timmy Bascom laced his running shoes. Lawrence Bergson pulled a cotton T-shirt over his head. No one said a word.

When the two long wails rose into the air above Bingham Academy and spilled out into the Kwolfe district, and the third fell like a pigeon shot from the sky, we didn't kid around. I tried to moisten my suddenly dry mouth as I closed the curtains, turned out the lights, got in line, and waited for our monitor to lead us in single file to the tunnel under Bingham's main building. We called it a tunnel because it had been dug out from a crawl space under the kitchen and dining hall. An unassuming tool shelf at the back of the basement-level workshop hid its only entrance — aside from the trap door that had been cut into the pantry to provide access to food and water. You would never dream there was enough room under those floors for a hundred and seventy

kids and their teachers. There, we were told, we would wait in silence till it was safe to come out.

Riot drill was serious business. I'd witnessed a riot downtown once, and it was no laughing matter. On a Friday afternoon a couple of months before, Dad had driven the hour and a half from Obi mission station to Addis to collect John, Marianne, and me for a weekend at home. On the way back, he had a couple of stops to make. This was bad news, because Dad could turn the quickest errand into eternity. A box of whitewash mix led to a backslapping confab with Señor Luciano at the hardware. A packet of stainless steel sewing machine needles required story swapping with Mr. Singh at Delhi Dry Goods. A bicycle tube from Ato Dawit's New and Used Raleigh turned into a decade of anecdotes.

Ato Dawit's shop was a low garage half a block down from the six-storey United States Information Service building, also known as the USIS. While Dad kibitzed with the bicycle man, the sun beat in the windows of our Volkswagen beetle, and our tempers rose with the smell of hot plastic car seats.

Our simmering tempers suddenly chilled, however, when a crowd of people rounded the corner by Addis Ababa City Hall, three blocks away. Banners waved above their heads, their slogans echoed by megaphoned shouts of "Go home, Yankee!" and "*Etyopia Tikdem*! Ethiopia First!"

Earlier that day, when Dad had picked us up at school, he and Mr. Reimer, the school manager, had been talking about the student protests.

"I can't disagree with what they want," Mr. Reimer had said. "Land reform is way overdue — way overdue."

"I just wish they wouldn't blame the West," Dad had replied. "It wasn't the US that set up the system of landlords."

Now, the marchers eddied in the street in front of the USIS, only a hundred metres from our Volksie. They wore all the signs of the radical student movement: Afros combed out as wide as the students' shoulders; young people in unEthiopian-looking Mao suits or dashikis; headbands emblazoned with the hammer and sickle; megaphones and placards and banners.

"Go home, Yankee! Go home! Go home, Imperialists! Go home!" A rock hurtled up from the crowd and arced through a window on the third floor of the USIS. Others sailed after it. Soon, a rainbow of falling

Roomates in the new dorm: Kenny Veer, me, David Iwan,
Philip Jackson, and Philip Neville.

glass shimmered between us and the American building. Its light flickered and winked to the thunder of the crowd.

I'd once been inside the USIS with Mr. Ricker on one of his weekly journeys to get movies for Bingham's Friday film night. I loved film nights. The grades one to four kids, dressed in pyjamas and bathrobes, would crowd the area rugs in the lounge, while the older kids in grades five and up were allowed the dignity of day clothes and chairs. We watched Vision USA films on Yellowstone National Park or the Florida Everglades. *Ninety Minutes of Comedy,* a collection of Laurel and Hardy,

Charlie Chaplin, and the Marx brothers, was a big favourite. USIS movies alternated with BBC productions of Shakespeare from the British Council and National Film Board features like *Neighbours* or *Paddle to the Sea* from the Canadian Embassy. We loved *Ti-Jean*, a National Film Board movie about a tiny man who ripped across Canada, stooking sheaves and felling trees at jerky, superhuman speeds. Frenzied piano music set the pace. When it was done, we begged Mr. Ricker to show it backwards, so we could watch Ti-Jean spool a huge basin of spaghetti out of his mouth with a fork.

Now the student rioters rained stones through the glass panes of the building where we got some of our favourite movies. Laurel and Hardy and the other stars were under attack, along with everything else American.

At this moment, Dad leapt into the driver's seat and fumbled the keys into the ignition, thumbed his glasses over the bump in his nose, and slammed the stick shift into reverse. He jerked the car back around the corner a half-block behind us. He then sped down a side street toward the Woliso-Jimma road and Obi. Had they come upon us, angry protesters wouldn't have taken time to find out we were Canadians. Pink skin and English voices would have been enough to tag us as the enemy. I tried to swallow the bile in my throat. We were lucky to get away unharmed.

Most schools have fire drills. Ours, in the early 1970s, had riot drill. I was glad we had riot drill. Before I had seen the students stone the USIS building, I had liked riot drill for its sense of adventure. The cool, red earth of the tunnel walls had made me feel like one of Aladdin's forty thieves. After witnessing that demonstration, I liked riot drill for a different reason. I liked it because it was serious. It made me feel good to think our teachers had soberly considered the situation and come up with a plan to keep us safe.

Therefore, when Mr. Dubois, with trembling neck muscles and lips stretched thin, collared a fourth-grader named Mark and delivered three sharp slaps to the face for horsing around at the workshop entrance

during one day's riot drill, I thought he did the right thing. I felt my thighs tremble when Mr. Dubois's hand reddened Mark's cheek, but I didn't join the other kids who backed Mark's complaint that Mr. Dubois was too severe. I knew that riot drill was a matter of life and death, and there was no room for monkey business.

A riot could come at any moment: Miss Willey might be in the middle of checking our long division on the board; Mr. Ricker might be telling us about the difference between Left and Right wings in politics — it didn't matter. We knew exactly what to do. At the sound of two longs, a pause, and a short, we would get up from our desks, pull down the window blinds, and march behind Marion Entz, our class monitor, to the basement workshop's secret door. No talking or running was allowed from the minute the siren rang. Orderly regiments of students from our various dorms or classrooms converged on the workshop and the tunnel behind the tool shelf.

Now, in the early morning, our teachers' careful training was having its planned effect. Our classroom drills had set a pattern we could follow even in half-sleep. This time, however, I was sure it was not a drill. Mr. Reimer would never get the whole school out of bed just for another practice. Timmy Maret, Philip Jackson, Timmy Bascom, Lawrence Bergson, and I lined up with the others at the door to our room behind Stephen Scheel, our dorm room monitor. Lawrence's sour night breath flowed over my shoulder.

Despite the rule of silence, someone whispered, "Have the others gone yet? Hey Scheel, look down the hall."

Scheel recited the monitor's rules: "We're supposed to wait for the knock! It might not be safe to open the door."

We shifted weight from foot to foot, fidgeted in our clothes. How could my tongue taste of fish when I hadn't eaten any in ages? I longed to be able to rinse my mouth. Philip Jackson stifled a sneeze, but the forced air squeaked through his fingers like a fart. Lawrence and Timmy Maret started to giggle. Someone whispered, "Shut up!"

The door swung open to reveal our dorm parent, Mr. Johnson, with his pyjama top stuffed into his workday pants. His tense lips offered not a word as he motioned us down the hall to the exit. Outside, early sun glittered in the dew that frosted the grass and drenched the cinders of the parking lot. No sign of rioters anywhere. The damp, red stones

grated under our running shoes on our march towards the workshop. Dogs barked in the neighbourhood streets. The sky was loud with bird traffic. A rooster crowed in somebody's yard. The dew had rinsed the air clean, and the morning sounds of Kwolfe district sparkled in the air, pristine as the beads in the grass.

I listened anxiously for the megaphones spitting out metallic shouts of *Etyopia Tikdem!* and "Land to the tenant!" I scanned the *bahir-zaff* woods below the gym for evidence of headbands and banners. Nothing. Where were the rioters? The silence made me grow as hot as I had in our Volksie that day the protestors had rounded the corner by City Hall.

Were they noiselessly collecting forces outside the Bingham gates? Or had the watchman seen them through the cracks in the corrugated iron fence and called Mr. Reimer from his bed? I wished Scheel would hurry up and get us to the shop.

Inside the tunnel, sleepy kids in rumpled clothes rubbed eyes adjusting to the dim passageway. Teachers and dorm parents wordlessly arranged us in classes for the monitors' count. As each class from grade one to grade ten was accounted for, it filed to its assigned bench along the walls of the tunnel's several chambers. The serious, calm faces of the adults and the grade nines and tens kept the younger kids from starting to chatter or cry.

After we were all settled, Mr. Reimer got up on a wooden crate in the little open space where the rooms intersected and motioned us to listen up. His calm voice assured us we had done very well. We had gathered in record time, everyone was present, and we'd hardly made a peep. While we waited for news about the situation, we would have a bit of breakfast. We would line up class by class and receive tea and buns at the table under the trap door. He asked the blessing and then motioned to the grade ones on his left-hand side to start the breakfast line. The oldest students would go last.

The laces of kids' running shoes dragged past me through the rust-coloured earth of the tunnel floor. How could there be dust when the air smelled damp and a little like blood? Naked bulbs swung from electrical cords. Their light leapt unsteadily from the tousled hair of filing kids. We'd had no time this morning for brushes and combs. Slouched against the dirt wall on our low bench, we sat in jerky shadows cast by six- and seven-year-old kids whose hair flickered and whose legs

disappeared in the gloom below their knees. They jiggled towards breakfast on dark dust.

Half an hour later, I was sipping comfort from my cup of milky, sweet tea and wondering when the riot would start. Suddenly, the shuffling silence was shattered. The grade nine and ten boys leapt to their feet from their bench.

"April Fools!" they shouted. "There's no riot! It's April Fool's Day!"

The electric bulbs jerked on their cords, making the light wink in the hubbub. Dust rose to our waists. It tickled my nostrils. Everyone was standing and talking and laughing. I sneezed and dropped my empty cup. When I tried to pick it up, I got my fingers squashed under Timmy Maret's heel.

I tucked my burning fingers in my mouth. "What?" I asked Lawrence. "What did they say?"

"It's all a joke!" said Lawrence. "Mr. Reimer was in on it, too! Don't you know? It's April Fool's Day. There's no riot. It's just a joke!"

"A joke," I said. "A joke?"

No rioters with stones and megaphones swarmed around the school outside? No protestors? No banners saying, "Imperialists, go home"?

The tunnel had burst into shouting and laughter. My ears grew hot and the fish on my tongue grew thicker. My stomach heaved once, twice. I tasted bile around my pinched fingers. Something buried deep inside me burned and wanted to break through my throat. Any second I would erupt into laughter or tears, I couldn't tell which.

One of the grade sixes, Robert Coop, thumped me on the back.

"Shwagged!" he crowed. "April Fools!"

"No kidding," I wheezed between hiccups. "April Fools!"

Shwagged. I leaned a hand against the tunnel wall, my eyes and brain swimming. I had been completely and utterly taken in. I could see a guy like Coop taking great delight in shwagging the rest of us. But Mr. Reimer?

It was our schoolboy code that you shwagged your friends and they shwagged you. You didn't go crying to a dorm parent or a teacher if you'd been shwagged. To tell an adult was to admit you'd taken it seriously and missed the joke. Shwagging was something between kids — mainly boys. Boys had fun. We could say and do things we didn't really mean, maybe because we didn't expect ourselves to know what

most things meant in the long run anyway. We relied on adults and older kids for that — like the time I said "fuck" in grade three and Reuben Flynn, a fifth grader, told me it meant something really bad and I should never say it again. Older kids and grown-ups knew the meanings of things, and their knowledge made them serious. The older you got, the more serious you became, and you left shwagging behind.

The ninth and tenth graders were held up as models of maturity for us younger students. I'd heard Mr. Reimer himself remind them of their responsibility. But here he was, helping them make a practical joke out of riot drill! I looked at Miss Willey, who was still wearing her curlers, to see if she was laughing. She smiled as she told Marion Entz what a good job she'd done as monitor for our class. Despite the smile, though, there were tense lines on Miss Willey's forehead and shadows under her eyes. Mr. Johnson came around, in his pyjama top and workday pants, offering seconds from the teapot. His face was kind, but he wore no smile.

I heard Mr. Ricker say to Mr. Reimer above the racket of kids' voices, "It's good to be able to laugh, for once! All this tension isn't good for anybody."

"It's the best medicine," Mr. Reimer replied.

I knew what they meant, and I wanted to join in the laughter with everyone else. I wanted to bury my raw emotions and act as if I was unaffected, that I hadn't been shwagged, but the humour eluded me. If our teachers made a joke of riot drill, would we be ready when the stones started to fly? I had taken comfort in the seriousness of adults. Their sober contemplation of all the angles meant I could live without worry. This joke, however, left me not so sure. Mr. Reimer's participation in the older boys' joke threatened my confidence that everything was under control. And, as politics in Ethiopia grew more dangerous, my uncertainty about adults' ability to manage the situation only grew.

Within three years of our fake riot drill, Ethiopia had completely changed. Haile Selassie had died in May of 1975. The *Ethiopian Herald* reported that he had died in his sleep, while *The London Times* claimed

he'd been smothered with a pillow. The USIS had been packed off to the States along with all American military personnel. The Provisional Military Administrative Council had won out over its partners in armed revolt, and now it was hounding them out. Those very students who had risked prison when they commanded Yankees to go home and demanded the end of the Emperor's reign were once again the enemies of the state. Before, they had been revolutionaries; now they were declared counter-revolutionaries.

The students had started the revolution with their calls for land reform and an end to corrupt government, but once Lieutenant-Colonel Mengistu Haile Mariam's junta elbowed its way into power, there was no room for protestors or dissidents. The military thugs snatched the Marxism from the students' lips and sugared their own tongues with it when they went begging for Soviet support. Then, after they got their MiG fighter planes and Kalashnikov rifles, they systematically hunted the students — and anyone else who might protest — from the streets; they rounded them up like so many sheep in a pen before opening fire with their shiny new guns.

The students, for their part, formed the notorious EPRP, whose armed cells targeted junta members and collaborators for sidewalk assassinations. The PMAC declared *Kai Shebbir* and a sundown curfew. At night, we would lie in our beds and pull sweaty sheets to our ears to try to block out the pop and snarl of single-action and automatic gunfire echoing around the city. *Kai Shebbir* was meant to keep the students, and anyone connected to them, underground.

The government wanted to shove the mission underground, too. The PMAC had declared itself officially atheist, and they targeted missionaries by refusing to renew their work permits and visas. When Bingham closed for summer holidays, we began weekly trips to the airport to say goodbye to family after family. "Lufthansa Thursdays," we called them, referring to the weekly departure of the one remaining international airline. Every Thursday afternoon at four-thirty, Paul Cumbers and I would lounge on the plastic airport chairs and watch our parents tearfully crush old friends to their chests. We weren't leaving because our dads worked in Administration at HQ and still had valid work permits. Through the big windows of the terminal behind our departing friends, we could see the rainy season's customary afternoon

shower slant across the city. Clouds would obscure the summit of Mount Entoto in the background, while in the foreground the fogged windows of the blue-and-white taxis hid their drivers, who read the newspaper while they waited for passengers to emerge from the terminal. Paul and I would mumble goodbye to our classmates around the Double Bubble in our mouths and try to appear unattached to the wet-faced people by the departure gate.

"Hey, Creighton!" I once yelled across the terminal to my friend Danny, who stood with his family as they waited to lift their luggage onto the scale at the Lufthansa counter. "Which suitcase did you put the bomb in?"

Paul's hoot of laughter was cut short when my dad took three quick steps to where we sat and rapped me sharply with a knuckle on the head.

"That's enough!" his voice was thin and tight. "Now go and say goodbye properly."

I did as I was told. The clench in Dad's jaw didn't leave room for argument.

The exodus of our friends had one benefit Paul and I hadn't looked for, and that was loot. People were packing up so quickly they didn't have time to dispose of their goods properly. More often than not, they would leave a box or barrel at the BD with a note asking that the contents be disposed of by any convenient means. Paul and I dubbed ourselves Convenient Means.

The general divestiture turned up some fine treasures indeed. The Coles' clapboard crate, for example, contained a real crossbow, with a catapult of tempered steel, cherry wood stock, and a stainless steel bolt. We took this beautiful, deadly thing out of its box, walked down a-blow past the L-shaped building that housed the dining hall, administrators' apartments where my family now lived, and guest rooms for down-country missionaries. We considered this part of the HQ compound our domain. The whole property was surrounded by a two-metre-high stone wall that stepped down from the white-tiled, concrete-block administration building, past the L-shaped *chicka* building, and descended to our kingdom. At the higher end of down a-blow, a small parking lot provided a few spots for visitors' cars, and off to the side, under a large, spreading pine, stood a low concrete-block laundry building. Potholes

filled with runoff from the rain we'd had just after lunchtime pocked the parking lot. A waist-high retaining wall of stone separated the parking lot and laundry building from a green lawn with a peach tree and another pine on one end, and this lawn was edged with beds of marigolds, lilies, roses, and hens-and-chicks. A hedge and another retaining wall divided this garden area from the two stone houses at the bottom of the property. One of these houses now functioned as Mr. Schmidt's workshop, while the other, the one I was born in, was still used as a residence.

Ato Debray, the gardener, had left a pile of weeds and culled plants in one corner of the lawn, and I lifted out a large, cabbage-sized hen and stripped it of its chicks. "We can shoot at this," I said, and leaned the round mitt of fleshy leaves against a stone step on the retaining wall. The water drops caught in its green ears rolled and jiggled, clear as mercury beads. Paul loaded the steel bolt in the bow and levered back the wire cable into cocked position. He swept his copper hair out of his eyes and sighted down the barrel at the succulent target.

He seemed to yell "Ouch!" before he pulled the trigger, and he dropped the bow gun, ringing, on the grass. He pulled his hand from his freckled cheek to show me a smear of bright blood. Something was wrong with the mechanism that aligned the cable with the bolt, and the bolt had kicked up at the back and cut his jaw.

"Doesn't look deep," I said when I turned his head to the light. "I don't think it'll bleed much."

We took the malfunctioning crossbow back to the Cole's crate in the BD and looked for something better. We hit a jackpot — a box of firecrackers in the Weisners' barrel. Fat Boys, Long Fellas, and Alamos lay in tantalizing rows of different coloured paper wraps. It wasn't hard to see the potential for some great shwags in this box. I'd never lit a firecracker before and neither had Paul. While he went up to his apartment to sneak some matches, I untangled the lines to each fuse. I'd heard Dad talk about dynamiting a well at Obi, so I knew all about fuses. All you had to do was light the end of the string and run for cover. After the blast, you came back to inspect the damage.

Paul and I lit our first one down on the wet parking lot below the main HQ building. After an anxious five seconds, a pop just a little louder than the discharge of a .22 rifle echoed off the stone wall surrounding

the compound. The Alamo cleared the sand and gravel from a thirty-centimetre patch of tarmac, but I was disappointed at the small diameter of the devastation. After Dad's story about dynamite, I had expected something more dramatic — a crater, perhaps, or maybe a rain of pebbles and dirt.

Just then Ato Debray squeaked his wheelbarrow around the building on his return from the compost.

"Hey! Let's freak out ol' Debray!" said Paul. Ato Debray didn't speak English, so we didn't have to whisper.

We walked casually by the spot where the man now stooped among the dripping calla lilies, weeding clover from around their roots. Ato Debray didn't seem to be paying us any mind. He was used to kids playing in his garden, and had developed a superior ability to tune us out — that is, until we stepped on one of his transplanted marigolds, when he would explode in Amharic and Oromifa epithets beyond our years.

One calla raised its white cup to the overcast sky only a metre from Ato Debray's bent back. Paul lit a Fat Boy and dropped it in the cup, and we scurried off. We turned just in time to watch the white lily leap into the air and shatter like shrapnel.

"*In-dey!*" Ato Debray yelled, bounding to his feet. "What the hell are you *jildésoach* up to?"

The two of us doubled over in hysterics by the peach tree.

His Oromifa-accented Amharic carried on. "What's wrong with you *dureeyay* boys? There isn't enough shooting on the streets already? Do you *ibdoach* have to make this garden a war zone, too? *Min ainet lidjoach!*"

Laughter heaved from my stomach and squeezed my breath. Salt tears burned my sinuses. Waves of laughter smashed against my ribs and tossed a bitter taste up my throat.

"Shwagged!" I managed to gasp. "Definitely shwagged!"

Paul whacked his thigh with a weak hand. Our glee steamed Ato Debray thoroughly.

"*T'abat!*" He grabbed me by that shoulder tendon of which he was absolute king. "*Ah-hee-yah!* What have you got in your hands?"

He marched us up to the parking lot, where we found a dry place between the puddles and showed him how a firecracker worked. At the bang, he shook his head.

"*Ferenjies*," he said. "So much money and invention on useless things. What are your parents thinking?"

We had no ideas about what they might be thinking. I hoped mine weren't thinking anything right now.

After Ato Debray went back to his lilies, shaking his salt-and-pepper head, Paul and I tried tying three or four firecrackers together to see if they'd all blast at once, or go off one at a time in rapid succession. We then compared the sizes of cleared circles on the tarmac after different combinations of Long Fellas and Alamos.

"Hey, boys!" a voice called out. We were so engrossed in our experiments that we hadn't noticed an adult's approach. It was Mr. Freeman, a down-country missionary we didn't know too well. His voice made me jump, but I detected no disapproval in it. "You guys could have all kinds of fun with those! Like, what if one of you climbs up on the compound wall over there, and the other one lights one of those firecrackers. Then the guy on the wall falls off just as it explodes. You could pretend you'd been shot by one of the *Kai Shebbir*! Wouldn't that be great?"

Paul and I looked at him *kift-afo*, as Ato Debray would say — open-mouthed. We watched Mr. Freeman's hands echo his speech: first the wall, then the burst of the firecracker and the fall to the ground, and finally the jab in the air for greatness. His flapping jacket lapels wafted Old Spice to my nostrils. Was this guy for real? A missionary, dressed in a black three-piece suit, hair shiny with Brylcreem and wearing aftershave like my dad's — for all intents and purposes an adult, but suggesting a shwag beyond the bounds of funny, even for us.

Sure, we had just shwagged Ato Debray, but that was part of a regular game. We were always terrorizing the poor man. There was something about the way his anger flared suddenly and then immediately diminished that egged us on. His curses deliciously tingled our ears. Our parents would never let us say the words he said. And, when he returned so readily to his work, talking to himself and humming, we knew his rage was really a wonderful act. He was beating us at our own game.

Besides, for us, Ato Debray wasn't part of the regular world of adults. He wasn't responsible for our safety or for anyone else's, as far as we knew. All he did was weed and water a bunch of plants. Anybody could do his job, we thought. We demoted him, as we did the other manual

labourers at HQ, such as the kitchen staff and laundry ladies, to our own level. None of us were responsible, like Paul's dad and mine, or like Ato Lakew or Ato Bereket. These two mission administration employees spent their days in government offices negotiating travel permits, visas, or the renewal of property leases. They were responsible.

Mr. Freeman, an adult *ferenjie* in a black suit, looked to us like one of the responsible adults, so we didn't know how to read his suggestion. Was it some kind of riddle? A trap? Was he testing us — proposing something obviously taboo to see how strictly we kept ourselves in check?

"Yeah," I said uncertainly. "That'd be great."

Paul went back to picking out three Alamos and two Fat Boys, our biggest combo yet. While he laid them out in a star shape, I scooped a bank of sand and gravel around our little powder keg. When this thing went off, we wanted to see something really fly. Paul then began to tie the fuses together. Attending to our game let us off Mr. Freeman's weird hook.

"Just a suggestion," said Mr. Freeman, clearly disappointed in our lacklustre response. He started to walk up the slope towards Mr. Fahnestock and Mr. Maret, who were talking by one of the BD cars. Good, the strange man was gone, and his Old Spice, too. These down-country missionaries who rarely came to Addis often assumed an uncomfortable familiarity with us HQ kids because they knew our parents. The best thing was to smile and nod but not encourage them.

Paul struck the match and cupped the flame to the woven strings. Acrid smoke began to rise. We leapt back a couple of metres. The blast was our most impressive so far. Just as we stepped towards the spot to check our circumference, Mr. Freeman keeled over. He lay on the damp asphalt, hand clutched to his chest, grimacing in pain. One of his shiny brogues jerked spasmodically at the edge of a puddle slicked with a rainbow of motor oil.

Mr. Fahnestock and Mr. Maret dashed over to the prone man. Mr. Fahnestock tried to pull the convulsed hand away from the chest to look for the wound, while Mr. Maret spoke in a clear, loud voice: "Kermit, what happened?"

"On the wall," wheezed Mr. Freeman. *"Kai Shebbir."*

With his two thumbs, Mr. Fahnestock tried to open the fallen man's clenched eyes. When he peeled one eyelid back, we could see only the white. The iris was rolled back.

"Did you boys see what happened?" Mr. Maret asked, looking up at Paul and me. "Hey, what's so funny?"

Paul had his hand over his mouth, and I was trying hard to keep the spasms in my stomach from surfacing.

"What are you boys laughing at?" Mr. Fahnestock demanded.

Now the laughter would not stay in. It sprayed up the back of my throat and burst out my lips like a sneeze.

"You guys gave it away!" said Mr. Freeman, sitting up suddenly. "It was going perfectly well until you started to laugh."

My ribs bounced so hard they hurt. Paul began to hiccup.

"Oh, so you're okay!" Mr. Maret spoke with relief.

"Yeah. The boys and I thought we'd play a little joke. Eh, boys? But they didn't do their part." The sitting man turned to Paul and me. "How come you gave it away? You can't laugh if you want it to work."

"Some joke, Kermit!" Mr. Fahnestock said, brushing damp sand off the back of Mr. Freeman's wool suit jacket as they helped the man to his feet. "You scared us half to death!"

"No kidding," Mr. Maret added. "I thought one of those stray bullets had got you."

"Well, it's either laugh or cry," said Mr. Freeman, "and I'd rather laugh."

"All right, you let me make the jokes," Mr. Fahnestock said, "so you can laugh. I'm not so sure your humour gets my funny bone."

Despite our laughter, Paul and I weren't so sure either. Mr. Freeman's joke, like Mr. Reimer's before it, unsettled me. We kids were constantly told that *Kai Shebbir* meant no fooling around. When the riot drill siren rang, you went straight to your place in line. If the school bus got stopped at a checkpoint, you courteously opened your bag for the soldiers. We knew that any silliness from us could be misread at any moment by the men in the leather boots and green camouflage, and then who knew what might happen? Only maturity and precaution stood between me and those piles of bloody clothes we sometimes saw in the streets. My parents and teachers had those lines around their eyes and lips because they were constantly alert to what might occur.

Mr. Freeman's and Mr. Reimer's jokes, however, showed that adults succumbed to pressure and did silly things, too. Adults could misjudge their own behaviour, just like kids. I could no longer rely on grownups

to know what was right at any given moment. From now on, I would have to look after myself. I would have to keep silliness and shwagging in their proper place. There could be no more kidding around.

Thick Skin

"Forgive me for blubbering," Mary Amalia said. She dabbed her eyes with a tissue and then blew her nose.

Mary was one of my favorites among the missionary ladies, even though she wasn't one of the women who worked in the two hospitals at Sheshemane — one for leprosy patients, the second for patients with other diseases. I'd met her when we used to live in Addis, before Dad was transferred in 1973 to Sheshemane to serve as administrator. Everyone called her "Mary Amalia from Somalia" because of her many years with SIM in Mogadishu. Though she hadn't seen me since we lived in Addis and was just here on a visit, her tanned face had lit up when she saw me, and her dark eyes had regarded me seriously as I told her about the tree house I was building and the ride Ato Warhana gave me on one of the mission's farm tractors.

Now it was Sunday evening prayer service, and with the smells of our recent potluck supper lingering in the living room of the nurses' apartment, Mary gave a report on the medical trip she had made into Wollo and Tigray provinces. She told us for the first time about the widespread famine in the rocky and, to us, remote country of the north-central highlands.

"So many people, thin to the bone, and so little being done!" she said in a strained voice. "All the years I spent in the Ogaden and Somali deserts — none of them prepared me for this. You have the constant feeling that it's too late. Many of the people we tried to feed in the camp south of Mekele couldn't digest a thing. Their stomachs had gone so long without food, they simply threw it back up."

She told us about meeting an old woman on one of her first days there, who told her the story she soon realized she would hear dozens of

times a day. Her daughter had died on the trek to the camp; the two kids with her were her grandchildren. There hadn't been a crop for two years. After the first year, they traded their cattle and donkeys for seed grain, hoping, if it were God's will, that they would get rain and be able to plant the next year. Apparently it wasn't God's will, she said, for they never got a drop.

Mary blew her nose into her hanky. She took a drink from the glass of water one of the nurses had brought her.

"Everything was 'God willing' with those people," she said. "I winced every time I heard it, and they seemed to say it without fail. Everybody would say they had hoped for rain or crops, 'God willing.'"

She had another sip of water to clear her throat and returned to her story. Having traded their animals after the first rainless year, the old woman and her family couldn't plough the second year — but it never rained anyway. So they ate the seed grain, and, when that ran out, they tried anything that had once been a plant: dried tubers pried from the dust, the bark of shrubs that had survived their now-dead goats, the spongy leather of cactus leaves, the softer twigs of the leafless eucalyptus.

"I've seen those dried-up trees," Mary told us. "Eucalyptus has to be pretty dry not to have a scent. I can't think what it was like to try to eat it."

Then the old woman had heard a rumour about a relief camp, so she roused her daughter and her two children, and they followed the story for five days until the camp materialized out of the rocks. By then, she had left her daughter's corpse drying by the footpath, and one of the two children was permanently coiled in the fetal position from weakness and from having been bound in a *shemma* on his grandmother's back for days on end. Both children were barely holding on.

The heaviness within Mary must be told, could not be told. It dammed up in her throat. She pushed her voice past the blockage. "It was as if the old woman were telling someone else's story," she said. "As if she were listing so many inert facts. She showed no emotion as she spoke. After she died that night, one of her neighbours told me she was around forty years old. I had thought from her wizened face and trembling hands that she was seventy or eighty."

"Is it true that the grain donated by other countries is being used to

feed the army instead of being given to the hungry?" one of the other nurses asked.

Mary twisted a Kleenex in her hands and said, "I wouldn't know about that for sure. I've heard people say it's happening. But the mission is trying to stay out of politics and concentrate instead on helping people.

"The thing is, there are too many. You try to find a vein in the dry stick of a woman's arm that moments ago was pried loose from a dead baby. Ten minutes later, it's a different mother's arm, hollowed of its child. The sheer quantity of arms and the same, repeated story wears you down. And you don't have time to learn their names, to address anything but the bare demands of their bodies. Porridge. Water. Blanket. Needle."

Silence held the room. Mary drank more water.

Then her voice burst too loud from her chest: "How is a child supposed to get strong again after she has seen her mother tossed into the pit at the back of the camp, where they throw down a shovel full of sand between each layer of dead? Why would she want to?"

Mary's tears were the closest contact I'd had with the famine that spread, when I was in my early teens, through Wollo and Tigray provinces in the north, as well as parts of Bale and Gomo Gofa in the south. We knew that Haile Selassie's fall from power in 1974 was due, in part, to widespread frustration with his government's sluggish response to the disaster, but because the new Provisional Military Administrative Council censored the press, we learned only of the old monarchy's failures from the newspapers or radio reports. We heard rumours of the army commandeering donated food and medicine, but these were over-shadowed by more sensational stories about the execution of all sixty deposed cabinet ministers or about Haile Selassie's corpse being embedded in concrete under Mengistu Haile Mariam's office desk.

My family had always lived on the verdant plateau of central Ethiopia. Whereas Obi and Addis were high and cool, Sheshemane was perched on the lush green lip of the arid Rift Valley that extended all the way from

the Red Sea to the Serengeti plains of Tanzania. Of the three places where we lived in Ethiopia, Sheshemane was the most fertile. Outside the living room where Mary pressed her voice through tears, irrigation ditches fed our garden of pineapple, carrots, passion fruit, potatoes, rhubarb, Swiss chard, and papaya. We had cut down the mulberry tree because its canopy leaned so densely over the garden shed that it trapped the little building in a pocket of warm, moist air, which rotted the roof beams and walls. Before the gardener cut it down, Mark Rogers, Danny Creighton, and I used to have rotten mulberry fights that tallied each direct hit with a red stain on the other guy's T-shirt. An avenue of scarlet-haloed flame and crow-infested avocado trees alternating with sweet-smelling loquat and peach trees led past the missionaries' front lawns to the hospital entrances beyond.

Mom and Dad told visitors that the combination of reliable rains and volcanic ash in the soil made Sheshemane one of the most beautiful places on God's green earth. The mission had come by this wonderful place back in the 1950s, when Dejazmach Asrat Kassa, governor of Arsi province, had been so taken with the mission's proposal to establish a leprosy treatment hospital and farm in south-central Ethiopia that he had donated some of the richest land in the country to the project. Such donations were standard practice under Haile Selassie's feudal regime; the emperor regularly rewarded his *Rasses'* loyalty and service with prize tracts of down-country land. Dejazmach Asrat Kassa had simply followed suit. The big difference in the mission's case was, of course, that rather than collecting half of the peasants' crops each year, as the Addis-based nobles did, the mission put all the profits back into the Sheshemane project.

The system was meant to be self-sustaining. The farm provided work for leprosy patients, who were ostracized in their own villages. Its grain and beef provided hospital meals, and any extra was sold in Addis to support the two hospitals, the elementary and secondary schools, and the TB clinic. The experiment didn't really work. Although the farm did turn a small profit, it couldn't make enough to pay for the hospitals' medicine and the orderlies' salaries, and so the mission had to work out a formula with the Ministry of Health that shared between them the remaining expenses.

It fell to Dad, as Sheshemane station manager, to negotiate this

formula with the new government. "Nobody disagrees that land reform is way overdue," I had heard Dad say to Mr. Creighton, the farm manager. "Those rich Addis Ababa *Rasses* could have afforded to skim less from these poor country folk. But the military government's determination to return all the land to the people really leaves us in the lurch. I've been to the municipality offices in Zwai every week this month, and they're still not telling me if they're going to go with the old formula. I sometimes wonder if some of the higher-ups in the new government have their own eyes on these fields."

The farm operation included five or six imported Massey-Ferguson tractors, which were driven by men from the community. Among the drivers, I liked Ato Warhana best. His eyebrows would arch high on his coffee-coloured forehead when he saw my thirteen-year-old form standing hopefully at the edge of the yard where the drivers got their daily assignments. His hand would cup air towards his chest as he beckoned me to the space between the fender and his driver's seat. Once we arrived at the field designated for that day's ploughing or sowing, he would pat the seat and switch places with me. He operated the hydraulics of the disc-plough or seeder while I steered down the furrows.

The windblown rocks and sand in Mary Amalia's stories seemed impossibly far from the pungent Sheshemane earth that arced like dolphins under the plough's blades. Earthworms and grubs wriggled frantically in the overturned sod as they struggled for cover from the flashing beaks of crows and starlings. The screeching of birds easily bested the chug of the Massey's diesel motor.

"*Aizo!*" Ato Warhana exclaimed when the tire hit an off-centre bump and the steering wheel jerked viciously. "*Indezee*" — and he showed me how to avoid a sprained wrist by keeping my fingers from curling around the wheel.

I was concentrating on the new technique, watching my front wheel trace the edge where the emerald sod met the black earth of our last turn, when something made me look up. I was surprised to see Ato Warhana, who I hadn't seen jump off the tractor, at the edge of the field, where he grasped a seven- or eight-year-old boy's arm and struck his buttocks smartly with a broken walking stick. The boy wriggled, lithe as a gymnast, in the tractor driver's grip. Tears glistened on his copper cheeks, but his eyes flashed merry fire as he twisted out of Ato

Warhana's clutch. The moment he was free, he leapt, fleet as a gazelle, over two hurdles of steaming earth and vanished into the pungent *bahir-zaff* trees at the field's edge. The tractor driver tossed the broken staff into the woods after him and swung up on the fender when I made the turn at the end of the row.

"*Dureeyay!*" Ato Warhana spat into the weeds that grew between the field and the eucalyptus. "He was trying to throw that *dula* under the plough each time we made the turn. Just to see the wood snap when the blades came down. Any closer and he'd have got a leg caught underneath."

I watched the discs slice great peels of green-furred sod and expose its shiny undersoil to the air. I could hardly conjure up the images of desert Mary Amalia had put in my mind. My family had once made a holiday trip south and east all the way to Harar and Dire Dawa and onwards to Jijiga, a city on the edge of the Ogaden desert. I recalled fields of dust where, it seemed, only thorns and ragged goats could live. Even though I had seen nobody starving there, I was still glad we lived here at Sheshemane, where the earth was green and the children sleek. I was afraid of being overwhelmed, as Mary Amalia had been, if I lived in a place where the earth burned and the people starved.

On the return trip from the field to the tractor shed that afternoon, we picked up Ato Anisi, the truck driver who ferried Sheshemane wheat and *teff* to the Addis Ababa markets. The man flagged us down from the side of the dirt road and swung up onto the other fender while the wheels were still turning.

"*Aiye, cus-cus!*" Ato Warhana said. "You could catch your *shemma* in the treads and be pulled under the wheel! Then what would we do?"

"*Minnim aidelem,*" Ato Anisi said in an excited voice. "It's nothing. I wanted to show you something." He reached into his belt and pulled out a dull, black pistol. He flipped it back and forth between his hands, eagerly testing the grip in each palm. "I got it yesterday from a cattle trader. He said it works fine."

"*Indey!* What is this?" Ato Warhana asked. "What would you want with a thing like that?"

"It's crazy out there," said Ato Anisi. "A lot of mad *ibdoach* on the roads these days. All these unions run by firebrand *zemecha* teenagers, and then they've got kids with machine guns manning the checkpoints

on the highway between here and Addis. You never know who's a thief and who's a government officer. Nobody's going to push me around."

Ato Anisi's fingers swarmed the pistol's contours like ants. "Isn't it a beauty?" he said, turning the weapon on its side. "The safety is somewhere over here . . ."

Then, without warning, the thing went off, sending a chip of steering wheel flying between Ato Warhana's two hands.

A second passed before my brain registered what the sharp crack of the pistol meant. I was sure I felt the bullet breeze past my stomach, it was that close.

"*T'abat!*" shouted Ato Warhana. "What are you trying to do? Get one of us killed? You put that thing away before you murder somebody! Talk about *ibdoach* and crazy soldiers with guns! That bullet chipped the wheel right where my hand was sitting a minute ago!"

Crestfallen, Ato Anisi stuffed the gun back in his trousers, and we rode on in grim silence, the whiff of gunpowder still in our noses. The tractor bumped up over an irrigation ditch culvert and onto the gravel road that led into the tractor yard. We pulled up by the grain terminal, where Ato Anisi's truck would load its gunny sacks of Sheshemane *teff*.

"I didn't mean any harm," muttered Ato Anisi. "*Yekirta.* It's just since the political change, you don't know friend from foe."

"*Minnim aidelem,*" Ato Warhana replied in a low voice. "You didn't mean any harm, but you've got to be careful."

After Ato Warhana parked the tractor in its spot in the diesel-smelling shed, I trotted down the fragrant avenue of flower and fruit trees to our house and was surprised to find the back door locked.

"You can't go in there for a while," Mom explained when I came around to the front. "I've set up the tin tub in the back room so our visitor can take a bath. Steve's one of the famine workers who's just come in from a camp in the south. They don't have running water down there, so the first thing he said when he got here was, 'Can I have a bath?' Hadn't had one for a month, poor guy. He's been soaking for a couple of hours already — he'll be wrinkled as a prune."

I was glad we had a visitor for supper that night because the distraction meant I could avoid telling Mom and Dad about Ato Anisi's pistol. With Steve here, the conversation would centre around him.

I took an immediate liking to the young Minnesotan who was here on summer break from college in the States. His subdued voice, mild grey eyes, sandy-blond hair, and tall, athletic build gave him a quiet magnetism. He had been working flat out at the camp, seven days a week, every waking hour for five weeks, he said. Any and every job that needed doing, he did it. He unloaded grain sacks, stirred steaming barrels of porridge, and lifted people too weak to walk. He replaced the corrugated iron roofs of some of the shelters and dug new latrine pits. After he blacked out one day while carrying buckets of water to mix into the porridge barrel that bubbled over the fire, the camp director told him he'd better get away for a weekend's rest. So he caught a ride to Sheshemane on a grain truck. He would hang out here for the weekend and then ride back when the truck returned with another load on Monday.

Steve seemed glad of my offer to show him around the mission station after breakfast the next morning. For such a young, sporty-looking guy, however, he dragged his feet on our tour. We'd only walked through the antiseptic-smelling corridors of the two hospitals, poked our heads into one of the men's wards, circled around the TB clinic, had a quick look at the elementary school, and stopped by the water filtration system — that's all we'd seen when he asked if we could sit down to rest. I was disappointed to pause so early. I still hadn't shown him the leper village, the wood shop, the tractor sheds, the cattle pens, or the shoe shop where Ato Worgessa and Ato Bekele made sandals for the lepers' misshapen feet.

I quelled my enthusiasm and squatted beside him in the grass. We could hear the water whisper softly as it flowed from the spring and into the first of the pools. Upstream from the actual filters, a large concrete square the shape of an unbuilt house's foundation was subdivided into rectangular sections with spillways, through which the upper layer of water could trickle over the dividing wall and into the next rectangle. Sediment stained the bottoms of these rectangular tanks a terracotta red, and the spillways ran clearer and clearer as the water descended through each successive pool. The system, however, was far

from perfect. Even after the settling pools and the filtration, and even though the box of Mom's Omo laundry powder promised clothes of brilliant white, repeated laundering gradually turned my undershorts orange.

The water here in the settling pools gurgled as contentedly as a well-fed baby. Steve selected a long, green shoot of grass and chewed on its sweet, white end. He ran his hand absently through the furry tops of the foxtails beside him as he watched the water descend from pool to pool.

"I could get right into one of those pools," he said, pointing with the end of his grass stem. "That water looks like heaven."

"Yeah," I said, looking at the silty water. It was fine, but not as enticing as the dark green Bishoftu Lake or the aquamarine swimming pool at the Ras Hotel back in Obi.

"It's like being in another world here," Steve said, forgetting my presence. "I can't believe I'm sitting in green grass, listening to running water."

Another long silence. He chewed his grass stem. I didn't know what to say.

"You know, this water in these pools? If we could load it in a truck, it would be enough to give every person in our camp enough to drink for a week."

There was a catch in his voice. His grey eyes were red around the rims.

But we need this water, I thought, for our laundry and drinking water. You can't run a hospital without water.

"When I think back to how I wasted stuff in the States," Steve went on, "I just cringe — flush toilets, swimming pools, even watering the lawns, for crying out loud. In Minnesota, everywhere you turn, there's another lake.

"One day Seifu, the guy who translates from Oromifa, told me that the nine- or ten-year-old kid we were talking to had never seen rain fall from the sky. Not a drop. The only kind of water he knew came from the ground — a river, a well, or some kind of water hole — that's it.

"It's as if the world is divided into cells or something, just like these pools. All the good stuff goes to one place and all the crap to another. If you're at the good end of the system, you get clear water, and if you're

at the bad end, you get the muddy stuff. Whether you get the good stuff or the crap depends on which cell you were born in."

I had turned this thought around in my mind before: when we lived at Obi, my friends' houses had dirt floors and ours had polished cedar. Or when Mulugeta's mother went around their yard picking up fresh cow patties with her hands so she could lay them out in circles in the sun, where they would dry and make fuel for their fire. Or when we stopped at a red light in Addis and the beggars surrounded the school van with their hands extended for a coin, *sillah-Mariam*. You couldn't have enough coins. Furthermore, how would we cook on our wood-stove if we gave Mulugeta's mother our own firewood? What would be gained if we walked on dirt instead of cedar?

Still, Steve was right. We did live in different cells. You did have to develop thick skin if you lived in close contact with people from another one. Otherwise the unfairness would drive you crazy. When we lived at Obi, we were the only ones within kilometres who had a car. Dad was always being asked to drive someone somewhere: a pregnant woman to the doctor, a kid with a broken ankle to the clinic, a drunk home to his family, a casket to a funeral.

"I could run a taxi service and make a good profit," Dad joked to cover his frustration. "I guess I just need to get thicker skin, to learn to say no."

He needed to say no, but he couldn't always say no. When Ha'da Biru looked as if she might die in childbirth, he drove her straightaway that night to Princess Tsa'hai Hospital in Addis, no questions asked. But when Ato Gaytacho asked Dad to take him to Woliso town because he'd twisted his ankle, Dad said no. He felt badly about it, too, even though Ato Gaytacho could afford a horse-drawn *garri* if his ankle couldn't bear the walk to town. Even if your skin was thin, you had to pretend it wasn't, or you would be at everybody's beck and call.

"You have to have thick skin," I now said to Steve beside the chuckling water pools, "to live in Ethiopia."

He didn't seem to have heard me. He chewed his grass stem for a minute longer. Then he pushed himself up and walked over to the concrete edge of the pool system. He leaned over the waist-high wall and dipped one hand in the water.

I remembered the time I'd seen Kassa, the bent old man who kept

the wood-fired water heaters at Bingham constantly burning, pick a red-hot coal out of the fire with his bare fingers and drop it into a tin can so he could restart the fire in another heater. When I expressed amazement, he lifted another coal out and rolled it around on his callused palm, chuckling at my astonishment.

"*Sir-ra,*" he said in broken Amharic. "Work."

He grabbed my hand and pressed his horn of an index finger into the pink membrane of my palm.

" *Yeh hitzahn idjoach,*" he said. "Hands of a baby."

Steve straightened and ran his wet fingers around the back of his neck.

"Yeah, I can see why you do need thick skin," he said. "But what do you do about the unfairness in the meantime? There's a military checkpoint on the way down past Negele, where they always stop the grain trucks on their way to the relief camp. The soldiers make the driver unload any bags of *teff* before they'll let them pass. So the people at the camps get porridge or *injerra* made only out of corn, without any good quality *injerra* made with *teff*. I once asked the director why he didn't complain, and he said that if we wanted to get any grain to the camp at all, we had to stay out of politics."

"That's right." I was on sure ground because I'd heard Dad say this was the mission's official policy. "We missionaries have to remain apolitical if we want to stay in Ethiopia under the new military government. Some missions have had to leave the country because they got too involved."

Steve stretched and yawned. "That may be true, but do you think it's right that the soldiers skim the best stuff off the trucks, and the people who need it most get the dregs?"

I didn't know what to say. I'd never heard anybody ask Dad that question before, so I didn't know the right answer.

"All right, tour guide," Steve said after a minute. He pushed himself back from the low wall and turned to face me. "You wanted to show me the shoe place and a workshop. Want to head out?"

Steve caught his ride back to the camp the next day, and I never saw him again. I thought of him often, though, over the next few years. For, as the conditions of the famine grew worse under the added complications of Ethiopia's two wars — with Eritrea in the north and Somalia in the southeast — so, too, did the political situation grow more and more volatile. The divisions between the cells grew higher and wider.

To draw Soviet support away from Somalia, the PMAC declared the nation an out-and-out Marxist-Leninist state. It worked. Over the next decade, eleven billion dollars' worth of rocket launchers, MiG fighter planes, and Kalashnikovs rolled into Ethiopia as the Soviets switched their support from Said Barre's regime in Somalia to Mengistu in Addis. The roads running north and south out of Addis became potholed from the heavy traffic of military transport trucks. We saw more and more Cubans in fatigues driving half-tracks and rocket transports toward the front lines. For the Soviets, the Ethiopian-controlled Eritrean ports of Massawa and Assab on the Red Sea were strategically closer to the world's major oil-shipping lanes than anything Somalia had to offer on the Indian Ocean.

Since most of our mission's personnel came from NATO countries, the new government suspected us of being politically opposed to their Communist platform. They weren't far from right. Official atheism constituted a major component of the new government's Marxist-Leninism, and the censored press proclaimed religion unscientific and anti-progressive. Our religious propaganda, opium for the masses, sapped people's will to improve their own conditions.

Thus, we were numbered among the country's undeclared enemies. As Dejazmach Asrat Kassa's grant of land for the Sheshemane farm still demonstrated, the mission was associated with the old, corrupt system of absentee Amhara landlords.

The new rulers couldn't dismiss us missionaries outright, however. Because their coffers were completely consumed by the Eritrean and Somalian conflicts, they couldn't staff the hospitals and schools the mission had established throughout the country. Not right away. In the resulting game of smiling resentment and grudging negotiation, the municipality dragged its heals over deciding whether to contribute its share of the subsidy agreed upon between the Selassie government and SIM.

After a year and a half of repeated trips to the regional offices in Zwai, which produced only delayed and partial payments, Dad and the mission's Addis administrators informed the Health Minister that, with the shortfall in funds and the difficulties with hospital employees, they would have to shut down the Sheshemane hospitals if the subsidy was not maintained. The officials countered that if the mission closed any of its operations, the Ministry of the Interior would not renew any missionaries' visas, and SIM would have to leave the country entirely. Concerned about what would happen to the Kalleh Hiwot churches and Bible Schools in the absence of foreign observers, the mission suggested that if the Ministry of Health couldn't afford the old subsidy and help the mission deal with its labour problems, then it would have to scale back the size and complexity of some of the medical operations. The government agreed to reconsider and invited the mission to enter into a series of discussions about how the current arrangements might be revised.

The labour unrest rose from a fundamentally good scheme. The Ministry of Education had established *zemecha,* a nationwide literacy campaign in which university and senior secondary students were required to teach literacy and the basic principles of Marxism throughout the rural provinces. The campaign was a huge success in raising the nation's literacy rate in a very short time, but the young student-teachers that came to Sheshemane also taught the lepers that the missionaries were underpaying them and taking the profits back to their homelands.

"Look at all those cattle they feed with the grain from the farm!" the Addis Ababa-born cadres told their listeners. "Do you get beef in your meals every day? And where does all that *teff* go? The white missionaries are just another kind of landlord. They take the fields Dejazmach Asrat Kassa stole from you and plant them with their big tractors. They make you work on what should be your own land and tell you that it's for your own good — that all the profits go into the hospital and the medicine you take. But do you live in houses with flower gardens along a tree-lined avenue? Do you have shiny cedar floors in your houses?"

The cadres' agitation got more personal yet: "Haven't you noticed what happens every few years? Almost without fail, every three or four

years, Sheshemane gets a new station manager. Why does the old one leave? They tell you they've been transferred, but that's just a cover. What really happens is that each one fills his suitcases with money from the farm and the hospital. It takes only three or four years to fill them up, and then he goes back to America or England and puts it in the bank. Each one tells you that he came here to help you, but it's all big business. That's how these *ferenjie* imperialists think: everything for them is money and profits. Their mouths are full of God and Jesus, but their noses are always sniffing out cash."

Thus, with the young cadres' help, the farm and hospital workers, many of them under long-term treatment for leprosy, formed a union and presented my father with a list of grievances and demands. They wanted shorter hours, more sick days and holidays, and, most of all, a substantial wage increase. Dad tried to explain that, in fact, the farm and hospitals lost money and that the whole operation was under greater financial restraints than ever, since the government was withholding its contribution. Just at the moment, in fact, the Sheshemane operation was so short of fuel that the tractors hadn't run for a week. He and Dr. McClenny were anxious about not having enough diesel to run the hospitals' emergency electrical generators. The new union leaders, however, saw this explanation as another lie, so the missionary could fill his suitcase.

Relationships with the farm workers grew more and more tense until, one day, Dad had to lay off a night watchman because some power tools had gone missing during his shift. The man came after Dad with an axe.

"What did you do?" I asked Dad when he told us about it over supper that night.

"Ato Channi shouted out to warn me," Dad said, in a voice that seemed much too calm to me. "He grabbed the axe, which made the guy lose his balance. When the man fell, I put his head between my shins to hold him still until he calmed down."

Too bad Ato Anisi wasn't there, I thought. He could have pulled out his pistol. That would have put the axeman in his place. Better than shins.

I looked down at my own legs. Were they strong enough to hold a man down who was bent on murder? I'd heard of full-nelsons and half-nelsons, and I'd heard of twisting somebody's arm behind his back,

but I'd never heard of holding someone down by gripping his neck between your shins. I wasn't convinced it would work very well.

"By then," Dad continued, "the hospital *zubunya* and another watchman who was just coming on duty arrived, and they took the fellow out of the crowd that had gathered so he could cool off. Ato Channi thought we should call the police and press charges, but the man's got a history of insanity. He was under the influence, too, so I thought we should let it go. When I got in the car to come home, however, he ran out from the crowd and threw a brick that dented the driver's door. The *zubunya* grabbed him again and said he would take the poor man home to his family."

Dad's calm voice was meant to keep Marianne and me from being too frightened of our Sheshemane neighbours, but we could see that he was far from being at peace himself. Several mornings in a row, when we sat down at breakfast to our steaming bowls of oatmeal, Mom explained that he was in bed with a headache.

"Sinuses," she said. But it was stress.

Mom and Dad hadn't signed up, when they first became missionaries, for the kinds of problems they were facing now. They had joined the mission out of a desire to help — to bring love, healing, and hope to people. They had come to tell them about Jesus. They were proud of the schools, clinics, and hospitals that embodied Jesus' love in social and physical terms. They certainly hadn't planned on playing the role of management in disputes with an angry labour union. They had come to give things away, not parcel them out in stingy contracts resented by disgruntled workers.

As negotiations with the new government in Addis grew more and more tricky, the mission council asked Mom and Dad if they would move to SIM's central office in the capital city, where Dad's quiet demeanour, added to his proficiency in Amharic, would be a big support to the Ethiopian church leaders in the constant jockeying with the new government officials. They also wanted Mom to help in the treasury department while the full-time accountant went on sick leave back to Britain. Although Mom and Dad knew it was a move from the frying pan into the fire, they reluctantly agreed to go. All of this was a far cry from the church work and Bible School teaching they loved, but they reasoned that these trying jobs needed to be done if the mission was to

stay faithfully alongside the Ethiopian Christians during increasingly ominous times. After Marianne and I had returned to Bingham for our school term, Dad and Mom packed up our house and booked Ato Anisi's grain truck to haul our furniture to Addis.

"See?" cried the cadres at the farm workers' union meeting. "Here we go again! One day, the *ferenjie* manager tells you he can't afford better wages or beef *sigga* in the hospital meals, and then the next day he's packing his suitcases full of money to smuggle the profits back to America. The barefaced hypocrisy of these religious freaks! It makes you want to laugh out loud!"

Thus, the morning Ato Anisi's diesel-belching Trente-Quatro Fiat growled to a stop in front of our house to load up, a delegation from the union growled in, too. They impounded the vehicle and all our household goods to stop our escape with suitcases of cash.

That is how my family departed from the paradise of Sheshemane, and, as with so many things in those days, I heard about it only second-hand. It seemed all the major events of my life occurred offstage. Somewhere across the city of Addis, a power struggle was taking place between junior and senior army officers for control of the ruling military junta. Somewhere in Tigray and in the Ogaden, people desperately awaited grain trucks often held up by Eritrean and Somali guerrillas. Closer to home, but still unseen by me, my family's dresser drawers and mattresses mouldered for two months in an empty house at Sheshemane, while the union looked carefully through the mission's accounts, hoping to find the suitcases of money that would bring higher wages and better benefits. Finally, when the account books revealed no such skimming, the truck was released. Now, here we sat on the gold brocade loveseat that had traveled with us from Obi to Addis to Sheshemane and now back again to Addis, while Mom told us sadly about the dark cloud under which we'd left that beautiful green place.

Not that Addis wasn't green. The *bahir-zaff* woods at Bingham Academy still threw a lovely mottled shade whose menthol scent once inspired me to build brushwood forts when I was in the lower grades

and now energized my workouts for the cross-country team. Likewise, the HQ gardens, where Paul Cumbers and I had scared the dickens out of poor old Ato Debray, were still splendid with marigolds, nasturtiums, and bougainvillea. During my next school vacations, when I was sixteen and seventeen, I would spend long afternoons cross-legged on the asphalt of the parking lot, just above Ato Debray's hens-and-chicks and roses and in almost the exact spot where Mr. Freeman had once played dead. There I handed wrenches to Yared Lakew while he worked on one or another of the R&R vehicles in preparation for its next trip to the famine areas in Wollo or Tigray.

"R&R!" he would joke as he lay on his back under the oil pan of a Fiat truck. "It's all rest and relaxation in the R&R! See? All I do is lie about at work all day long."

In response to the famine Mary Amalia had told us about several years earlier, the mission had raised funds among its supporters in Europe, North America, Australia, and New Zealand for a new Relief and Rehabilitation department. R&R served two purposes at once. It addressed the primary needs of starving and displaced people in the drought-stricken areas. It also made the SIM indispensable to the new government, which had so many troubles on all fronts at once that it needed any help it could get to deal with the famine. The mission received special rations of diesel to fuel the trucks going north as well as free access passes so our drivers could bypass the time-consuming inspections at the military checkpoints along all highways leading out of Addis. In return, the SIM was required not to proselytize or offer Bible classes in the relief camps.

"By jingles!" Yared said under the Fiat. "These vehicles must have been designed by a drunk! Hand me that spanner, will you? A guy practically has to take off the whole manifold just to reach the oil filter. Crazy Italianos! Compare this to one of those new Toyota Landcruisers — you can pretty much do the whole job just by opening the bonnet. Those Japanese don't want to get dirty doing a simple job."

He'd learned his mechanical terminology by working with Ian Rendel, a retired Aussie farmer who could fix anything from a water pump to a Daihatsu truck. The skills he learned from Mr. Rendel and from mechanics classes at technical school made Yared indispensable to getting the R&R operation up and running.

"Feh dinkum!" Yared would say, rolling out from under the Fiat and rubbing grease from his hands on a rag. "One more R&R pleasure vehicle at your service, sir!"

The vehicles Yared worked on were our closest contact with the famine raging in the north. Having no televisions in our homes, neither Yared nor I had seen the images of stark-ribbed mothers and bloated babies that flooded news screens from Australia to Europe to North America and swept people like Ian Rendel and Steve out to Ethiopia. What we saw, instead, were the brand-new vehicles that flowed into the R&R parking lot with door decals proclaiming their sponsors: TEAR Fund, World Health Organization, World Vision, Baptist World Alliance, UNICEF. The dusty, rivet-ridden Land Rovers and rickety Willys Jeeps that had defined four-wheel drive throughout my childhood were suddenly eclipsed by tough, fuel-efficient Toyota Landcruisers and sleek Mazda pickups. The tottering Trente-Quatros that had been the only trucks on the road in my younger years gave way to Daihatsus, Volvos, and Mercedes.

R&R was big money. At the same time that it introduced me to a level of poverty I'd never imagined before, it also gave Yared a job — and it showed me luxuries beyond my dreams. In so doing, the famine of the mid-1970s taught me a division that has troubled me ever since. From its one voice, I heard the contradictory calls of opulence and social responsibility.

"Want to come for a drive?" Yared asked. "I've got to pick up some gas and then deliver it to the people over at R&R."

Any drive with Yared was welcome. Sometimes, when we were on back roads, he even let me take the wheel of one of the swanky new machines. As well, the R&R compound, a quiet, perfumed paradise in the midst of the honking, stinking city, was my very favourite destination. I jumped at any chance to go there, simply to absorb its green, unhurried calm.

Yared and I hopped in the Landcruiser he'd been working on, and we headed off to the Shell station down by the stadium, where he thought the line-up might be shortest at this time in the afternoon.

I settled into the new-smelling vinyl seat and gazed lovingly at the instrument panel encased in pebbled, lustrous plastic. Not a crack anywhere. When I fiddled with a little silver toggle on the passenger's door,

*Pupsi and me, Paul Cumbers, and Yared, with
Yared's Balilla at HQ.*

I was amazed to find that I could adjust the side mirror without rolling down the window.

"Check this out," I said. "They think of everything!"

"Can you have a look at the ration book?" Yared asked me, while he braked for a red light. "How much can we collect this week?"

A group of beggars who had been waiting on the meridian fanned out among the cars that had stopped at the light. Of course, they came not to Yared's window but the one where I, the pink *ferenjie*, sat.

"*Gunzub yellegnyim,*" I muttered at the woman and two old men who thrust withered hands towards me. "No money." I opened one empty palm helplessly to the heavens while I used the other hand to roll up my window. The glass protected me from the sour smell of their sores as well as the din of their voices — "*Sillah Mariam! Meestair! Beh Cristos sim!*" It also kept them from grabbing anything out of the glove compartment when I rummaged in there to find the ration book. Mr.

Maret had told Dad just the other day that a beggar at a traffic light had stolen a flashlight off his dash when he'd leaned over to the glove compartment to find some tickets to Hope Enterprises, a mission that served meals to homeless people from the city streets.

There had always been lots of beggars in Addis — old men with polio-shrivelled legs, young women carrying sightless babies, or girls with twisted feet. Several years before we moved to Sheshemane, Dad and I had taken a city bus early in the morning and seen a dozen or so beggars commuting downtown in time to swarm the cars of white-collar workers arriving at their jobs in government buildings, legal offices, and banks. The numbers and the poverty, however, had increased radically in the past couple of years as people from the famine areas gradually followed the legends of wealth to the city. We saw more and more people with missing arms and legs, which they'd lost to land mines after the fighting in the north had shifted battlefields.

And then, periodically, when Castro or some other foreign dignitary planned a state visit, army trucks would curry the streets, the soldiers loading ragged folk into the backs at gunpoint. The streets would empty ominously for a month or so until more displaced people arrived from areas beleaguered by famine or war.

"Looks like we can get fifty litres," I said, checking the dates of the ink-stamps in the Landcruiser's ration book. "And if we add the R&R allowance for the Volksie van, we can put another fifty in the jerry cans in the back."

Yared slapped the steering wheel as we came around the corner at the stadium. "*T'abat!*" The Shell station queue trickled way down the street and around the corner. "I told Ato Solomon at R&R I'd bring the *benzine* over before three o'clock! With this lineup, I'll never get there!" He drove along the bumper-to-bumper chain of Volkswagens, Peugeots, Opels, Fiats, and Datsuns. His head wagged at our bad luck.

"I guess we'll have to go around the block to find the back of the line, eh?" I said.

We came up alongside the pumps, where a cab driver leaned against his blue-and-white taxi, talking to a guy in Shell station coveralls.

"*Simma!*" Yared yelled, leaning out his window. "How long was the wait?"

"Fifty minutes," Ato Taxi responded.

Just then a cream-coloured Lada at one of the other pumps started its engine and began to inch away from the station.

In a flash, Yared backed the big four-wheel drive in the exit ramp and stopped beside the empty pump.

"*Inat-kin! Mihn te sarallih!*" the guy behind us shouted. He shook his fist out the window of the Peugeot 504 at the front of the long line. "Your mother! Get in line and wait like everybody else!"

"International Aid priority!" Yared replied, slamming the door and pointing to the TEAR Fund decal on the Landcruiser's shiny green panel. "I've got to get these *ferenjies* to a meeting at the Ministry of the Interior." He pointed at me. "Big money for the famine, you know."

I wanted to shrink down to the floorboards, but I sat as tall as I could instead and pretended not to know a word of Amharic.

In the side mirror, I could see the man in the 504 look uncertain. These days, nobody could tell the difference between a government dignitary and a street urchin. The new authorities all looked like kids. The TEAR decal on the door also gave us a legitimizing stamp.

The station attendant screwed out the gas cap and slipped in the nozzle, and Yared gave me a big wink as he sidled up to the attendant. My friend muttered, "These *ferenjies*! Everything with them is 'right now,' 'right away.' *Tolo, tolo*. They can't wait for anybody. But one day soon, once the revolution is firmly in place, we'll be rid of them. And there won't be any rich people, *ferenjie* or *habisha*, leaping to the front of the line, eh?"

"Right on, *Guadenya*," said the Shell guy. "*Etyopia Tikdem*. Long live the revolution."

The smell at the gas pumps made me somewhat nauseous. It didn't used to. I used to find the smell of gasoline exciting — it had always meant going somewhere in the car, or learning to drive the tractors down at Sheshemane, or helping Yared with the R&R vehicles. But ever since I'd accidentally swallowed a mouthful while Yared and I had been siphoning gas out of a VW van and into one of the R&R jerry cans, the merest whiff recalled the sulphurous burps I'd suffered for two days after that mouthful, and the Shell station brought back to my tongue the taste of rotten egg that had infused every bite of food.

"It's a new kind of mathematics," I had said to Yared, after I'd rinsed my mouth out at the garden tap. We were lugging the jerry cans from

the VW van to one of the Landcruisers so it would have enough to make the long trip to the relief camps in Wollo: "Famine plus revolution equals siphoning gas, and gas ration plus R&R equals a rotten taste in my mouth!"

In fact, gasoline had played a major role in the change of governments. When the world price of oil skyrocketed during the 1973 energy crisis, the Haile Selassie government, which had regulated the price of gas throughout the country, announced that it would have to raise the price per litre. Addis was immediately gridlocked by a city-wide strike of taxi and bus drivers. The Ministry of Transportation protested that it had no power over the new price — the problem was worldwide, not local. The drivers had no ears for these excuses. Whatever the world price might be, they couldn't pay this much per litre and still make a living. Therefore they stayed home, and the city was shut down for days on end. Nobody could get to work. Offices had no secretaries at their desks, businesses had no employees, and schools had no teachers. Finally, the Ministry of Transportation caved in and said that it would find a way to return to the old regulated rate.

When disgruntled junior army officers saw that a general boycott could intimidate the tottering Selassie regime, they took the hint. Several divisions holed up in their barracks and refused to carry out any orders until their wages rose. When the old government capitulated to them, too, it wasn't long before students had taken to the streets to protest the limited number of seats in higher education. By 1974, those junior officers had taken not only the new wages but also the purse strings themselves as they formed the new government. Then they turned their guns on the students, who rebelled against the idea of a military state.

The new government still had to deal, however, with the hard reality of international gasoline prices. After considerable debate, it came up with the proposal that had resulted in my siphoning of gas. It would subsidize the price to keep it at its former rate, so the taxi and bus drivers would go happily back to work. To keep a cap on how much it had to spend on the gasoline subsidy, however, the new government would have to ration the overall distribution of fuel. Public carriers like taxis, trucks, and buses would receive a more generous allotment, but all other vehicles — whether private, business, or civil service — would be rationed to thirty litres a week. There were some exceptions for

special circumstances, such as international agencies' vehicles, which got a larger ration so they could drive back and forth to the famine areas in the north. From that point on, every car license issued by the Ministry of Transportation included a ration book, which had to be examined and stamped before each week's infusion of thirty litres.

Benzine, therefore, became one of Yared's and my main occupations. I would help him change the oil or drain the radiator in one of the R&R vehicles in the morning, and then we would spend long afternoons sitting in line for gas and getting the ration books stamped for the mission's or R&R's various cars. Then we would siphon off any extra litres from the local vehicles so they could be used to get country-bound vehicles farther afield. I learned a lot from Yared.

I learned that if you didn't want to taste sulphur and rotten eggs for the rest of your life, you needed to get a length of clear rubber tubing, make sure it was long enough to reach easily from the car's tank to the jerry on the ground, and then place your head close enough to the mouth of the can that you could get the tube from your lips to the can the instant you saw the gas rise over the bend in the tube and start down towards you. I got that first horrid mouthful because I'd used a length of solid green garden hose to do the siphoning, and I'd sucked in a whole mouthful before I knew it was coming down the tube.

After that, Yared took me to the pharmacy, where SIM workers prepared simple capsules and food supplements for the famine relief camps, and we each got ourselves our own length of clear surgical tubing so we'd never be caught unprepared again. We found a spot at the back of the shed where the jerry cans and steel barrels, kept for transferring and storing gasoline, were stored, and we hid our tubes there so we'd always know where to find them. It had been a long time since I'd tasted any gas, but the smell at the Shell station still had the power to turn my stomach.

Yared stepped up into the Landcruiser and slammed the door. "So! Now we can still get over to R&R on time! Thanks to you, Mr. *Ferenjie* International Aid priority!"

As he pulled forward to the exit, he waved at the man behind us in the 504 who, in reply, placed one hand over the biceps of his other arm, which he vulgarly pumped.

"Mees-tair! *Ferenjie!*" a grizzled young man slurred at my window

when we paused at the light on Churchill Boulevard. "*Sillah Yesus Cristos.* For Jesus Christ's sake." One leg of his ragged army pants was tied off at the stump above his knee. The lump of the narcotic *ch'at* he was chewing poured a sweetness into the sour smell of sweat that flowed from his clothes.

When I rolled up my window, he hobbled on his homemade crutches to Yared's side of the car: "*Sillah Mariam, wondimé. Guadenya.* Have pity on a wounded veteran. *Yeh agirachin watadir!*"

I watched Yared empty his face of expression as he rolled up his window. He stared straight ahead. Then the light changed, and he pulled slowly away from the man's extended palm.

Once we'd traveled a block, he suddenly hit the dashboard with an open palm, like you'd slap a child's face. "By Jingles!" he shouted. "What are we still doing here? That guy could have been me. They used him till he lost his leg, and then they tossed him aside. It's not right! Nothing works like it's supposed to in this place. We've got to get out of here, Dan."

He fell into a smoky silence as we drew to a halt at another light, and mothers with babies on their backs, young kids with dysentery-swollen bellies, and more discharged amputees surged into the traffic. We sat wordless in our seats with the windows rolled up and stared straight ahead.

I knew what Yared was thinking. R&R had saved him from having to choose, as my mom would put it, between a rock and a hard place. With his high school diploma and his certificate in auto mechanics from technical school, Yared was among those who had to choose between the two forms of national service: the military or *zemecha*. Either choice meant taking his life in his hands. We saw more and more ancient-looking young men on the city streets, whose missing arms or legs witnessed to the fact that, despite the celebrations of victory that filled the government-run *Ethiopian Herald* every day, a young man's chances of coming home unscathed from the Eritrean front were next to nil.

The other option was no better. Yared once told me that of the four friends who'd been sent out to rural areas on the *zemecha* literacy campaign, he'd seen only one of them since. The others had simply vanished. Their Addis Ababa families had no news about them — whether they were alive or dead, whether they'd defected to the rebels

or to Sudan or Kenya, or whether they simply couldn't get word out to their loved ones.

While most people agreed that the *zemecha* campaign was a good idea in theory, and it was only fair that students should give back something to the country that had given them a free higher education, the problem was in its execution. The new government was anxious to prove that despite the coinciding adversities of war and famine, it was committed to bringing about major social reforms. The *zemecha* campaign would not only demonstrate this commitment, but its student-teachers could also help to explain to the populace how these reforms would work. In its eagerness to launch the program, the government forced young people to ship out to their postings sometimes even before the host communities had been contacted and proper arrangements made. The lucky ones had only minor wrinkles to iron out when they arrived at their assignments, such as where they would sleep or get their meals. The unlucky ones might encounter a community vigorously opposed to some young person dropping in from nowhere and attempting to teach his or her elders that they must change their ways. More often than not, there were no supervisors to go to if arrangements didn't work out. And the young teachers ran the risk of being labelled counter-revolutionaries if they complained.

One day Yared had pulled out his wallet and shown me a picture of a soft-eyed girl in a white blouse with a frilly, embroidered collar. "Turunish," he had told me. "That's her name. She was in my chemistry and mathematics classes at St. Joseph's. She got sent to Gambela province — somewhere towards the Sudanese border, you know, where people don't wear any clothes. Her parents never heard what happened to her. That's eighteen months ago."

R&R spared Yared from this choice between *zemecha* or the army. His dad worked for the mission as a legal advisor, and when he told the missionaries about his oldest son's impending national service, he and the mission leaders came up with the idea of hiring Yared to assist Ian Rendel with R&R maintenance. Since his job contributed to famine relief, it qualified as national service and saved him from both lousy choices.

The problem was that no solution was permanent. We had all heard about the place north of the city popularly known as *Siggah Mehda* —

"Meat Meadows" — where boys as young as twelve and thirteen were handed a bolt-action Remington rifle and given a week of parade-ground training before being packed into buses bound for the front. When they arrived, rumour had it, the officers sent them in first to clear the minefields before sending in the regulars. These rumours looked pretty accurate when you added up the missing sons and husbands among families we knew plus the missing arms and legs on the city streets. It was also clear that, as the war dragged on and the casualties mounted, the military government was growing more desperate for more *siggah*. The mission couldn't shelter Yared forever.

We wheeled up to the gate at R&R and he beeped the horn. I was glad we had arrived. The open sewers of Addis streets and fly-ridden eyes of beggar kids seemed far away once the guard opened the wrought-iron gates and we pulled into the walled one-and-a-half-hectare park that surrounded the stone mansion that served as R&R housing and offices.

"Okay, it's my turn to be Mr. *Ferenjie* Aid and your turn to be the chauffeur," Yared said, opening his door.

We traded seats and I slipped behind the richly padded steering wheel. The Landcruiser lurched when I shifted into first. He and I rolled down our windows to let in the sweet, green air. Now that we were rolling, the Landcruiser purred sedately along the paved drive that wound underneath jacarandas, guavas, and thornless acacias. All these trees had been imported and carefully planted by a landscape architect. Not one was on its way to becoming indigenous, like the *bahir-zaff* so common elsewhere. Golden sunlight fell through the canopy of leaves and dappled the lawns in moving patterns of emerald and jade. We approached the low stone stables that now served as a garage for R&R vehicles. This is where we would drop off the jerry cans, but it was our habit to tour the whole looping drive before stopping. As we passed the building, Yared reached out a hand and lightly brushed the petals of one of the burgundy tea roses that bloomed along the stable's foundation. Next came the brilliant orange flowers of a trumpet vine that massed over one end of the building.

We then approached a long, low bungalow, once servants' and gardeners' quarters, whose three apartments now provided living space for the families of doctors who'd left their British or Canadian practices to work in the relief camps for a month or two. Wine-red bougainvillea

formed an arch over each doorway, and the garden borders around their flagstone porches teemed with calla lilies, marigolds, and nasturtiums. Beyond the bungalow, tall reeds with round, spiked crests nodded above the lily-padded surface of a pond, in which we occasionally caught sight of an orange carp. The skirling song of frogs rose steadily from its marshy banks.

Neither Yared nor I had known that this kind of opulence was possible in Ethiopia until the famine had come along and attracted big money to the mission. Even the flame trees and pineapples of Sheshemane couldn't match the green majesty of R&R.

Just as the images of skeletal babies on North American, Australian, and European television screens had brought into our world new Landcruisers and Volvo trucks, so also the famine brought this estate. As part of its land-reform campaign, the new military government had nationalized all second properties owned by Addis Ababa's elite. I wondered how such a luxurious place could be someone's *second* property. What must the first look like if the second was this grand? I couldn't imagine.

Part of the mission's negotiation with the government over establishing its R&R department had involved renting property that could house incoming groups of volunteers, provide a mechanic's shop for the new vehicles, and include spaces for the new administrative offices. Strangely, the coincidence of socialist nationalization and famine relief had produced this mansion for us.

The drive curved into a loop at the base of stone stairs that rose to a terrace, where massive teak doors hung in a vaulted stone frame. The mansion introduced me to proportions and dimensions I'd never before experienced. It was surrounded on all sides by generous stone terraces, some covered by tile-roofed porticos and some open to the sky. These terraces, two or three metres above the ground, provided commanding views of the drive we'd just taken, the lily pond across the lawns, the stables and servants' quarters, and the grove of imported peach, guava, and cypress trees that shaded the grass. Low concrete railings, composed of bench-high arcades supporting a forty-centimetre-wide cap, lined the periphery of the terraces. While Yared and I waited for instructions on which truck would need the gasoline, we sat on the stone railing and dangled our feet over the bougainvillea, poinsettia, and cedar sculpted

into shrubs at the base of the terrace walls. Turned any direction, our eyes fell upon green, colour, modulating light.

As we sat there, thunder rumbled low over the city. Clouds rolled across the sun in preparation for the rainy season's afternoon shower. At the first few spits of rain, Yared and I moved to a stone bench under one of the porticos and watched the drops grow heavier and whiter until they became pellets of ice that shredded rose and hibiscus petals in the bushes below. The hail leapt like crickets from the shiny, black tarmac of the driveway. We could hear its roar as it ripped leaves from the trees, but the thickness of the portico overhead reduced its violence to a hiss. The smells of torn flowers and damp grass drenched the air as the ice water danced from the roof.

I sat and watched the hail turn back to rainfall and then to scattered drops while Yared went inside for instructions for the gasoline. I'd been inside lots of other times and had marvelled at the three-metre ceilings of the huge rooms whose grandeur jarred against the summer volunteers' bedrolls rumpled on the floor and the office manager's dented metal desk. For now, I just wanted to watch the last of the storm. By the time Yared returned, the squall was over and sunlight reflected in rainbow colours from the water beads on leaves and grass.

I got back behind the padded wheel of the Landcruiser and concentrated on letting out the clutch slowly so the vehicle wouldn't lurch. I guided the car back along the drive to the stables. "In that kind of house you don't have to worry about storms," I said. "It's almost like there's no bad weather."

"Yeah," Yared said. "Rain comes down and you don't even have to run inside. And on hot days, those stone walls make it all cool within."

At the stables, we each lugged a full jerry can into the locked room where the fuel was kept.

"A guy who came to work in the famine told me that it's as if the world was divided up into different cells," I said. "Over here you get lots of rain and over there you don't get any at all. It's just luck which cell you're born in."

Yared inserted the surgical tubing in the Toyota's tank in preparation for siphoning. "Just like us," he said. "We're dry after the storm because we had that stone roof over our heads. Meanwhile, that guy with no leg on Churchill Boulevard is soaking wet."

I sucked on the tube and kept a careful eye on the bend where the gas would start to flow down. When it did, I jammed the tube into the mouth of the jerry can.

"I hate it," I said. "This constant rubbing. The minute we drive out those gates, we'll be hassled all the way home by beggars. Problem is" — I gestured around the grounds — "this green park is what I like best. I'd take this any day. So would the guy with one leg, I bet, if he had the chance. But you have to have a wall and a guard at the gate to keep the beggars out. Otherwise, it'd all be trampled in about five minutes."

I latched the cap down on the jerry can and lugged it into the gasoline room, while Yared wound up the tubing and got back in the driver's side.

I settled into the passenger's seat and continued. "Mary Amalia from Somalia told us that the desert system of the Sahara — she called it the Sahel — is moving south. That's why there's the famine in Wollo and Tigray. So everybody from up there keeps on moving south to avoid it. But then they overcrowd everything down here, too. It's like they bring the famine with them."

I knew it wasn't right to think this way. I didn't like where it led.

"You have to have thick skin to live in Ethiopia," I grumbled, thinking again of Steve at Sheshemane.

"Huh?" Yared said. "What does 'thick skin' mean in English?"

"It means like the calluses you get on your hands from working with tools — tough and hard."

"But don't people need it everywhere? I mean, wherever people work with their hands?"

"Yeah, but we use it like a saying, too. Thick skin can also mean you have to act tough and hard — like nothing's bugging you, even if it is."

"Like when we roll up the windows when we stop at a light downtown?"

"Yeah," I said, "like that."

The Spiritual Geographies *of* Time

The nights of my youngest years resounded with drumming. Across the fence from our compound at Obi mission station, an erratic pulse emanated from the round, thatch-roofed *tukel* where Ato Angassu lived. His drums tattooed the night air of my dark bedroom and sped the heartbeat in my throat. Rega'ah, the young man who worked the garden for Mom and Dad, had told me enough about what went on over at Ato Angassu the *qallicha's* house at night to make me beg Mom to leave the door open just a crack so the band of light from the kerosene lamp in the living room would steady the quivering darkness around me. Ato Angassu's drums were the vocal cords of the *ayana* spirits. These drumbeats spattered crazily or lumbered in deliberation when Ato Angassu called upon his own *ayana* to discern the *gurri* dance of his patient. Bone-deep rhythms far beyond the daylight world of reason resounded from the goatskins stretched across Ato Angassu's wooden cylinders.

Ato Angassu's spirit drums exemplified the ancient era my family had entered when we moved in 1962, from Addis Ababa to Obi, in the rural highlands of south-central Ethiopia. His drums syncopated the time signatures that grounded my early sense of when and where I lived. Even now, I live between time signatures, in the offbeat between primordial animism and modern-day rationality.

One afternoon as I helped Rega'ah pull weeds from the pungent earth, he had warned me, "One of the forty-four *ayana* can grab you any time. You might be out for a *shir-shir*, just walking along and minding your own business. You might pass under a sycamore, and one might drop down upon you from the branches. So keep away from Ato Angassu's place. There's an *ayana* over there that makes people eat little

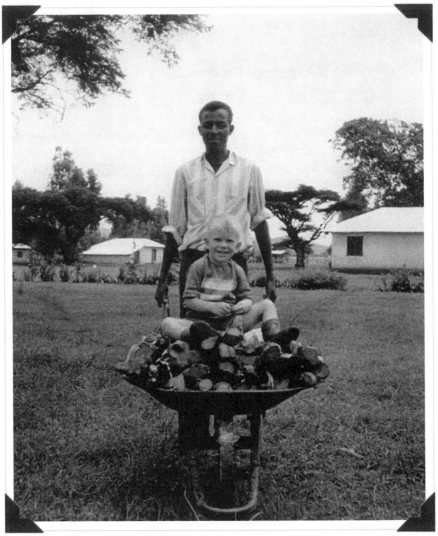

Rega'ah and me at Obi.

children. Do you hear the voice of a baby crying over there every day? It's the *ayana* of the baby-eater crying for more."

As Rega'ah beat iron-smelling clay from the weed roots, he explained that you must be constantly alert. When you cross a stream or pass by large boulders in the Chebbo hills, you'd better not forget to offer a handful of *tchokorsa* grass to the *ayana* of rushing waters or rocky fastnesses, because if you didn't appease them, they would overtake you. You could become like Abebe's mother, frothing at the mouth like a *ferruss* that's been overridden. For that is exactly what happens; you become the *ayana's* horse. He will spur you through convulsions and hallucinations. You'll be like an unbroken colt in a thunderstorm. Ha'da Abebe's relatives had to tie her in bed hand and foot to keep her from bashing her head against the walls of her house. Some people who become the *ayana's ferruss* must be constrained from running out at nights to make love with hyenas or from throwing themselves into fire.

I knew it was all true. Mom once had told us kids about the day she visited a household near Ato Kumbi's place down by the river. She and her Oromifa translator, Ayellech, had gone the rounds of the neighbourhood in an effort to get to know our neighbours — particularly the women. The minute they stepped into this one home, she felt something was wrong.

"I was wearing my *nettella* over my arms and shoulders as usual," she said, "but my skin went all prickly anyway. Outside, the sun was shining brightly. I'd been too hot in Negussie's father's house, but it was as cold as a winter's night in this place. I thought I might see my own breath. The air was charged — like those few seconds between the thunder crack and the flash of lightning. It was thick and smelled like rotten eggs. You had to pull hard to get it down into your lungs."

As my mother's eyes adjusted to the smoky darkness inside the *tukel*, she saw that a bed had been pulled out from along the circular wall and placed next to the fire in the centre of the house. A young girl poked sticks into the blaze, but this made no warmth under the sooty thatch. In the bed, the woman of the house was curled in the fetal position. Her face was puffy and battered. Mom didn't know what to say or do. She felt her own brain pound in time with the thud of the girl's pestle in the coffee mortar. Had the woman's husband beaten her? Should she inquire about this? Ayellech wasn't offering any leads, and so Mom

received the steaming *seeni* of coffee from the girl in silence. The minute she stepped out of the house, Mom took a deep breath of the warm, light air. It took several hours for the heavy taste of sulphur in her lungs to disperse.

Mom later learned from Ayellech that the woman had been over-taken by her *ayana* some nights before their visit. She had beaten her head against the centre pole of the house. She had cast herself on the floor, her body rigid in a cataleptic arch. She then emitted high-pitched screams alternating with deep-voiced commands in an incomprehensible language. Finally, she had grabbed live coals from the fire with her bare fingers and swallowed them.

The neighbours said she was somewhat better now. The night after Mom and Ayellech's visit, the woman's family had taken her to Ato Angassu for diagnosis. Her family said that, at the insistence of his drums, her *ayana* had risen up and the *qallicha* had been able to identify its voice and *gurri*. After they had learned its name and established communication, he and his retainers had been able to negotiate with her *ayana* the necessary price of peace. If the family slaughtered a tawny-coloured goat in honour of the *ayana's* lion avatar and agreed to pay a monthly tribute in care of Ato Angassu, the *ayana* would let her alone. The woman herself must attend the half-moon rituals of the secret *moyat* society and devote herself yearly to the major ceremonies of *meskel* season. For now, she could go in peace. However, if she or her family were hiding anything, if they had resources they had hidden from Ato Angassu, he was helpless to protect them from the *ayana's* rage.

And it appeared that perhaps they had tried to deceive Ato Angassu. For, the very next week, when Mom passed by that same compound, she heard a great commotion rising from the thatch-roofed house. Shouts and screams and curses from a dozen different voices chilled the afternoon air.

"It's the woman's *ayana*," a neighbour girl explained in halting Am-haric. "That woman died three days ago. Though she's starting to smell sour, her body is still the *ayana's ferruss*, and it refuses to stop riding her. She'll quiet down in another day or two. Then her family can bury her."

Sure enough, a couple of days later the funeral was announced and the neighbourhood summoned to attend the mourning.

"They live in such dark superstition and fear," Mom had said. I'd

called her from marking students' papers on the dining table because, once again, Ato Angassu's drums were frightening away my sleep. "But you don't need to be afraid. Jesus is in your heart. He'll keep you safe."

"Why does Ato Angassu hate us, Mom?" I persisted.

"He doesn't hate us, dear." Her soft hand smoothed my sweaty hair, and the golden band of lamplight fell from the partly opened door across my darkened bedspread. "He's just afraid. He thinks we'll threaten his position in the neighbourhood."

She was talking about the clinic, the school, and what the teachers did.

Before the arrival of missionaries, a *qallicha* like Ato Angassu had immense power in the community. His knowledge of the occult world of *ayana* made him even more necessary, feared, and highly paid than a physician is in Canada. People walked carefully around a *qallicha's* property. They didn't dare even to cut brushwood for their fires from the hedgerows around his lands. Tax collectors were afraid to demand the usual taxes. You never knew what dark laws you might transgress in the proximity of a *qallicha*, so it was best simply to keep your distance. Missionaries undermined Ato Angassu's pride of place because we brought the Bible and opened a school so people could learn to read. The Bible taught that there was no dark mystery. Everybody could read God's word for themselves if they wished. God was not a distant trickster who dished out adversities and pleasures in a confusing jumble. Nor was God subject to the chaos of personalities represented by *ayana*. Instead, God was intimate, logical, obvious. You could live confidently in the daylight and need not fear the dark workings of the night.

The clinic operated by the same logic. Human health was not a dark secret to be augured from the lining of a cow's abdominal cavity. You could study it, like God's voice, in a book. Miss Ott, the mission nurse, proved this true when she put a white lab coat on the shoulders of young Terefa and took him on as her aide-in-training. Every night this local boy, whose mother and father were known to everybody in the neighbourhood, read his medical books by the oily light of a tin *kuraz*. Every day he helped the nurse dispense tablets, ointments, and bandages. Someday soon, he would be a nurse himself. Anybody could do it. All you had to do was learn to read for yourself.

The clinic, therefore, was a threat to Ato Angassu's livelihood. Each

morning, a growing crowd hobbled their mules and horses outside the door to the clinic and waited for Miss Ott to arrive from the missionaries' morning prayers and open for business. Relatives of the sick passed the time in the shade of umbrellas, trading gossip and flicking their hands at blue-green horseflies, while Miss Ott and Gashé Terefa donned their white coats, turned on the reel-to-reel gospel tape, soaked balls of cotton in sharp-scented antiseptic, and set to work on ulcerated wounds, tubercular lungs, and intestinal parasites.

"There's no harm in trying the *missyonawi's* treatments," I heard a man say to the elderly woman beside him. He swished the long white hairs of his fly-whip over his shoulder. "If the *qallicha* can't negotiate with the *ayana* in your body, it's okay to give the *missyonawi* a try. But only after you've given Ato Angassu a chance."

"As long as you don't mind listening to that tape machine blasting their religious talk all day long," she replied in a gravely voice. "The *missyonawi* nurse in the white coat can't speak Oromifa herself, so she gets a machine to do it. It's like her medicine. She doesn't speak to the *ayana* directly, but approaches it sideways, with machines. She listens to your chest with one tool and then looks in your ear with a flashlight."

"But her prices are okay, so what's there to lose?" the man said. "She's not like the *qallicha* — no lifelong tribute, no demand for this kind of ox or that kind of goat. In fact, I've heard if you don't have the money to pay the *ayana* to stop blocking your wife's womb and hassling the baby, the *missyonawi* might even apply her medicine for free!"

"But she never haggles with *ayana*," the woman rasped. "She might as well be fixing a broken plough or a dented cooking *mettad*. She asks if your throat hurts, or how long the baby's been puking, but she doesn't want to know much else. Don't you think it's weird that the *missyonawi* claims to be so religious? She asks you all about your body, but looks right past the spirit."

Over the years, the Obi people gradually developed a way to accommodate both missionary clinic and *qallicha*. In the first months after my family moved to Obi, the women of the *moyat* secret society had trotted around the station at dusk, waving freshly cut eucalyptus branches. It had been some kind of ritual. Every so often on their route, they would turn and rush at our fence, making sweeping motions with the branches and uttering hisses to frighten our spirits away from their homes.

Back then, Mom and Dad had been deeply troubled by it all. They were so new in the neighbourhood that they didn't realize Angassu and his *moyat* society didn't represent the neighbours' views. Ato D'aybo, the village *balabat*, later told Dad that they were tired of Angassu's threats and domination. They wanted to see him, not us, pack up and leave. Our Oromo neighbours gradually came to welcome the mission station, not because they shared our religious beliefs, but because we brought with us both the clinic and an elementary school. Ato D'aybo himself proclaimed that these two institutions would make Obi region a beacon of the future for the surrounding districts. It would usher the young, particularly, into the modern era. Look already at young Terefa. He was just the first of many who would lead the community forward. However, this new era posed difficulties for the representatives of ancient traditions such as Ato Angassu.

The mission school had been open only a short time when the first direct confrontation occurred. Gashé Fergassa and Gashé Achalu, the two single men the mission had hired as teachers for the grades one-to-four school, lived in a dormitory on the mission station. For their evening meals, they had made a contract with a widow across the road from the school. Every night they would return in the dark from eating their *injera* at Ha'da Gallani's home, pause for Bible study with my father, and then spend the rest of the evening in preparation for the next day's classes.

The teachers were young and earnest. The Bible clearly ruled out spirits other than the Christian God: "Regard not them that have familiar spirits, neither seek after wizards, to be defiled by them: I am the LORD your God." Yet Fergassa and Achalu woke red-eyed each morning from long nights listening to Ato Angassu's drums of divination. Finally one evening, on their way home from supper at the neighbour woman's house, they stopped by Ato Angassu's compound just as his rituals were about to start.

From the entrance to Ato Angassu's yard, Gashé Fergassa shouted, "There shall not be found among you any one that useth divination! Not an observer of times, or an enchanter, or a consulter with familiar spirits, or a wizard, or a necromancer! Deuteronomy 18:10-11!"

"A man also or woman that hath a familiar spirit, or that is a wizard,

shall surely be put to death!" Gashé Achalu yelled. "Thou shalt stone them with stones! Leviticus 20:27!"

"The Holy Bible forbids the incantations of a *qallicha*," added Gashé Fergassa. "Come out of your house, Angassu, and hear the words of God about your *ayana* chicanery. Your ancient methods are a thing of the past. Come out and see the path of the future."

Two days later, at the inquiry to which *Balabat* D'aybo had summoned my father, Ato Angassu complained, "They came to my house at night with sticks. These young hoodlums that the *ferenjies* brought into the neighbourhood threatened to beat me just for practising my trade! They have no respect for these greying hairs on my head, nor for the poor people to whom I minister."

The *balabat's* role was to negotiate a compromise. Ato Angassu was middle-aged, not old enough, strictly speaking, to claim the grey hairs of a *shemagilay*. He was a good deal older than these teachers, however, so his point did carry some weight.

What did Ato Angassu want? That the young men should be given a curfew. They shouldn't be allowed off the mission station after dark, when they could go around threatening peaceful people in their homes.

"But how will they get their suppers?" my father reasoned. "They eat their *injera* every night at the widow Ha'da Gallani's home across from the mission compound."

The *balabat* suggested that perhaps Ha'da Gallani could bring the teachers' *injera* to them in the evening. But what did the missionary want in exchange?

Dad was more than ready with his demand: "No drumming at nights."

"No drums at night!" Ato Angassu said. "What does this *ferenjie* expect me to do? Starve? How can I make a living if I can't treat patients and read the book of the cow's peritoneum? Everyone knows that the drum is the tongue and the ear of *ayana*! It's like telling this *missyonawi* not to study his Bible!"

The meeting broke up in disarray. Ato Angassu couldn't actually prove that the teachers had done him any harm. Everyone carried walking sticks to fend off dogs or hyenas at night. As well, the teachers needed to get their suppers. They were entitled to their beliefs. Though no one said so directly at the meeting for fear of his dark powers, the com-

munity hoped Ato Angassu would move away. It was a good thing to be able to consult a *qallicha* when you were in trouble, but it was always a tricky business to have one in your neighbourhood. You never knew when you might fall afoul of his obscure laws.

An informal compromise did gradually evolve. The scripture-wielding teachers never bothered Ato Angassu again, and he, in turn, turned down the volume on his nightly incantations. In fact, he began to farm part-time to supplement his dropping income. As a result, we slept more soundly in the quiet nights. Ato Angassu remained troubled by the mission, just as we on the mission station continued to be troubled by him, but we agreed to disagree and tried to get along as best we could, even though our different versions of the spirit world remained rivals. This kind of compromise, or at least a willingness to try to translate between opposing views, was an everyday fact of life in Ethiopia. Sometimes the translations were severe and disapproving, such as when we strained the world of *ayana* through the taboos of Christianity. Other times these conversions seemed more mundane, such as when we calculated the time of day or identified the year. Even these less sensational transpositions, however, took place between very different spiritual geographies.

We reckoned time differently, for example. Ethiopia followed the Julian calendar of the Eastern Orthodox Church, while we followed the Gregorian reform of the Western church — which meant that *ferenjies* always had to subtract seven to figure out what Ethiopian year we were in. The holidays and months were different, too. The Orthodox calendar celebrated Christmas about seven days after the European New Year. Ethiopian New Year itself came in what *ferenjies* call September; it marked the end of the long rains, when the earth garbed itself in the new clothes of the yellow *meskel* flowers and farmers sowed the year's new crops.

The concept of the year itself was different, too. The Ethiopian year included an extra month. The Tourist Service posters on my bedroom wall advertised "Thirteen Months of Sunshine," and the claim was not

hyperbole. At least, not with respect to the number of months. The country's official calendar observed thirteen months a year: twelve equal months of thirty days apiece, and a short thirteenth lasting five days — or six in leap year.

It made sense for Ethiopians to have their own delineation of months, for the equatorial seasons had nothing at all to do with those of northern or southern climes. For that matter, because most of the country spreads across a high and mountainous plateau, its relatively cool and wet seasons had little to do with the desert conditions of the countries surrounding its borders: Kenya, Somalia, Djibouti, Eritrea, and Sudan.

The enigma of seasons first occurred to me when I was in the fourth grade at Bingham and our Sunday School teacher, Miss Forsberg, introduced "Quarterlies" into the curriculum. These newsprint booklets, published in Grand Rapids, Michigan, contained weekly lessons that consisted of a reading from the Bible, a short meditation, and a page of questions for discussion. Our first Quarterly proclaimed "Fall" on the front cover, and the subsequent ones, "Winter" and "Spring." The Fall Quarterly cover displayed a forest whose lurid leaves I disbelieved. No September I knew consisted of these jarring yellows and reds. We gazed at pictures of ripe pumpkins and squash, and then we looked out the windows to see farmers rejoicing over new shoots that were half a year away from harvest. Just six weeks ago we had seen the same farmers defying veils of rain and tramping behind yoked oxen through the red muck raised by their ploughs. The approach of dry season and sun-cracked clay made it urgent they spread the *teff* seed at the height of the heavy rains, while the scent of minerals rose from the steaming humus. Now in September the recent rainy season had greened every growing thing, and the water lapped in lakes on the soccer field. Not a yellow blade or a brown leaf interrupted the verdant world.

The Fall Quarterly also told of the American pilgrims greeted at Plymouth Rock by Indians bearing corn. We read a Psalm of thanksgiving for the abundance of harvest, and we puzzled over questions such as "How do we know that God cares for us, even when the trees and bushes all around us seem to be dying and the world is getting ready for winter?" Meanwhile, the windows of our classroom shook with the cacophony of ravens vying for dominance as they dipped and struck at

the winged termites driven out of the ground by moisture. The ground seemed to be blooming insects, sending out masses of new life. If I had known the word, I would have called September fecund.

The Quarterlies spiritualized the geography of our Northern homelands in a way that completely misfit the Ethiopian seasons we knew. In the Winter issue, we tried to envision white Christmases and sleigh bells while sway-backed nags pulled two-wheel *garries* down the dusty gravel roads of Addis's back streets. We got out the cotton wool from our Christmas decorations box and spread it over cedar boughs to evoke snow, while poinsettia trees outside our classrooms wilted in the hot sun and leaned against the eaves. With the Spring Quarterly, we gathered at dawn on a chilly hilltop on Easter Sunday and sang "Up from the Grave He Arose." Here, though, it was the middle of dry season, when nothing new was likely to spring out of the baked earth, least of all a lily.

The disjunction between the Sunday School Quarterlies and the local seasons strengthened my growing awareness that time was determined by standards, and these standards were usually set somewhere else. There was the Western Christian standard of the Gregorian calendar, and even within Ethiopia, there was a standard. We used the Julian calendar because Orthodox Amharas ran the government. If Muslims were in charge, however, we would have a different one. *When* depended, then, not just on *how* your people counted religious history, but also on *whose* religious story was strongest.

Every misfit season, we learned again that we did not inhabit the standard. Our Ethiopian time signature was not as strong as other time signatures. Not being as strong meant we must do all the adjusting. For instance, there was the standard of the BBC World Service, called "Greenwich Mean Time." When the BBC World Service delivered its time signal, we added three hours to locate ourselves in the East African time zone. However, if you lived in England, Dad once explained to me, you didn't have to add or subtract any hours because you lived in the meantime. When we phoned Grandma Coleman in Ontario, we subtracted eight hours from our time to make sure we didn't get her out of bed. We must always add or subtract hours to make contact with the larger world.

Every day, we converted from *ferenjie* to Ethiopian time and back

again. Though the Ethiopian way of numbering the hours of the day made more sense to me, every *ferenjie* I knew set his or her watch to European time. Ethiopians rose at dawn and numbered this dew-drenched moment the first hour of the day. They paused for lunch and siesta at six o'clock when the dust and lethargy of midday made work pointless. Then they worked through the hours of the afternoon until twelve o'clock, when dusk sent them home in search of their *injera buh watt* and an evening's rest. They began the evening at one o'clock, and climbed into their blankets to sleep around four or five at night so they would be rested when they woke between twelve and one, when the sun's first rays coloured the horizon. *Ferenjies*, by contrast, preferred to hide the transitional moments in the middle of things: the drama of sunset and sunrise occurred somewhere in the middle-hours between five and seven, a.m. and p.m., and the date on my Swiss-made Oris wristwatch tripped forward in the secret hour of midnight.

When I was an infant, John and Sharon had two pitch-black rabbits whose names are the earliest puns I can remember: Half-Past Eleven and Midnight. I recall seeing pictures of the rabbits in John's photo album when I was six or seven and suddenly getting the joke: how clever to name those inky bunnies after the darkest hours of the night. Then I got to wondering. Why didn't they name the second bunny "Five-Thirty," a half-hour before Midnight, instead of Half-Past Eleven, which was when the sun started coming up? I supposed it was because pets and rabbits were a *ferenjie* idea in the first place, so that's why they should be named by the *ferenjie* way of counting time.

The differences between Ethiopian and *ferenjie* time did not mean, however, that spiritual events were restricted to the world of *ayana*. The miraculous was as real to us missionaries as it was to those who consulted *qallichas*. The life we shared between time signatures meant that our worlds leaked into one another.

When I was just turning five, I rounded the corner from the living room in our house at Obi and found my mother hanging by the neck from the doorframe of my parents' bedroom closet. Shock stabbed from my

head to my toes. I tasted something sour on the back of my tongue. What was she doing? From a hook in the solid wood of the door lintel hung a canvas sling that fit snugly under Mom's skull. She had her knees bent so her feet didn't touch the floor, and she swung gently in front of Dad's blue-grey suit and her floral Sunday dress.

Just two weeks before, Rega'ah had told me about the public hanging that had taken place in Woliso, the closest market town. A public defender, realizing that he was about to lose the case, drew a pistol and shot the prosecuting lawyer dead right there in the court-room. There had been over twenty eyewitnesses. The sentence of hanging for first-degree murder was handed down only a few weeks later.

"His body went down hard, ka-dah!" Rega'ah mimed the fall and jerk of the body with his hands as he spoke. "And then he went like a chicken after you cut its head off — flopping and jiggling like crazy. Without the blood, of course. That's why they kill them that way. The blood stays inside, and they don't have to clean anything up after-wards. They let the body hang all day, and they bury it later. Anyway, he was jerking around, and finally, after a few seconds, he went still. His head stayed bent way over, like this." Rega'ah tilted till his ear touched his shoulder. He let his tongue loll out of the side of his mouth. He drooled and made drowning, gurgling noises. Then, before my terrified eyes, he reached up with both hands, flipped his eyelids inside out, and came after me. I ran screaming, while he fumbled theatrically at the gate I'd slammed on my flight from the garden.

Rega'ah's story was two weeks old, but I'd relived it at night on my sweaty pillow ever since. Now here was my own mother, swinging like a murderer in her open closet door! The sour flooded my tongue.

"Mom!" I cried. "What are you doing?!"

"Shh," said Dad. I hadn't seen him sitting on the bed as he watched her sway in the closet. "It's okay. Mom's got a sore back again, and the doctor said she should try this."

I had seen adults doing other weird things because of Mom's bad back. Like the time Mom lay on her back across the bed, Miss Ott had her in what looked like a headlock, and Dad grabbed one of her ankles in each hand and pulled steadily. I thought of the woodcut I'd seen in *Foxe's Book of Martyrs* showing how they stretched saints on the rack. John had told me their bones pulled right out of their joints. Mom's

backaches made her submit herself to disturbing indignities, but this hanging in the doorframe was the strangest I'd seen so far. I turned to leave as soon as I could because I always felt queasy when Mom's back hurt. I needed fresh air.

Within a few days I became accustomed to my mother's hanging ritual. Oh yeah, there's Mom again, hanging by the neck in her closet.

Then big changes took place in our house and pushed Mom's back remedy out of my mind. Grandpa Coleman was very sick, Mom told me at supper one night. She spooned green mush into Marianne, who smacked a sticky hand on the tray of her highchair. That's why Dad was in his bedroom putting clothes in a suitcase instead of having supper with us. He would be catching the bus to Addis before dawn the next day and then a plane to Toronto. We'd be on our own for a month, until John and Sharon finished their school term, and then the rest of us would fly to Canada and rejoin Dad.

A plane ride! My older siblings could remember flying when we went on furlough four years before, but I'd been only months old and couldn't remember it at all. Now I would see what clouds looked like from the top! Maybe the pilot would let us come up to the cockpit.

During the intervening month, Mom spent long hours climbing the stairs to the attic and packing clothes, dishes, and furnishings into the steel barrels we'd saved from the last time we'd sent things by ocean freight. Usually, Dad would have done this heavy lifting, but with him gone, it was all up to Mom. The house filled with the sharp smell of mothballs from her labour. Because other missionaries would be living in our house while we were gone, everything had to be put away.

One day Mom learned by telegram that Grandpa had died. She solemnly told Marianne and me the news over our steaming oatmeal at the breakfast table. Her quiet, even voice made me realize that Grandpa's death was a serious matter. I had no memories of him, however, and Mom had no tears in her eyes when she told us the news, so I heard and dismissed it like other solemn news that got passed around the table during our after-breakfast prayer time. The mission printing press's VW van had finally broken down for good, and they needed money for a new one. A missionary down at Bonga had contracted malaria. We called these bits of sober news "prayer requests" and mentioned them one by one to God during our devotions after breakfast. This time

Mom prayed that God would comfort Dad, Grandma, and Auntie June. As soon as prayers were over, I squirmed out of my chair and headed for the door.

"Uh-uh, Danny." Mom's sharp voice stopped my busy feet. "Plate and silverware to the sink, and then there's the woodbox to fill, and don't forget to brush your teeth before you go out to play." Morning had a routine, and it didn't matter how restless you were to get on with the day. Chores had to be finished first.

One morning, however, Mom plunked my bowl of semolina porridge on my placemat and nearly skipped around the table to her own chair. My mother. I looked at her with interest. She was glowing. Positively radiant!

"Oh Lord our God." She began to bless the food. Then she stopped. "I'm too excited to pray properly!" she said before my startled face. "I'm healed! God's done a miracle. You know how I used to hang in my closet before Daddy went away? Because of my back, right? Well, with Daddy gone, I just didn't know what I'd do. How was I going to pack up this whole house? How could I go up and down the stairs all day to the attic and lean way over to put every blessed thing we've got into those high barrels? I started to pray about this. I couldn't do it! So I asked God to do something.

"And you know what? I've been praying each day that my back will be okay. I've run up and down those attic stairs. I've leaned over at the hip for five days straight. And I keep expecting the ache. But I haven't felt a thing! I wake up in the morning and wonder if I'll be able to get out of bed. Five mornings in a row I've lain there checking every sensation in my back, and there isn't a shred of pain! Not a twinge. I used to have trouble just lifting down one of those mixing bowls from the kitchen cupboard. And now I've packed most of the kitchen, and all the clothes from you kids' closets, and I've even packed up Dad's tools in the *ickabait* and lugged them up to the attic. Not a thing! It's like I have a whole new spinal column. I'm almost afraid to say it too early, but I think God's healed me!"

After breakfast prayer that day was different than usual. We didn't read the monthly prayer list sent out by the mission. We didn't read the little lesson from *Our Daily Bread*, the devotional guide we used every morning. Instead, with the guava jam still sweet on our tongues, we

sang together, Mom and I, with Marianne hooting and banging her spoon to keep time with our noise. First Mom chose "How Great Thou Art," and then I got to choose my favourite: "How Did Moses Cross the Red Sea?" Mom helped Marianne do the actions that went with the chorus:

> *Did he swim? No, no!*
> *Did he fly? No, no!*
> *Did he sail? No, no!*
> *How did he get across?*
> *God blew with His wind, puff, puff, puff, puff.*
> *He blew just enough, nough, nough, nough, nough.*
> *And through the wind, God made dry land,*
> *That's how he got across!*

I loved it. Devotions that morning were like a party. We sang louder and louder. We got out of our chairs and did the actions as we circled the table. I puffed my table napkin right onto the floor with a mighty wind. My mother sang and glowed, and tears ran down her face. Her back was healed. God did miracles, not just in the Bible, but in our own time, 1966 *anno domini,* right here in Obi — non-standard, non-Greenwich, non-Mean Time. God cared about us. He healed my mother and made her happy. Even as I write this now, all these years later, my mother's back has never pained her again as it did in those early years before she was healed at Obi.

I am sure that Mom's healed back can be explained medically. Maybe she had a partially herniated disk or a persistent subluxation. Perhaps the constant stretching and leaning over those steel barrels pushed some misaligned vertebrae back into place. Maybe, too, the woman with the *ayana* hadn't been inhabited by spirits. Possibly she was suffering an extreme form of psychosis. A psychiatrist would likely rationalize such spirit possessions as some kind of schizophrenia or a form of epilepsy. Explanations exist for such things. In fact, the woman could have been still very much alive when Mom heard her screaming those few days later, and she died afterwards simply because her family neglected her during a series of massive seizures. The world of reason has ready explanations for the phenomena of the spirit world.

The missionary culture in which I was raised placed one foot in each of these worlds. We believed in both spiritual powers and presences *and* in medical science and rationality. We lived in the time zone of the clinic and school, and also in the time zone of the supernatural. We believed that God healed people sometimes through doctors and nurses and sometimes through miraculous means. We lived between the clinic and *ayana*, between Canada and Ethiopia, between reason and spirit.

Since moving to Canada as a young adult, I have observed how persistently Canadian society chooses one side over the other. The time signature here is ordered and moderated by the intellect. I say this not just because I have become a university professor, and at university, reason is god. Everywhere in our larger society you can see the priority given to the organizing, rationalizing powers of the mind. Look at the lines painted on the roads to keep cars in orderly rows, the signs that tell when and where to smoke, the organization of grocery stores into produce, dairy products, baking supplies, and meats. From these mundane details to the use of a referendum rather than armed struggle to decide who will constitute our nation, it's rationality that keeps our world predictable, efficient, and safe. There are, of course, pockets in which spiritual or mystical life are practiced: football players praise Jesus when they win the Grey Cup, environmentalists shout Amen when First Nations claim the sacredness of old growth forest, and you occasionally spot advertisements in the paper for a psychic fair in your city. These pockets, however, remain outside the rational systems that define our society's modernity.

There's a flip side to our rationality, though, that suggests that this modernity isn't as absolutely removed from the spiritual as we might want to believe. The orderly categories of a bookstore, for example, include "Occult" alongside "Humour" and "Biography." In addition, every paper across the country runs a horoscope column alongside the comics and the crossword puzzle. We have our own dark spirits, but we contain them in special categories. Whereas the rational occasionally poked through the spiritual when I lived in Ethiopia, here in Canada,

it's the spiritual that only rarely pokes through the rational. Thus, it still surprises me that the only exorcism I've ever witnessed took place not in Ethiopia but in Saskatchewan, Canada in 1980, Gregorian calendar, when I was in my second year at the University of Regina.

The phone rings at three o'clock one morning, and I rub sleep out of my eyes while I listen to Craig, a friend I've made through the campus chapter of Intervarsity Christian Fellowship, asking me if I'll go with him over to Susan's apartment right away. Something about Susan's boyfriend, William, acting strange. Craig's voice sounds thin on the line. "I don't feel good about going over there by myself, Daniel. You know about these kinds of things from Ethiopia, don't you?"

Half an hour later we knock on Susan's door. When we follow her down the hall to her living room, I notice two large kitchen knives stabbed through the carpet and into the wood floor by the door to her bedroom. William is sitting on the couch with his elbows on his knees and his face resting on his fists. His shoulder-length brown hair hides his face. A third knife glints on the carpet by his foot. He's rocking back and forth in time to the rock music blaring from Susan's radio. Even over the music, I can hear him grinding his teeth.

"Hi, William," Craig says over the radio's steady pulse. "Susan phoned us to come over. Sounds like you're having a bad night."

"Fuck off," William growls as he lifts his head out of his hands. His eyes, red and bleary, are intensely focused, his craggy cheeks are unshaven, and his body perspires rancid alcohol.

"That's no way to talk to a friend," Craig says. His stocky figure steps to the couch and sits beside William. "We just came over to make sure you're all right — maybe pray together a bit, ask Jesus to be close to you and Susan."

William yells, "Don't talk about Jesus!" He shoves Craig away with a stiff arm on the shoulder. "Don't fuckin' talk about Jesus!"

I startle when the doorbell rings.

"That'll be Pastor Gord," Susan explains. "I phoned him, too."

"Sure, invite a preacher!" William shouts after her as she walks down the short hall to the door. "Invite a whole fuckin' congregation!"

Craig puts a hand on the trembling man's knee. "She just didn't feel safe, William. She wanted us to come over and talk with you. You were making her scared."

"Don't touch me!" William leaps up, grabs the knife, and stabs it into the floor between Craig's feet on the carpet. "And don't talk to me about Jesus, either!"

"Why not?" Craig asks. He stands, and, though he's twenty-five centimetres shorter than William and the top of his red hair only reaches William's chin, he steps between the troubled man and the knife. "Isn't this the best time of all to talk about Jesus? When things are out of hand? Come on. Susan asked us to come over here to pray together."

Pastor Gord and Susan are in the room now. I see the tall, bearded pastor take in the knives in the floor. His mild gaze lifts to William. Seeing he's preoccupied with Craig, he pulls the knives out of the floor and takes them into the kitchen. When he comes back, he turns off the radio. Suddenly the room is empty of drums.

William swings a fist at Craig's chest. "No Jesus!" he screams. "No fuckin' prayer!"

Craig steps into the punch so it lands before it gathers force. I come up behind William, and before I know it, Craig, Pastor Gord, and I have William on the carpet, Craig and Gord holding an arm each and me holding his legs. We're trying to keep him still without hurting him while he calms down. Susan looks on wide-eyed from the kitchen door.

"Don't talk about Jesus, don't talk about Jesus!" William yells, and he flings his head from side to side. Then suddenly he goes still. He cocks open one eye at Craig and says in a strange, deep voice, "How come it takes three of you guys to hold us down? Are we that strong?"

"What do you mean, us?" says Craig. "Who are you?"

"Heh," William leers. "That's for you to find out. We're not saying anything."

"Well then, in the name of Jesus Christ I command you to come out of William!" Craig intones in a calm, strong voice. "With the authority of . . ."

"Don't mention that name!" We're back to William's voice, but this

time it's more a plea than a yell. "Please don't mention that name. Oh God, Craig, please don't say it anymore."

"But it's only by the power of Jesus' blood that you can be free of Satan's grip," says Craig. "So, I say again, in the name of Jesus and by the power of his blood, I command you to leave William and not return."

William arches his back in a wrestler's bridge. The small of his back lifts fifteen centimetres off the carpet. I'm holding his shins with both hands and sitting on his ankles, and when his back snaps down, he kicks me off the floor. I taste blood from having bitten my tongue. Then William surprises us all by spitting out dentures. With them gone, his stubbled jaw collapses. He's a young man — mid-twenties, I'd guess — but there's not a natural tooth in his mouth, and without his false teeth he looks tired and old. The thin, sarcastic lips fall into a fleshy crater in the middle of his skull. William's body sinks to the floor, and I can feel his calf muscles go slack. Pastor Gord takes the dentures from William's chest and places them on the glass-topped lamp table by William's head.

"Dear Jesus," Craig resumes in a conversational tone. "I pray that you would deliver William from Satan's power. That you would give him peace of heart and quiet of mind. I ask that you would protect him and Susan and all of us from evil influences in our bodies, minds, and hearts. Be with us now. Give William a settled spirit. And may we all be able to sleep well tonight and wake refreshed to the new day that is your daily gift. Amen."

William lies quietly. We're still holding his arms and legs, uncertain of when he might go into another frenzy. Susan is crying quietly at the kitchen door.

Pastor Gord starts to pray. He asks God to bring peace and calm to all of us. He asks for rest for the remainder of the night. He asks God to be especially close to William and Susan. He prays all these things in Jesus' name.

The room falls quiet again for a few minutes. I begin to relax my grip on William's legs. Then he begins to pray himself.

"Jesus," he lisps without his teeth. "Jesus. Forgive me, Jesus. I've done wrong, Jesus. Forgive me. I drink too much. I smoke dope. I go out of my head, Jesus. I — "

He interrupts himself. "Do you guys mind letting me sit up?" His voice is quiet.

We let go of his arms and legs, and he rolls over, gets up on hands and knees. He crawls to the couch and kneels there beside the lamp like a penitent.

"I've hurt people, Jesus. I've hurt so many people — my folks back on the island, my friends at work here, Susan . . . I need you to make me better, Jesus. Please make me a better person."

And so it goes. He prays, kneeling at Susan's couch in a circle of golden lamplight. We follow suit and kneel beside him, our elbows on the nearest piece of living room furniture — coffee table, armchair, couch. I pray briefly with the iron taste of blood receding on my tongue. We all ask God to help William make the changes he desires. I get home at about six a.m. and collapse on my bed just as the sun begins to rise.

Over the next few weeks, I see William a lot. He's at prayer group on Tuesday, he's not just at church but at Sunday School, too, and he and Susan show up for Thursday evening Bible Study as well. There seems to be nothing left of the howling madman on Susan's living room carpet in the quiet, receptive guy he's now become.

The Sunday after that night at Susan's, Pastor Gord calls Craig and me aside after church. "I thought we should talk a little bit about last Wednesday night. I'd say we should keep that evening to ourselves, okay? I just don't think it would do William a lot of good — or Susan either, for that matter — to spread the story around. It could become a sensation. And I'm not sure we have the whole story, anyway. I'm not sure how much of what we saw was spiritual, how much was alcohol, and how much was psychological."

To this day I'm not sure either. Dissociative reaction? Schizophrenia? Just plain substance abuse? I don't know. Was Pastor Gord trying to create some distance from an embarrassing event he didn't understand? I know I'd rather pretend I'd never been there. Still, I can't deny that in

the space of half an hour, I saw a man full of violence become reasonable and contrite. And I did see a person who went ballistic at the mere mention of Jesus' name calmly pray that name only minutes later.

If we were Obi villagers, we might say we had discerned the *ayana's* voice and delivered William from being its *ferruss*. There was no slaughter of a tawny-haired goat, no reading of a cow's peritoneum. Nonetheless, the distance between Obi and Saskatchewan seemed small that night. How many hours did I need to add to three a.m. in Regina to calculate the correct time in Ethiopia? How many hours apart were Saskatchewan and Greenwich Mean Time? I wondered if old Ato Angassu was still alive and if he continued to sound his drums now that he had moved away from Obi and Ato Terefa's thriving clinic. Despite the many rational explanations for William's behaviour, despite Pastor Gord's concern that we not let it become overblown, and despite the medieval ethos of the whole thing, I can't dismiss it all as psychomedical. My Ethiopian past will not let my *ferenjie* present remain so sure of itself, so reasonably smug.

In this case — and in the case of Mom's back, too — the dissociative reactions and misaligned vertebrae of the modern present seemed to need help from the ancient past of spirits and miracles. Such moments of temporal overlap serve as another reminder of the relativity of time. *When* depends on *how* we measure time's units, on how many beats fill a bar. The time signature that tells us how to count the beats, in turn, depends on *whose* music, *whose* stories we've got ears for. It's the musical framework that makes meaning out of noise, just as narrative charts a path through the chaos of events. These sense-making structures are powerful, because they give us faith that we understand what passes before our eyes. We need them. They enable us to put one foot confidently in front of another. They let us walk upright, assured that our feet will meet solid ground.

But it's also a good thing, occasionally, to encounter moments of overlap, when the rhythms of another time signature muscle into our mundane measure, our familiar terrain. The resulting syncopation, if we're willing to adapt to it, can help us improvise a flexibility that enables us to dance between the spiritual geographies of time.

Broken Word

On November 8, 1985, mere months after his release from the prison popularly known as Alem Bukagne (No More World for Me, or, in looser translation, the End of the World), Negussie Kumbi broke off a piece of scripture and sent it in an aerogramme to my brother, John. It was a kind of Biblical *goursha*. In Ethiopia, a good host shows concern for a guest's nourishment by tearing off a large piece of sourdough *injera*, wrapping it around the choicest piece of chicken or lamb in the hot-pepper *wutt*, and delivering it gently into the mouth of the guest. Negussie's father, Ato Kumbi, used to take particular delight in filling my mouth so full when I was little that it was hard not to bite his fingers when he placed the *goursha* there.

Now, in 1985, Negussie had learned about an obstacle John had encountered in his dream of returning to Ethiopia, and he showed his concern by placing in his letter a choice portion from Psalm 37:

> *Yahweh guides a man's steps,*
> *they are sure, and he takes pleasure in his progress;*
> *he may fall, but never fatally,*
> *since Yahweh supports him by the hand.*
> *Now I am old, but ever since my youth*
> *I never saw a virtuous man deserted,*
> *or his descendants forced to beg their bread.*

Though I love the taste of the Psalmist's confidence in God's care, I cannot read this Biblical passage without a bone sticking in my throat. For, while Negussie used the Psalm to assure others, its assurances did not play out in his own life: he could honestly say in 1985 that God

had protected his steps, even in prison, but eight years later, uncomprehending, I held his hand as his own fall turned fatal. I've seen Negussie's wife, Fantaye, widowed and his two little boys, Nat'nael and Mikias, orphaned. I have seen his family made to wonder where their bread would come from, and I cannot help but wonder why God would break his word to Negussie.

"Maybe he was cursed!" his sister Almaz speculated when John went to visit her. This from the long-suffering sister who, for six years, had taken Negussie's supply of food every Sunday to Alem Bukagne, which had earned its End of the World nickname when the sixty members of Haile Selassie's demoted cabinet were executed there by firing squad in 1974.

"He must have been born under some kind of evil sign, with his bent back and his endless troubles," she said. "Did you know my father didn't even want him to go to the mission clinic for TB treatments when he was little? Mother used to sneak off with him to the clinic when Father was visiting the second farm or preoccupied with village meetings. The rest of us children used to wonder: why do all the bad things happen to Negussie? He was always so gentle and happy — you know? But trouble came to him like flies."

Negussie's life does this. It throws those who knew him into an anxious search for explanations.

For the members of my parents' SIM, who heard terrifying stories about the imprisonment and torture of many Ethiopian converts during the *Kai Shebbir*, Negussie is a hero of the faith. He was tested in the fiery furnace and found true. He remained faithful under enormous pressure, refused to compromise his beliefs, and emerged victorious from the Red Terror. Far from being cursed, he was himself a blessing. To the very end of his life, his constant delight in God's goodness lifted the spirits of anyone who knew him. His life demonstrates how simple joy under enormous adversity becomes a saint's legend.

I can't bear to think Negussie was cursed. To do so, I'd have to deny what he himself believed. But I also think that making him into a saint sprinkles sugar all over him in a desperate attempt to make a cupcake out of the course grain of his life.

My family met Negussie shortly after Dad and Mom were posted to Obi mission station in 1962. Some months before our arrival, Betty Martin, the mission nurse, had found Negussie huddled on a pallet in Ato Kumbi's house hard by the mission station. Tuberculosis had attacked his spine when he was a baby, collapsing several vertebrae and leaving him unable to stand erect. The boy, whose name meant "my king," had been housebound his whole childhood. Treatment at the TB clinic in Addis, followed by a regime of physiotherapy over the next few years, liberated Negussie from his bed and allowed him to run and play like other kids. The only signs that remained of his youthful disease were the curve of his spine near his right shoulder blade and the disparity between his long legs and shortened torso. To look at the highly arched eyebrows of his cheerful, gentle face, you would think he'd never seen a day of trouble in his life.

No one in our family remembers the moment when Negussie became a virtual fifth child. He just grew into us, more or less. The feeling was not merely on our side, nor was it limited to those early years in Obi. In August 1989, for example, he wrote to John in Saskatchewan, "I received a letter from Mr. and Mrs. Coleman. They told me about you, Sharon, Daniel, and Marianne, so I have some knowledge of you all. I count you as my second family." There were other kids we spent time with at Obi — Alemu, Mulugeta, Zenebech — but a combination of circumstances made Negussie our most regular companion. He lived nearer than Alemu, and his church involvement and attendance at school brought him onto the mission station more often than Mulugeta and Zenebech. Most of all, we warmed to his amiable self.

Though he was Sharon's age and older than John, Marianne, and me, he entered gladly into our childhood games. He invented a game called "Stone Tag," which combined Hide-and-Seek with the conventional tag game. He converted the sycamore tree into a Saturday market, where, with John, Marianne, and me, he established a bartering system in which moss stood for *kibé* butter, unripe berries for *inqulal* eggs, bark for *inchet* firewood, and leaves for *birr* money. On rainy days, he joined us in games of Monopoly. He once famously scammed me by showing

Negussie.

empty coffers when he owed me rent. I let him go, only to find, when his turn came, that he had hidden three five-hundred-dollar bills in his sock, with which he proceeded to put new hotels on his properties.

Negussie animated our imaginations. If we weren't playing Monopoly or Stone Tag or Tree Market, we would be seeing how long we could swim underwater at the Woliso pool at the Ras Hotel. If none of these, then he would spark our fancies with John's and my favourite — an animal fable. Negussie's gentle voice savoured the parts of his story as if each were the finest morsel of spiced beef *tibbs*.

"I read this story in school," he began one afternoon after a day at the pool. "It's a Showa folktale." We three boys were riding in a horse-drawn *garri* from Woliso back home to Obi. The roadside was crowded with people walking home after Saturday market. The smell of the horse's sweat mixed with the reek of its saddle sores and drifted back to us on the *garri's* bench seat. My hair was still wet, but the breeze of movement would dry it quickly. The horse's iron shoes clacked tiredly on the tarmac of the Woliso town road.

"It was nearing the end of Saturday market, and Donkey was nervous about returning home after sundown. He knew Hyena and his band of thieves often hid in the dark along the road back to his house, and he knew he didn't have the teeth or claws to defend himself. He wavered over what to do. Should he set out anyway and take his chances? Or should he wait until others were heading home and fall in with them?

"'What's up, Donkey?' growled Lion, who passed by as Donkey worried over his problem.

"'Make some good sales today?' grunted Lion's friend, Leopard.

"'Oh, sirs! Thanks be to God, I did manage to sell a few things. Now I wish to go home to my wife and children, but I've heard that Hyena and his gang have been lurking along the road. Have you heard this news, too?'

"'You've always been such a coward!' said Lion. 'Who cares if Hyena's skulking in the bushes with fifty relatives? One swipe of my Lion's paw and they'd all be crying for their mothers, eh, Leopard?'

"'But perhaps our brother Donkey needs protection for the road home,' said Leopard. 'Am I right, Donkey?'"

Negussie paused. Donkey was thinking over his reply. John and I were thinking over Donkey's situation. What would be best: risk Hyena

in the bushes, or trust the intentions of Lion and Leopard? Our *garri* passed a man on the roadside whose feet swam, wildly searching for solid ground between each step. When Dad saw drunks teetering home from market, he always grumbled about their wages going straight to the *tej* sellers instead of the wives and kids. The man's walking stick saved him. It gave him a third leg, so he could always keep two contacts with the ground while the mobile limb searched for its next elusive home.

Negussie watched the man, then returned to his story. "'Oh, masters!' Donkey cried in a thin, high voice. 'Please don't concern yourselves over me. I'm sure you have more important business here at the market. I've no doubt I'll find a safe way home.'

"But Lion and Leopard insisted. Before he knew what was happening, Donkey set out for home in the early evening light with the market's two most powerful characters for his chaperones.

"Just barely out of town, Lion spied a goat in a farmer's field by the road. He leapt on it and ate it. When he saw the horror on Donkey's face, he said, 'I absolutely must apologize. I have committed a major sin. I have no quarrel with this farmer or with his goat, yet even though they've done me no harm, I couldn't help my hunger. I am a murderer and a thief.'

"'Oh, sir!' pleaded Donkey. 'Please don't berate yourself. You are a big and vigorous fellow. You need to eat great quantities to feed your powerful muscles. So it is your nature to kill and eat. This is not a sin. You were simply following your instincts!'

"They had hardly taken ten steps along the farmer's pasture when Leopard pounced upon an unsuspecting calf and gobbled it down. When he returned to the roadside and saw the terror on Donkey's face, he said, 'I, too, must get this great crime off my chest. To my knowledge, this farmer and calf have never insulted my family or wished me harm in any way. Yet I have killed this innocent creature and robbed his rightful owner. I am a great sinner.'

"'Oh, my masters! How can you accuse yourselves in this way?' Donkey squeaked. 'You are predators in your very bones. This is the core of your being. It cannot be a sin to follow the dictates of nature! Please do not feel you must confess guilt over these minor mishaps.'"

"He's such a coward!" I burst in on Negussie's story. "Why doesn't he tell the truth?"

"What else could he say?" John reasoned. "He needs to keep Lion and Leopard friendly. If he makes them angry, they might eat him, too!"

We passed a woman and a young girl walking on the shoulder of the road. The young girl had a baby tied in the soft cotton *shemma* on her back and a chain of hen's eggs tied in *insett* leaves dangling from each hand. The woman tilted heavily over the hand in which she carried a full, bucket-sized kerosene tin. The sound of the liquid rinsing the inside of the silver cube wobbled in the air. The late afternoon sun threw her long, grotesquely bent shadow down the road; the sharp scent of the kerosene briefly displaced the horse smell, over-rich in my nostrils.

Negussie nodded a greeting to the woman and girl, then returned to his story.

"The threesome passed by the farmer's field. It seemed that Lion and Leopard had to stop at every slight distraction along the way. They paused at a stream to drink. They conferred about the kinds of trees they passed. They stopped to observe the direction of the wind. The shadows lengthened. Donkey grew more and more concerned about the lateness of the hour. He also grew hungrier and hungrier, as he'd missed lunch in the busyness of the market. But his companions brushed off his hurry as they paused to examine the dust of the road for signs of Hyena's tracks. When they paused yet again to discuss the best route over the Jarsa River, Donkey could restrain himself no longer. He wandered over to the side of the road and began to crop the green blades of grass that grew there.

"'Hey! What do you think you're doing?' shouted Leopard. 'Are those your blades of grass, that you can cut them off and eat them without a qualm?'

"'Do you think this whole country belongs to you,' Lion added, 'that you can devour its flora indiscriminately?'

"'Please forgive me, sirs!' squealed Donkey. 'I did not think anyone would care about these few blades of grass on the public road. No one told me it was a crime to eat them! Have mercy! Please, forgive me!'

"But Lion and Leopard did not have mercy. They pounced on

Negussie and the Coleman children.

Donkey then and there and ate him, tip to tail, for they were the most powerful figures in the land, and it was their duty to make sure that sins and crimes did not go unpunished."

Negussie's voice descended to its resting note just as we entered the mission gate at Obi.

"Is that the end?" I burst out. "That's not fair! Donkey forgave them, so they should forgive him! And he didn't even do anything wrong!"

"What's fairness got to do with it?" asked Negussie. "Leopard and Lion didn't choose to be carnivores, nor did Donkey choose to be an herbivore."

"What's a carnivore and an herbivore?" I demanded.

"Meat-eaters and grass-eaters," said John. "And anyway, it's just the way things are."

He always took Negussie's side. Just because John was older, he pretended that he knew all the right answers.

I climbed indignantly out of the *garri*. "I still don't think it's right," I grumbled, and I stomped off into the house, not staying long enough even to say goodnight to Negussie or to watch John give the driver the money Dad had given him for the trip.

Later that night, when we were lying in our bunk beds in the dark, John asked me how I could be so dumb. Didn't I see that Negussie, of all people, did not expect everything in the world to be fair? He never chose to get TB. He didn't choose to be a hunchback. He also didn't choose to be the child of Ato Kumbi's second wife, who lived up in the Chebbo hills. He didn't choose to leave his own mother and come to live in the house of the first wife in Obi, where he did chores around the house to help the older lady. And did I know that his father had been reluctant to pay for Negussie's clinic treatments or his school fees, because the money spent on a crippled child was an uncertain investment? None of these things were fair.

"But Negussie isn't bitter," John said. "In fact, he's thankful. He's thankful that the mission station brought a clinic and school to Obi and for the treatments he got from Miss Martin. Most of all, he's thankful that Dad and Mom brought the Bible and the story of Jesus' love for everyone."

I wished I weren't so dumb. And I hated John for always being right.

Little did we know, as we lay there under our warm blankets, how suddenly the continuity of our lives at Obi would be broken. Later that year, Dad was transferred by the mission to Administration in Addis, and that move disassembled our happy life at Obi. In comparison to the ready welcome from the Obi neighbours, where my parents had formed strong friendships, Addis was unfriendly, dirty, and cold.

Chaos was the major reason for the city's lack of welcome. Some army officers had arrived at the palace one sunny afternoon in 1974, shoved Emperor Haile Selassie at gunpoint into the back seat of a Volkswagen beetle, and spirited him away to an undisclosed prison cell. Months later, he was dead. We had entered the terrifying period of the *Kai Shebbir*, when gunfire crackled back and forth between government troops and the EPRP in the night, and nobody asked any questions about the bodies next morning.

John started his Negussie file during this period. Later, he would add two detailed accounts of Negussie's imprisonment written by separate missionaries who interviewed him after his release, but he began the file with the letters Negussie wrote to him in Canada. John had completed all the grades at Bingham Academy and had gone on to Prairie Bible College in Three Hills, Alberta. Not only had we left the simple, happy years of Obi behind, but also our family was now divided: Marianne and me in Ethiopia with Mom and Dad, Sharon and John in Canada. We who remained in Ethiopia saw Obi friends only occasionally, when they came to visit us in Addis.

Negussie came to see us once, during summer holidays when John was visiting from Canada, and told us about his experiences in Asmara at the Teacher Training Institute there. Little did we know at the time how much he left out. He didn't tell us that he had been evacuated from the city when it was besieged by the Eritrean army and that he had walked several weeks through rebel-controlled country. He didn't say that he had nearly died in the town of Munz from wounds he sustained when he intervened in a fight between a drunken soldier and a barmaid.

Despite these troubles, he retained his characteristic pleasure in God's care for him. Before he left our house, he and John walked together to

the compound gate, where they promised each other that they would serve God together one day in the Ethiopian church. In spite of their best efforts to keep it, however, that promise was broken. When at last — after years of schooling, hope, disappointment, and prayer — John returned to Ethiopia in 1994 to begin his ministry with the church, he arrived just months after Negussie had died of complications from typhoid fever. The partnership they dreamed about was never realized.

It's one thing to die in the interrogation cell for refusing to deny your faith. This is the extreme but comprehensible death of a martyr, and stories of martyrs affirm our confidence in God's word. Look how their faith made them triumph over their persecutors, we tell ourselves. Faced with even the most horrific threats, they didn't knuckle under to those who rule by terror and brutality.

However, to return from Alem Bukagne, the End of the World, having survived the most inhumane treatment imaginable, and then to die in a time of peace from a common, treatable disease is darkly ironic. In comparison, God's terrible game with Job in the Bible ends on a sunny note, for at least Job is rewarded with peace and prosperity for his patience. Bad timing makes the irony. In Job's case, God saved the doubling of flocks and the restoration of family for the end, when rewards should properly be dispensed, while in Negussie's case, a minor but devastating adversity squeaked in after the encouraging penultimate scenes of reward. He triumphed over his captors and went on to marry Fantaye, the woman who had bravely waited six and a half years while he was in prison. She waited five more while he tried to get back into the workforce and then finally got a coveted scholarship to Scott Theological College in Kenya. Finally, she was able to get a visa to join him in Kenya, where they were married, and over the next four years, they sang God's praises as their two baby boys came safely into the world. It seemed as if God had rewarded Negussie for his loyalty.

Then, like a storm lantern that gutters and dies, not when it's out in the hurricane, but when it's brought back into the safety of the house, his life was suddenly snuffed out.

Though many storms threatened the flame of Negussie's life at various times, the harshest of them struck in 1978, when the Ministry of Education posted him to a tiny rural school in the village of Amaya, just months after he met Fantaye at a home fellowship group in Addis. Ironic timing once again: before they had time to explore the meaning of their attraction to one another, he had to go to his new job as director of the little school seventy kilometres beyond Obi on a minor branch off of the Jimma road. They would explore the rest of their twelve-year courtship by letter and through brief, unsatisfying visits.

The two missionaries' reports in John's file suggest that the Amaya posting was trouble from the start. Negussie later told his interviewers that all the teachers were new recruits, and the others could see no reason why the hunchback should be chosen over them for the position of director. Even so, because they were all newcomers to the region, the teachers were thrown together for company. These close quarters allowed the others to observe Negussie's daily pattern of Bible reading before bedtime and at first light. They therefore asked if he would let them have one of the little booklets of Key Scriptures he was always ready to pass on to anyone who showed interest in his faith. One afternoon, just a few months into the school year, two police officers and a government cadre stormed into his classroom, threw him against the blackboard, and handcuffed his hands behind him. His captors had planned their entry to occur an hour after school was out, so there was no one to witness his seizure except the teachers who had reported him.

A handsome young cadre who seemed to be the leader of the party shouted in Negussie's startled face, "You are suspected of carrying out counter-revolutionary activities. We're taking you to Woliso town for questioning."

It would be the beginning of six and a half years of questions, with no real answers sought.

At the police station, Negussie was flung, still bound, into a wooden chair beside a staff officer's desk. The cadre brandished Negussie's Amharic Bible like a hatchet over his head. "Don't you know that superstitious crap like this has kept the workers of our nation under oppression for centuries? Kissing the priests' rings, or the missionaries' asses — it's all the same, isn't it?

"You have a big responsibility. You're a school director — a shaper of young kids' minds. And here you are, teaching them to lean on day-dreams, instead of standing on their own feet. *Aheeyah!*" He smashed the book down on Negussie's head. The binding split with the force of the blow, and several sections of New Testament slipped askew. "Once you become a donkey, all you can do is teach others to stagger around under the heavy cargo of the fat kulaks!"

Negussie couldn't match the rage in the thin voice with the beauty of the young man's arched eyebrows and high cheekbones. "Our nation has always allowed freedom of religion . . ." he heard his own voice begin. But the long, tapered fingers of the cadre had flung the broken Bible on the desk and gripped a dozen airmail envelopes.

"And what are these? Letters from your Imperialist friends! Now we know who owns the donkey!" The carefully manicured fingernails curled into a tight fist that punched Negussie's jaw broadside. He tasted blood on his gums and two molars loosened beside his tongue. "You have been given a public trust, but then what do you do? You use it to undermine the people's revolution! Have you always been like this? Betraying your own family and friends to get a few crumbs from the *ferenjies?*"

Each statement was accompanied by the smell of sweet garlic in the cadre's mouth, by spit from the delicate curve of his lips, and by blows from his convulsed fist.

"You would think, wouldn't you, that the hump on your back would make you sympathetic towards your neighbours who are poor or sick! But no, you're one of those bastards who would sell his mother for a few *birr*. It's *shermutoach* like you — I mean it — that have prostituted this country to the decadents and bloodsuckers of the West. Not any-more. Your day has come, you bent freak. The new Ethiopia has caught on to the likes of you."

By this time Negussie's nose and mouth trickled blood, and his ears burned from the cadre's blows. One of the policemen came into the room to report that the sergeant had arrived, and so the cadre left with him, saying as he left, "I'll be back to see you again, *Aheeyah!*"

The other policeman remained at attention by the door. He had witnessed the cadre's harangue and now turned to Negussie. "I've seen

him in action before," he said in a fierce whisper. "He's a devil. Just tell him what he wants to hear. Tell him you were mistaken about that God and Bible stuff. He goes crazy on people!"

If only he had had taken this advice, I think, as I read the accounts of Negussie's beating in John's file. What's a white lie on the surface of things? That's all the interrogators cared about — that the prisoner should feed them stock answers. Negussie could still believe whatever he wanted to inside.

This option didn't occur to him. Apparently, the surface and the inside, for him, were not so readily divisible. Negussie was about to thank the man when the first policeman returned to escort him to a cell.

The cadre and the sergeant, a corpulent man with fleshy rings around his neck, awaited him in this concrete-block room. Its furniture consisted of two tables, a long eucalyptus pole, a chair, and a box of ropes. The men ordered him to strip down to his underpants. They took a nylon rope from the box and roughly cinched his wrists to his ankles.

While they inserted the pole under the ropes, the cadre leaned close to Negussie's face, which was pressed against the cool cement floor, and brought his garlic-laden breath close to Negussie's ear. "You're a teacher, so you know that sometimes troublesome students need discipline, don't you? The minute you say you're willing to reject this medieval religion of yours, we'll stop. But if you persist, I tell you right now, you'll feel pain like you've never felt before."

Negussie's voice echoed, unnaturally loud in the concrete box of the cell. "Even if I die, I won't deny my faith in Jesus."

The sergeant and the cadre swung the pole up onto the two tables so that Negussie's body hung upside down in the space between. His hands and the soles of his feet faced the bare electric light bulb that swung from the ceiling above. The cadre bound a gag around his mouth and muttered in his ear, "If you change your mind, just wave a finger. I'm a reasonable man."

The sergeant took a whip made of an old radio antenna and began to beat the soles of Negussie's feet. The cadre sat on the chair and pulled a package of Nyalla brand cigarettes from his jacket pocket. He struck the match and drew the smoke deep into his lungs. He calmly watched the smoke rise to the ceiling, even when, after five minutes of energetic whipping, the sergeant paused to remove his uniform jacket. Dark

patches of sweat marked the armpits of his khaki shirt. Ten minutes later, the sergeant mopped his forehead with a handkerchief from his jacket pocket. His breath rumbled in his fleshy throat. Large blood blisters covered the bottoms of Negussie's feet.

"Ready to change your mind?" The cadre had risen from his chair and stood over Negussie's suspended body. Negussie's head slowly shook: No.

"All right, hand me that whip. I'm going to show this little hunchback what real punishment is about!" The cadre ground out his cigarette on the back of Negussie's hand and reached for the whip. He carefully hung his suit jacket over the back of the chair and turned the whip with new fury upon Negussie's feet. The blood blisters broke and bright scarlet trickled down Negussie's arms and shins. The whip cut deep and turned the soles of his feet into ground meat. The cadre's finely contoured arm descended again and again in a blur. He stripped off his shirt to his singlet. Soon it, too, was soaked. The room grew rank with the mix of smoke, blood, and sweat.

When he paused for breath, he again asked Negussie to change his mind. Again Negussie indicated no. Something stretched taut inside the cadre seemed now to snap. He began to kick with his sharp-toed brogues at Negussie's head, shoulders, sides, and back. The whip fell everywhere: feet, hands, legs, buttocks, face. It fell like an endless hailstorm with no promise of letting up.

When the young man asked Negussie again and received the same response, he changed tactics. Chest heaving, he turned to the box, selected a length of thin nylon string, and wove this over and under Negussie's fingers. He then pulled on the ends, forcing the string to bite into the soft tissue. The string disappeared into Negussie's knuckles, but still no indication of a change of mind.

Having regained his breath, the cadre returned to the whip. Finally, during one of the moments when the cadre stopped to change whip hands and take some deep breaths, the sergeant, who had slumped in the chair through it all, said it was useless.

"If we keep this up, he's going to die. It's too late to bury him tonight, and I don't want Captain Tilahun to find a body here in the morning. We've got to quit."

"I know, I know!" the panting cadre said. "I just thought we could

get a statement out of this donkey. But believe me, if he'd rather die than cooperate, I'll give him what he wants!" He reached into the box for a wooden truncheon.

The sergeant, however, had had enough. He outsized the cadre easily, and, though he had less stamina, he had more bulk muscle than the younger man. He grabbed the club and wrestled it out of the other's grasp.

"That's enough," he said. "If you want to kill the guy, go ahead, but not during my hours. Come back when the captain's on duty tomorrow morning!"

He threw the club back in the box, lifted down first one end and then the other of the pole, and began to untie the glistening red knots at Negussie's wrists and ankles. The cadre banged out of the room, while the sergeant gathered up Negussie's pants and shirt from the floor. He tossed the clothes on Negussie's semi-conscious body, lifted him in his arms, and carried him to a cell three doors down, where he deposited him in the company of two dozing prisoners. He wiped the blood from his arms and chest with Negussie's shirt and tossed it back on the broken body.

He told the two groggy men, "Make sure he gets some water when he wakes up. If he dies from lack of something to drink, I'll come looking for you two."

Negussie later told his missionary interviewers that he had been numb throughout the whole interrogation. For all the strokes of the cadre's whip and the blood that ran down his arms and legs, he never felt a twinge of pain. It was as though it were happening to someone else. He didn't see his refusal to recant his faith as bravery because he hadn't been in pain.

The pain started later, when he lay feverish in the damp cell over the next week. His legs swelled up as if he had elephantiasis. He couldn't see out of his swollen eyes, and the click in his jaw sent a stab of fire up the side of his skull when he merely swallowed, let alone opened or closed his mouth. His fingers were thick as bananas, and the tendons in his wrists screamed when he tried to make his thumb and fingers close on anything. He needed his cellmates to carry him to the latrine when the guard unlocked their door in the mornings, for he couldn't stand

on his feet. He had to crawl across the concrete floor of their cell to get to the water bucket.

The third day of Negussie's incarceration, a policeman swung open the door for the captain, who stood in the doorway and gazed upon Negussie where he lay, curled and shivering on the floor. The captain silently shook his head. He asked Negussie's two cellmates if he was getting any food. They said he was drinking water, but so far no relatives had brought food. The captain swung on his heel, and the door was refastened.

Over the next few weeks, Negussie did manage to keep down the milk and porridge brought to the prison by his church friends from Obi. Over a couple of months, the swelling decreased, and the soles of his feet mended enough for him to hobble about in the sandals he got from one of his cellmates in exchange for his leather shoes.

I'm guessing from the reports in John's file that the captain disapproved of the beating, but he was afraid of the cadre. He presented Negussie again with the evidence of his counter-revolutionary activities: the Bible and the letters from our family and other friends in the West. He explained, once again, that all Negussie needed to do was sign a statement that he would no longer speak about religion and that he repudiated his foreign friends. Then he could go free. It was so simple. He could always believe whatever he wanted in his heart. This statement was just a formality.

Once again, Negussie refused. He explained, in his quiet voice, that to deny these things would be to falsify himself. It would be like agreeing that he was not Negussie Kumbi, he was not his father's son; like swearing that he had never existed and promised never to exist in the future either. He would rather die than deny his faith in Jesus Christ.

I still ask myself why Negussie couldn't be practical. Why not compromise, just a bit? Where was the Negussie who hid the Monopoly money in his sock? Why couldn't he see that he was involved in a deadly game and play it cleverly? After all, even Jesus advised his disciples to be as smart as serpents as well as harmless as doves.

Everyone involved — the captain, the sergeant, and the cadre, too — played a part, a role assigned under the new political game. The captain and the sergeant had to show the cadre they were loyal officers

of the revolutionary regime. They had to prove they were not just leftovers from the Haile Selassie years by enthusiastically enforcing the values of the new government; any reluctance could put them in the very cells they guarded. The cadre, too, caught in the same scenario, needed deviants like Negussie to demonstrate that he was one hundred and ten percent for scientific socialism. The more fiercely he punished the enemies of the people, the more noteworthy his dedication to the revolution. He might even be promoted from this Woliso backwater and return to his university friends in Addis.

Who knew what the cadre truly believed? Who knew what the captain and sergeant really thought? Most Ethiopians, despite the new government's official atheism, still privately held their religious views. It would take more than a simple government prohibition to expunge instincts that had animated Ethiopians for thousands of years. Still, the men at the Woliso police station had learned the rules of the new game, and they knew the difference between public declarations and private beliefs. They knew how to stay alive. Why couldn't Negussie learn this, too, and play along?

Seeing that he was not going to adapt to these rules, the captain suggested that Negussie might get a fairer hearing in Addis than here in Woliso, where the cadre and his *kebele* friends held the reins of power. The accusation against Negussie had been reported "anonymously" — that is, the teachers who had brought Negussie to the cadre's attention had withheld their names from the statement. Maybe in a different jurisdiction, a reasonable judge would see how skimpy the charges were and simply let Negussie go.

Negussie took the captain's advice and asked for a transfer to Addis. He was taken to the notorious Number Three Police Station in the city. However, his case never came before a court, and so the accusations were never examined. Instead, the interrogations started again, with bamboo canes and electric wires, and he still refused to compromise his position.

Years later, he looked back at his time in the Addis jails and wrote to John: "When I was in prison I was sick. I thought I was almost about to transfer to the glory of His presence. I thought it was perhaps the last breath, and with a deep inhalation I said, 'Lord, is this the time when I finish my earthly course and come to you? Thank you, for I will come

and see your face!' It did not happen as I thought. . . . It is often the time when we feel we are not fit, or are not strong, that the Lord uses us in a mighty way. Be encouraged, my beloved brother!"

He was referring to the way his experience in prison reinforced, rather than reduced, his faith. Three months of beating and questioning at Number Three Police Station produced neither a confession of anti-revolutionary activity nor a rejection of religion, and Negussie's captors realized he was hopeless. They were wasting their time and decided simply to put him out of the way. To release him would require an admission of wrongdoing, and higher-ups might try to scrutinize the non-existent paper work. The best thing to do was send him to Alem Bukagne, where disease and neglect would likely get rid of him without anyone's having to commit a further crime.

Alem Bukagne was a cattle yard for men. Petty thieves, political prisoners, fratricides, embezzlers, and prisoners of conscience alike were shoved into makeshift barns built of galvanized iron sheets supported by eucalyptus pole frames. These crude structures had sprouted up quickly around the older concrete buildings of the original jail to contain the increased numbers of prisoners. The sheds were separated by trodden patches of red earth, mud, or dust depending on the rains. Although, compared to Woliso and Number Three, at least there was outside light and air to breathe when the prisoners were taken out for exercise or latrine breaks. The whole compound was surrounded by high stone walls to keep out curious eyes. Broken bottles embedded in the concrete on the top of these walls made sure that anyone who tried to escape paid the price in lacerated hands and knees. Machine gun emplacements punctuated the walls at fifty-metre intervals. Aside from the rude schedule of visiting hours and latrine times, the motley crowd of inmates pretty much shifted for itself.

Negussie had managed to send occasional messages out to Fantaye to let her know where he was. She had even arranged to see him for an agonizing five minutes at the Woliso police station, but security at Number Three in Addis had disallowed any contact. Alem Bukagne was

an improvement, for Negussie could look forward now to weekly visits with Fantaye and Almaz. These were the women who waited — the first eventually becoming his wife, then his widow; the second who wondered if he had been cursed. He could speak with them for a few moments only through the chain link fence on Sunday afternoons, but at least he had moments of contact with someone on the outside who knew he was alive. As an official relative, Almaz was expected to bring Negussie food, but since Fantaye had no officially recognized relationship with the prisoner, she could only come and offer greetings during the last few minutes of the visiting hour. Negussie offered to break off their relationship, as he had no assurance he would ever be released, but Fantaye shared his hope that there was a future for them together. So, every Sunday, she rode the bus to the end of its line and then took a taxi to the prison for those last few minutes.

It didn't take long for Negussie to discern the presence of other believers in Alem Bukagne. The sincerity behind certain men's ritualistic statements of *Igzabier Yemesgen*, "thanks be to God," when they greeted him, and their quietude through days of immense tension were dead giveaways. That's how he knew, without asking, that Tadessa was a fellow Christian.

Unpredictability was the name of fear in Alem Bukagne. On any day, a detachment of guards with cocked automatic weapons would enter their shed, read out a list of names, gather the group, and herd them out the rough gate. Sometimes bursts of gunfire from the restricted zone on the other side of the main building echoed off the galvanized roofs of the barns, and the rounded up men were never seen again. Other times, the gate swung wide and the bruised and bleeding prisoners were dumped like so much dirty laundry on the red dirt. It was Tadessa's silent hand, clasping Negussie's as they carried one of these semi-conscious men to a pallet, that gave Negussie assurance to say, in a conversational tone: "If this is how they treat the Shepherd, why are you surprised that they treat the followers in the same way?" To which Tadessa replied, "He was wounded for our transgressions, but by His stripes we are healed."

In this way began the Invisible Fellowship Church at the End of the World. Negussie had asked Almaz if it would be possible to hide a pocket-sized New Testament in the parcel of food she would bring on

Sunday. In the weeks after it arrived, he carefully tore the sections from the binding and separated the long books — the four gospels, the books of Acts, Romans, and Revelation — from each other. He then divided the remaining epistles in two chunks. With Tadessa, Negussie met two other men whose refusal to reject their faith had brought them to Alem Bukagne. On Thursdays, during the half hour when they were taken to the latrine, the group quietly exchanged these broken bits of Word. It seemed a desecration to rip the holy book in this manner, but this was the only way everyone could get a section each week, and, if any one of them were caught with this illicit material, they wouldn't lose the whole testament.

The missionaries' accounts in John's file wax triumphant during this part of the story. Here, in the bleakest of conditions, Negussie and his friends nurtured tender life among their cellmates. The number of fellowship members grew, and the fragments of Bible were broken again and passed between more pairs of hands on Thursdays. After three years, there were seventy participants in the Invisible Fellowship, and, to meet the needs of so many readers, the Bible pieces had been divided and subdivided into a few pages rather than whole books. Every Thursday, Biblical *gourshas* passed in silence, where the brush of a hand or a meaningful meeting of eyes meant the exchange of the broken Word. The reek of latrines became for these men the sign of food for the soul.

The numbers continued to grow. Negussie and Tadessa assigned three men who had worked as government clerks under the old regime to collect notebook pages and to make fair copies of the epistles of Peter and of Paul's letter to the Philippians, which contained particular encouragement for prisoners. The original worn pages were like the loaves and fishes, they said. From these, many baskets full were gathered.

One day, the nightmare squad with the automatic weapons entered and began to read off a list of names. It consisted of the Invisible Fellowship to the last man. Negussie, Tadessa, and their group of seventy were shoved at gunpoint through the gate and down the rutted jeep track towards the central buildings.

Negussie took Tadessa's hand and whispered, "For me to live is Christ . . ."

". . . and to die is gain," his companion finished, loud enough for their friends to hear. In moments they could be lying, bullet riddled, at

the executioner's wall. Scripture was the only language for them now.

"When shall I come into the courts of the Almighty? When shall I see His face?"

"Where shall I fly from His Presence? If I ascend to the mountains or descend into the pit of death, still He is there."

The group of men was divided and shoved into three unlit cells in the main building, where, when the heavy iron doors were bolted shut, they found themselves in utter darkness. This was death row, where men's bodies emitted the stench of fear — urine and sweat. Negussie still held Tadessa's hand fast in his.

"My friends," Negussie spoke into the absolute dark. "We may soon be dead. There is no reason for us to be silent any more. Whether we live or die, whether we meet with kindness or injustice, God is with us. We might as well praise him and try to encourage one another, like Paul and Silas at Philippi. For me, I must say God has given me much grace. He has comforted me and healed my body in difficult times. He has restored my life when I thought I would certainly die. I am alive because of His love. I am alive in His love. I have nothing to regret and nothing to be ashamed of, for Jesus has given me a free heart."

Thus, the dark cell became a place of prayer and talk and song and even laughter. After years of keeping silent, these men no longer needed to remain quiet. It was clear their beliefs were known to the warden, and it was a matter of minutes until their fate settled upon them. A strange hilarity electrified the darkness. The walls of execution row echoed with men's voices singing old antiphonal songs, many of them written when the invading Italians had thrown Walaitta Christians into prison in the 1930s. The concrete-block hallway resounded with passages of Scripture, fervent "Amens," and songs.

These members of the Invisible Church, now on death row, had no way to mark the passage of time, aside from the motions of their bodies toward hunger or excretion. They could hear nothing beyond their walls, and they had no windows through which to chart the progress of sun or moon. The dark hours dragged. They leaned against one another and slept, some standing for hours to make room for others to lie on the floor, then switching places. At long intervals, the sound of liquid rinsing the inside of a metal container would wobble faintly in the hallway outside. Then the door would be unbolted and an old kerosene

tin filled with lukewarm vegetable broth would be handed to the first blinking man. This was food for the twenty-five in the cell, and it gave them their only glimpse of each other.

On impulse, one man handed the square tin to his neighbour and murmured, "The body of Christ, broken for you."

His mood caught on. "The blood of Jesus, spilt for you," each said to the next as the tin passed from lip to lip. "Eat and drink in memory of Him."

"By His broken body we are healed, and by breaking His Word and partaking of it together we are made whole."

"Amen. Amen."

They passed the tin until it was dry, each taking only a small mouthful so it would circle the room. Some days, there was enough for two passes, and these became their festival days.

Long hours of standing swelled the men's legs. Though the latrine bucket was passed out of the room when the soup tin entered, the stench of shit and urine grew heavier. The men invented a time-passing exercise. Each one was asked to recite a favourite scripture passage from Negussie's broken Bible. The reciter spoke a line and the group repeated after him; then he recited the next. Gradually, they learned the passages of each other's hearts. They punctuated these exercises with songs and hymns, one man singing the first line and the rest responding.

If we have little trouble here, we will have little reward there!

We will reign!

Why should we not suffer a little here and now?

We will reign!

We will reign with Him through all eternity!

We will reign!

Songs and scriptures filled the hours at the End of the World. The sudden flash of light at the exchange of buckets came and went. The men knew days had passed, but they did not know how many. Their tomb sealed them off from the living world.

Negussie, however, was not forgotten. The problem was that those in Ethiopia risked their own lives if they launched any kind of inquiry, and those of us who lived abroad had no idea what to do. John and I exchanged long-distance calls between Regina and Tisdale, Saskatchewan, in which we discussed and discarded possibilities.

"What about Amnesty International?" I suggested. "Maybe we could write to them about Negussie."

John's voice sounded tired. "I raised that idea with one of Negussie's Ethiopian friends who's now in the States. He thought that would be risky. It's so hard to tell how the Mengistu regime would react. On one hand, international pressure might make them look at his file and see how thin the charges really are. On the other, Westerners showing interest might confirm that Negussie *is* intimate with enemies of the revolution — and then he would be back in interrogation. The guy in the States didn't think it was worth the risk."

"The whole thing makes me sick," I said. "It's so unfair."

Finally, after an interminable miasma of darkness and time, the guards unbolted the doors on death row and shoved the squinting men at gunpoint down the hallway.

"If this is the end, my brothers," Negussie spoke aloud to the shuffling, stumbling men, "then let me say that these days of darkness have been full of great beauty and joy. You have been Christ's hands and feet to me and to each other over this difficult time. Be encouraged, for we will be together in God's presence soon, where there is no hunger or fear or suffering."

"Amen. Amen."

It was not to be as he expected.

The seventy men were ushered into a large room, where they were ordered to sit on the floor and wait for the warden. Negussie assumed this must be where sentencing took place, for a large desk, flanked by a row of tables on each side, dominated a low stage at one end of the room. The room smelled damp and dusty at the same time. Bare electric bulbs hung on wires from the ceiling and threw a harsh light that made his eyes water. Presently, a man wearing the insignia of a colonel entered the room and strode to the desk. Two guards with machine guns flanked the door at the back of the room.

The colonel's eyes swept the upturned faces of the prisoners gathered before him on the floor. "I have been observing you for the past weeks,"

he stated, without introduction or greeting. "You have a secret organization. You have organized an exchange of messages or instructions every Thursday at the latrines. You speak regularly with the same set of prisoners. You gradually incorporate new prisoners into your group. You capitalize particularly on the weakness of new or ailing prisoners — feeding them, caring for their wounds, tending them when they are sick."

The man paced behind the desk with his hands behind his rigid back. The fingers of one hand were white where they gripped the other wrist.

"You confirmed my suspicions when I had you put in the solitary cells. You are *Penties*, religious freaks, sowers of anti-scientific and anti-progressive thinking among the workers of the Revolution. And you are adamant in your misbegotten beliefs. I have had you tested in the interrogation rooms. Not one has dropped his resolution. Your minds will not be changed. Even now, when you know I could order your execution in the next few minutes, you remain silent. But" — the colonel paused for emphasis — "I have determined that I will not give you an opportunity to recant your beliefs or to deny your mistaken views. For I have decided that I can make use of you.

"Let us be frank. I know some of your leaders have committed no crimes. I have read the files of your ringleaders — Negussie Kumbi, Tadessa Beletta, and Alemaiyu Zewdineh. There is no case against any of you three that I can make out. Nonetheless, you have never once lodged a complaint for ill treatment. Instead, you care for other prisoners around you. The health of prisoners in your block — both physical and mental — is superior to that of prisoners in the other blocks. You teach your group members — whether criminals or prisoners of conscience to believe in mercy, to sacrifice their own comforts to help others, to make no trouble for the guards.

"So I have a use for you. In four months' time, my superiors wish to review my tenure as chief warden of this prison. I want you to work toward making this review a success. Here is my offer. I will guarantee you asylum from interrogations and harsh treatment from the guards. I'll even allow you to hold religious gatherings without interference. But on these conditions: you will separate into committees of ten to work in each of the blocks in this prison. You will organize the prisoners into cooperative units. I want my superiors to see a well-run prison. The inmates must be docile, inclined to work towards their own and others'

betterment, and aware of the basic doctrines of Marxist-Leninism. You might say I'm putting you under contract. The more improvement I see among the prisoners, the more freedom I will give your faith."

And so began a new phase of Negussie's experience at the End of the World. Rather than stepping into the hurricane of bullets he had expected, his candle was brought in to a sheltered place where its flame grew only brighter. The seventy members of the Invisible Fellowship Church agreed to the warden's offer — but asked for one concession. They asked if they might be allowed to find people among the inmates who might lead the classes in Marxist-Leninism, as they didn't believe in this Marxism, and so they weren't qualified to teach it fairly. The warden agreed, just as long as the prisoners would be able to answer questions intelligently when the review committee came to visit Alem Bukagne.

Thereafter, the seventy met each Thursday in the sentencing chamber, and, after an opening prayer, they discussed their strategies for prison improvement. They all knew that the inmates needed something meaningful to do through the long days, so they decided to organize cleaning, painting, and carpentry crews and to launch classes in crafts, bookkeeping, and literacy. They then dispersed in their groups of ten, and each group supervised a branch of the work. Soon there were classes in mending clothes, basket weaving, and sewing cloth caps for the hot days of the dry season. Prisoners learned to read and write from a marvellous combination of the New Testament and the *Communist Manifesto*. Soon there was no shortage of scriptures to be read, for multiple hands had copied out chapter and verse with ballpoint pens and exercise books supplied by the warden himself. In only a month, there were complete copies of the Gospels, the Book of Romans, and the two epistles of Peter. A translation of *Das Capital* was in progress.

The only letter John received from Negussie in prison resulted from the new conditions at Alem Bukagne. Given the improvements, it made sense that the prisoners' efforts to reform should be shown to the outside. They were encouraged to produce handicrafts that they could pass on to their relatives who came to visit on Sundays. Now all the world could see how humane things really were at the End of the Earth. The best of their hats or weavings were collected by the warden for a display that would greet the review committee when it came to

visit. Negussie crocheted a cap that he passed on to his sister Almaz for John. It contained instructions for its care, with this brief personal address: "To my beloved brother John and my whole family. Daily, it is my unabated joy and encouragement that He gives me the fullest health — greater than the demands of each day. The soap and bug spray you sent me through Almaz made me happy. God bless you. If it is God's will, after I receive a verdict, we will be reunited (Acts 20:24, Phil. 1:20). I am sending this small gift for my beloved brother John. Your son, Negussie."

The broken bits of Bible in his sentences had become the deep structures of Negussie's grammar. Both fragments in the hidden note came from the words of St. Paul. The first reads, "But life to me is not a thing to waste words on, provided that when I finish my race I have carried out the mission the Lord Jesus gave me — and that was to bear witness to the Good News of God's grace." The second is like it: "My one hope and trust is that I shall never have to admit defeat, but that now as always I shall have the courage for Christ to be glorified in my body, whether by my life or by my death."

Whatever I might think of the injustice Negussie had suffered under the revolutionary government, whatever Almaz might think of the bad luck of his life, he didn't see things that way. He had kept firm in his faith. He had offered simple acts of kindness to other prisoners. He had broken and distributed God's word among them like the bread of communion or like the *gourshas* of a generous host. Despite repeated attacks upon his body, he had maintained his courage. His spirit had never been defeated. Thus, when he finally emerged from prison three years after his bargain with the colonel, he left behind a warden who admired his integrity, guards who confided their family troubles to him, and a thriving Invisible Fellowship Church that now counted three hundred participants and that continued to grow throughout the years of the Mengistu government, right up to its fall from power in 1991. He never seems to have put the question of fairness or justice at the top of his list. What mattered to him was that his life bore witness to grace.

If I could only stop the story at this point, Negussie's life would rise like the eagles in the *goursha* from Isaiah he was always passing around to others. On eagle's wings, Negussie would lift above the brutal world whose jackboots bruised his flesh. I could celebrate the triumph of his faith. I could reassure myself again that God never deserts a virtuous man, that though he may fall, he will never fall fatally, since Yahweh holds him by the hand.

But Negussie's story will not be so easily settled. For one thing, his release was as arbitrary as his arrest. There was no moment when the injustices against him were recognized or acknowledged by his captors. Maybe the warden couldn't live with the daily knowledge that there was no case against Negussie. Maybe the review committee saw the lack of a coherent charge in his files. Maybe the overcrowding at Alem Bukagne finally became overwhelming, and the administrators simply pushed some inmates out to make room for new arrivals. Negussie himself never knew why he was released. Whatever the reason, in 1985, six-and-a-half years after his arrest at Amaya, he was led with a group of other prisoners to the front gates and told to go home to his family. It happened so suddenly that he had no time to discuss the future of the Fellowship with Tadessa or Alemaiyu.

The question of what to do after his release had no clear answer, either. He went to his sister Almaz's house, confident that the prison church would continue to thrive but completely at a loss about his own future. With the history of an ex-convict, he could never go back to teaching or to any other government job. Fantaye had waited all this time for him, despite her family's pressure to marry before she grew too old to have children. However, he had no profession or career prospects that would enable him to support a family. His prison experience made him more certain than ever that what he wanted was to work in the church, but he had no Bible college or seminary training, and he had no money to pay for it.

Over the following three years, Negussie lived in uncertainty, getting temporary contracts with World Vision and the Kalleh Hiwot Church, and then being laid off when the money ran out. One of his letters to John explained that he was working as a *tebaki* or shopkeeper for World Vision, while another explained that he had a short contract to

do the accounting for one of their food distribution centres in northern Wollo province.

Finally, his fortunes took a turn for the better when he received a scholarship to go to a seminary in Kenya. Here was the period of reward that he so richly deserved. Over the next three years, Fantaye came to Nairobi, they married, and they settled in at Scott Theological College. They soon started their family of two little boys, a year apart in age. It was all coming together. In 1991, Mengistu's brutal government fell from power and religious freedom was restored. Negussie would graduate in 1993 and then go back to Ethiopia to serve in the KHC. Fantaye's parents' anxieties would be put to rest when he provided her and the boys with a secure home. He would draw from his experiences at the End of the World to minister compassionately to so many who had lost family members or who had themselves been imprisoned and tortured during the years of the *Kai Shebbir*.

Negussie's graduation and return to Ethiopia coincided with Wendy's and my plans to return as well. The change of government, Mom and Dad's impending retirement, and Negussie's plans to be back in Addis made the time seem perfect. Wendy would see and hear and smell for herself the places that peppered the stories of my childhood. More than anything else, I hoped we could talk with Negussie, who had known my family years before, and who could help me understand what had happened to us in the terrible years of the revolution.

I did see Negussie, but we did not have the kind of conversation I had longed for.

In the final weeks before his graduation from Scott at the end of June, he had contracted typhoid fever. He visited the doctor there in Kenya and was told to take it easy for a while and get his strength back. But he had no time to take it easy. He had to complete his final assignments. He had to run about to embassies, travel agents, and government offices to arrange visas and airplane tickets for himself, Fantaye, Nat'nael, and baby Mikias. Fantaye had not regained her full strength yet after Mikias's birth, and Negussie had to pack and ship their household back to Addis. He would rest when he got home. When they landed in Addis, however, his temperature continued to climb. He began retaining fluids, and he found breathing harder and harder.

The day after we arrived in Addis in mid-July, Wendy and I visited Negussie in the clinic, where he lay on a gurney in the hallway awaiting tests. An old man groaned softly on a bench next to him. Antiseptic in the air and the smell of urine from the cut-down kerosene tin that served as a bedpan burned my nostrils. In one of the rooms off the end of the hallway, a nurse's aide was shouting orders to someone hard of hearing.

Negussie was in pain. When I took his hand, it was so swollen that he could not curl his fingers to fit the curve of my palm. Under his arched eyebrows, his cheeks and neck were bloated, too.

"Negussie," I said, leaning close to his ear. "It's Dan-ih-el," pronouncing my name Amharic style.

"Welcome home," he said, in a strained whisper. He seemed to have to concentrate to make his mouth form words. "God bless you. For coming to see me. God bless you and Wendy."

We didn't stay long. It hurt so much for him to speak, we didn't want him to tax himself.

People get sick in Ethiopia. Ever since my youngest days, I'd tagged along while Mom and Dad visited friends suffering from malaria, dysentery, or some undiagnosed fever. That disease lay everywhere seemed to be a condition of life. We went back to see Negussie the day before we began our journey down to Obi and then onwards to Hosa'ina in Kambatta region. He had managed to pass some water, and he seemed more comfortable on his gurney. He could bend his fingers more easily and was delighted with the clothes Wendy and I had brought for Nat'nael and Mikias.

I kissed him on both cheeks in the Ethiopian way. "We'll be back," I said. "In ten days. We'll see you then."

Two days later, Wendy, Mom, Dad, and I stared at one another with mute incomprehension when we heard over the mission radio that Negussie had died. He had seemed to be mending on that last day in the clinic. We had been confident that we would meet again soon. Now his flame had guttered just when the political storm had ceased. We couldn't understand.

By the time we got back to Addis, the funeral was long over because the lack of refrigerated morgues necessitates burial very close to the time of death. Negussie therefore slipped away in the brief moment when we

had gone from his side, and we missed our chance to say goodbye. I thought of John's bond with Negussie to serve together in the church — broken now, forever.

I cannot do the theological math that adds Negussie's faithful life to his absurd death and comes up with a loving God. On the face of it, Almaz seems to be right: maybe he was cursed. To my mind, his death in a time of peace after his return from the End of the World sums up the irony of human fate. God breaks his word. He does not keep the virtuous man from falling fatally. Instead, like Leopard or Lion, he devours the innocent person who finally has a chance to taste a few tender shoots.

But I cannot speak these bitter words and keep faith with Negussie as I knew him. To draw this conclusion to his story, I would have to discredit his own views entirely. Right up to the moment I held his hand on his deathbed, he remained convinced that God had showered him with grace. For me to insist that he had been abandoned would be the highest form of hubris. It would be to insist that I, who have lived all my life protected by pink skin and a Canadian passport, know better than he did. It would be to insist on the fairness he never demanded.

I therefore live between my own agnostic grief and a strange, vicarious hope. I vacillate between the incomprehensibility of Negussie's death and the conviction that animated his life. It's hard to see how God kept faith with Negussie, but Negussie's own consistent faith helps my unbelief. I believe in his faith, even as I stutter between hope and sorrow. And I realize that Negussie has become, for me, the broken word.

Cross-Country

Mr. Watson thumped me on the back. "You're amazing — four minutes and fifty-two seconds! Easily a school record for the 1,500 metres."

"Thanks," I gasped. I bent down to grasp my knees while my breathing slowed and my heartbeat settled.

"I don't know how you do it," he went on. "In all my coaching years at Viscount, we've never had anyone even make it to the city meets. And here you are: third in the finals with no training program, no track team, nobody to work out with."

"It's the elevation, sir," I said. I straightened my back and rested my hands on my hips as I drank air into my lungs. "I used to live at 3,000 metres above sea level. It makes breathing here in Calgary a lot easier."

"Well, whatever it is, it sure makes good runners. I've never seen anything like it."

There were all kinds of reasons why I should not have done well in the city finals that year in Calgary. My family had been passing through Alberta on a short summer furlough when, late in August, we learned that there was no room for me at Rift Valley Academy in Kenya, where I was to start grade eleven that September. I had completed all the grades available at Bingham, Good Shepherd School had been commandeered by the Mengistu government and transformed into a veterans' hospital, and Mom and Dad couldn't afford to send me to ACS, the American Community School in Addis. Desperate to find a school for me, my parents arranged for me to live with the Stinsons, missionary friends who had returned to Canada from Ethiopia a couple of years before. I would attend Viscount Bennett, the high school in their neighbourhood, while Mom, Dad, and Marianne went back to Ethiopia.

Crowds of teenagers ganged the hallways at my new school between classes. They banged locker doors open and dumped brand-new chemistry textbooks and spiral-bound notebooks inside as if sending these school materials down a chute like so much garbage. Boys in black T-shirts sported the names of rock bands such as Black Sabbath and Megadeth in gothic letters across their chests. Girls wore tight T-shirts and elephant pants whose legs were so voluminous you couldn't see their platform shoes. Separate herds of boys and girls roved from locker to locker and looked curiously at me as I tried to figure out the workings of the combination lock I'd been assigned.

Robert Kovach, who had the locker beside mine, showed me how to turn past the second number all the way around to the third before the combination would release. He had taped a poster inside his locker that replaced the maple leaf on the red and white Canadian flag with a cannabis leaf. The odours of his kielbasa, tobacco, and gym socks leaked into my still-empty locker.

Despite my initial nervousness, I managed, not just to survive, but actually to thrive during that year in Calgary. Although everything around me was completely different from Addis, a core inside me felt secure enough not to be overwhelmed by the newness. A good part of that security came from the Stinsons, whose home and church life was similar to the missionary world in which I'd been raised. Another significant part came from cross-country running.

Unknown to me, living and breathing on Addis Ababa's high plateau had so strengthened my lungs that, with the training I'd done at Bingham, I was uniquely set for distinction in Calgary.

Therefore, although everything about track and field in Calgary was unfamiliar to me; though Viscount Bennett had no organized track team, and Mr. Watson, who had noticed my stamina in phys. ed. class, had told me about the quarter-final track meets only a week before they were held; though this short notice left me with no time to start a regime of training; and though the Adidas spikes I'd used on the grass track at Bingham were too long for the hard rubber track here and bent my toes back uncomfortably at each stride, I won the quarters and semis, and I came in third in the finals behind two guys who belonged to a year-round track club. Given my belated entry into the competition, I was

satisfied with third place. I'd never done an under-five-minute 1,500 metres before, and anyway, third was my old position, the one I'd achieved against many odds.

Long-distance running allayed my sixteen-year-old's anxiety that my self might not be transportable. It assured me that I had abilities settled deep in my body, in parts like legs and lungs, and they could assert themselves wherever I happened to be. I was grateful, once again, for Mr. Porter, who had introduced me to the sport back in seventh grade at Bingham.

"Abebe Bekele!" a man had shouted from under his umbrella when we passed by on my first-ever workout. "*Bartah*! Keep it up!" The toes of my soggy Alligator-brand running shoes slapped the shiny pavement as I tried not to let Kenny Cole's mud-splattered calves get more than three or four metres ahead of me.

We approached a group of women who had taken shelter under a shop awning. I heard one say, "*Yehew inezee ferenjoach*. These foreigners think they can develop the legs of Mammo Waldé or Abebe Bekele simply by running in the rain."

"This last one's just a *hitzahn*," said one of her companions, "but the baby can keep up."

The compliment sent a spark of new energy down my thighs, but my lungs burned too harshly for me to say thanks. Just to keep Kenny Cole in view took all I had. Ahead of him, orange T-shirt dancing in a veil of grey rain, ran John MacLellan. Beside John ran our new track-and-field coach, Mr. Porter.

I'd met Mr. Porter just the day before, my first day of seventh grade. After I had unpacked my suitcase and placed my folded boxers, T-shirts, and socks in the pine-smelling dresser drawers I'd been allotted in my new dorm room, I had said goodbye to Dad and Mom at the school gates. I then realized that none of the other seventh-grade boys in my dorm had arrived yet. It felt odd to be back. My family had just returned from a year's furlough in Three Hills, Alberta, where John and Sharon

were at Prairie Bible College, and I was eager and nervous about seeing my old schoolmates again. Had they changed during the sixth grade while I was away? Had they filled my spot with new friends and interests?

I strolled down toward the gym, hoping other early arrivals might be shooting baskets in the wall-less, barn-sized building. Bingham looked pretty much the same. The red cinders crunched under my runners in the parking lot. To my left, the main building was still painted creamy tan. The double doors to the basement-level workshop stood wide open as they usually did on a workday. A table saw within whirred and sang as it bit the wood. Through the doorway I could see the tool shelf at the back that covered the tunnel's secret entrance. Outside the workshop, the familiar stone retaining walls curved around the raised area where we used to wait after morning Verse Group for the siren to ring for breakfast and the dining halls doors to open. Movement at the corner of my eye made me turn my head in time to see a striped green lizard flash across the top of the retaining wall. The smell of sawdust from the workshop mingled with the scent of fresh-cut grass. A silent lawnmower rested at the bottom of the slope by the gym, the gardener having finished his work on the lawn above. The gym's huge roof was supported by telephone-pole-sized *bahir-zaff* timbers, and though the galvanized iron kept the courts dry during rainy season, one or another of us still got drenched whenever a ball bounced out from under the roaring canopy.

A bright blue flickering attracted my attention in the deserted gym. A man with a welder's mask over his face knelt at the base of one of the volleyball poles. Each time he touched the wand in his gloved hand to the metal pole, a shower of sparks and blue-white light spread across his lap. The smell of sulphur and burnt metal stained the air.

The man's glove tipped up his mask as I approached. He was a stranger in his early twenties. He tugged the glove off one hand and ran his fingers through his ginger-blonde hair.

"Graham Porter," he said, and offered me the bare hand. "Just arrived last week. And you are?"

"Danny Coleman," I said. "Are you a new teacher here?"

"Uh-huh. Phys. ed. mostly, and a little science. Thought I'd work on getting some of this equipment ready for action."

A new teacher! And a young one, too: he said, *Graham* Porter, not *Mr.* Porter, like a friend, not just a teacher. Wow, the school might look the same, but things had changed here while I had been away.

Bingham had been my fixed point while I was in Three Hills. I had known we would be gone for just one year. If things didn't work out in Canada, if I didn't make friends or didn't like school, I could always count on returning to Bingham. This place would stay constant — with the same teachers, the same roommates, the same local men in the kitchen, and the same gossiping, soap-scented Oromo women in the laundry. I would be welcomed back from my adventures by people who had kept a place warm for me and who would envy my knowledge of the bigger world.

Mr. Porter's presence, however, made me shift my expectations. Not only did we have a new teacher, but he taught sports! He was tall and athletic-looking in a way that told me that phys. ed. would be a far cry from Miss Willey or Miss Wolman putting a whistle around her neck and taking us out to play kickball. Something about him — the steady regard of his eyes, his casual self-assurance, and easy conversation — made me look forward to the new things he'd bring to the place I had wanted to remain unchanged.

"You do sports?" Mr. Porter asked.

"Yep, in PT. And I played hockey last year in Canada."

"PT? Oh, I get it — physical training." Mr. Porter gave the volleyball standard an experimental tug with his gloved hand. "Not a lot of ice hockey here, Dan Coleman. You weren't at Bingham last year?"

"Nope. My family just got back from furlough. I did grade six in Canada. But I know the kids in my class, because I've done all my other grades at Bingham since grade one."

"So you're an old pro, huh? That's good. I'll bet you're looking forward to seeing your buddies again."

"Yeah."

"Help me wrap these cords around that cart handle, will you? Thanks. You do any other sports last year in Canada?"

"Ran the 1,500 metres in a track meet."

"Hey, now *that's* something you can do here. I'm thinking of getting some guys together to do some training. You interested?"

That's how I joined Bingham's first-ever cross-country team. We started right away the next day, when Mr. Porter came around to my dorm room after school and told me that, if I'd change into shorts and runners, I could join him, John MacLellan, and Kenny Cole at the school gates for our first workout.

It was the end of the long rains. A fine mist dampened our hair and shoulders as we three waited for Mr. Porter at the gate. I kicked my toe at some loose gravel where the asphalt met the damp grass, and I tried to avoid John and Kenny's questioning looks. When the new teacher had mentioned getting some guys together for training, I hadn't foreseen *this*. The whole school called John Magellan, because it rhymed with his surname and he had a marathoner's endurance that could circumnavigate the globe. He was in grade ten, and Kenny, who had shorter legs but equally powerful lungs, was in grade nine. There's no way they would have tolerated my company under any other circumstance — to them, a seventh-grader was a punk. When Magellan took off one of his socks to dislodge a pebble, I saw that his big toe was almost as thick as my wrist. The top of my rooster-tail stood no higher than Kenny Cole's chest. My voice was as high as my sister's and wouldn't change for another couple of years.

Mr. Porter, however, seemed not to notice how much smaller I was than the other two. Instead, he showed us how to stand with our heels together, place two hands on the fence, and lean forward, while pushing down through our ankles — this stretched our calves. Next he had us stretch our quadriceps by pulling up each heel to our buttocks with the opposite hand. After a few more stretches, he led the way out the school gates, and we trotted down the road into the Kwolfe market area.

Despite the rain, my spirits soared. Older boys like Magellan and Kenny were used to leaving the boarding school grounds. There was a sign-out sheet in the main dining room where grade nines and tens could indicate on Saturday that they planned to leave campus and take a taxi downtown or hike up Entoto Mountain on the edge of the city. In contrast, us littler kids never left the school grounds unless we were on a field trip or visiting with our parents — and then always in a car. This simple act of running off down the street gave me a thrill. Although the EPRP hadn't formed their cells yet, the city streets could still be dangerous, and there had been student riots long ago. This danger added to the usual

hazards of pickpockets and insane street beggars whose families couldn't keep them home. Going out for a run unprotected by a car, therefore, was risky and exciting. I was one of the big guys now, on our own in the city.

We ran in as tight a cluster as the taxis, donkeys, bicycles, and umbrella-bearing pedestrians would allow. There were no sidewalks, and the steaming mud beside the street meant that what pavement there was had to serve everything — animal, human, or mechanical — set upon a destination. Mr. Porter told us that we should keep each other always in view; this was our first run, and we couldn't predict our stamina. He himself wasn't yet accustomed to the elevation, he said, so he didn't know how long he would last. We could save energy by reducing the up-and-down chop in our stride. By concentrating on the arm-swing in our shoulders, we could produce a smooth forward and backward motion that would eliminate bounce.

He swerved around a little kid who carried a banana leaf overhead for an umbrella. "Two other things to work on," he said. "Try to take deep and deeper breaths. Especially extend the inhale, the exhale doesn't matter as much. I sometimes count footsteps for each breath, like this: in-two-three-four, out-two-three-four. See if you can increase the number: in-two-three-four-five, out-two-three-four. The deeper you breathe the more you increase your lung capacity.

"The second thing is about hills. When you're going up, drop your head, take smaller steps, and chug. With your head down, you get more air, and you give your legs a break with the smaller steps."

I frowned to show I was concentrating. In-two-three-four. Out-two-three-four. When Mr. Porter said we'd do some training, I had just thought we'd go running. Which is what I'd done in PT in Three Hills. We went out and ran around the track for a while, but nobody said anything about pacing your breath or pumping through the shoulders. I hadn't realized running had so much to do with air.

"Ayyy! *Ferenjie!*" a young man wearing a plastic slicker jabbed a hand towards Mr. Porter. "Abebe Bekele! *Comostaré!*"

"Hello," said Mr. Porter. "How are ya?" He shook the hand lightly and ran on. "I love the way they link us up with Abebe Bekele and Mammo Woldé. Maybe someday we'll be marathon champs, too!"

Earlier, while we had waited for Mr. Porter to arrive at the front gate, Kenny Cole had told Magellan and me that Mr. Porter was new

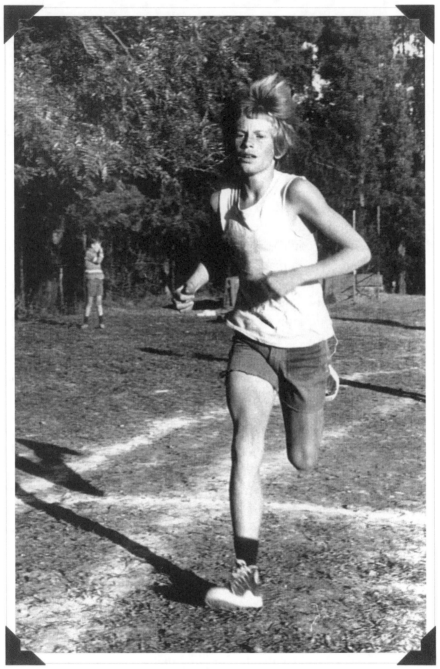

Running on the soccer field at Bingham.

to Ethiopia. He'd attended Kent Academy, our sister school in Nigeria, where his parents worked with SIM. Then he'd gone to college in the States, and now he'd come to Bingham to help out for a year. He was too new to know any Amharic, so he was unbothered by the derogatory nuance of the shouts of *Ferenjie!* or the way Ethiopians assumed we were Italians and greeted us with *Comostaré*.

Nonetheless, though he was new to the country, Mr. Porter led us through parts of the city I'd never seen before. We passed a small open area where people held a Saturday market. Then there was a pole yard, where donkeys unloaded varying grades of eucalyptus poles that would be sold for scaffolding or mud-and-wattle construction. Next came a string of roadside shops selling Japanese radios, Ethiopian-made running shoes like the Alligators I wore, or Taiwanese cloth. A tea shop, a hair salon. We turned uphill past a brick factory and a sign for a rock quarry. Next, a stand of *bahir-zaff* trees, which covered an area the size of a city block and reeked of human shit and urine. On a dry day, it wouldn't smell so bad, but today's rain doubled its stench.

This after-the-rain phenomenon used to make Timmy Bascom and me dig each other in the ribs in chapel when we sang:

> *Jesus, Jesus, Je-e-e-sus —*
> *There's just something about that name.*
> *Saviour, Master, Je-e-e-sus —*
> *It's like the fragrance after the rain!*

I grinned at the memory, and I tried to take smaller breaths until we were farther away from the eucalyptus grove.

Every once in a while, Mr. Porter would circle back to make sure each of us was doing okay. Any cramps? Any difficulty breathing? Side-ache? Sore joints? No? Well then, let's go just a bit farther. The joy of his body showed on his face. Even if I were on my very last legs, I would hate to cramp his style by admitting fatigue.

But I *was* tired. I kept looking down at my shoes to see if they were picking up clods of mud. Something must be making them feel so heavy. I bit my lip and determined that not one new centimetre would grow between me and Kenny Cole's muddy calves.

"Relax, Dan Coleman," Mr. Porter said as he dropped back to check on me. "You won't get there any faster by tightening up. Breathe-two-three-four; out-two-three-four."

We passed a woman with a plastic bag over her hair and a large pottery water jar slung on her back.

"Make sure your head doesn't tip back when you're tired," Mr. Porter said between his own deep breaths. "It restricts how freely you breathe. At first you have to tell yourself to do this stuff, but after a while it becomes instinctive. It gets into your bones and becomes second nature."

That first workout introduced me to three new pleasures. First, there was the pleasure of deserved exhaustion. Not just my legs and lungs, but my whole body sagged with relief when we stumbled through the Bingham gates and rested our hands on our knees, waiting for our breath and heartbeats to calm. As we leaned against the fence and pressed our heels to the ground, or pulled our ankles, one at a time, up to our buttocks, this relief settled deeply into my sinews. I pulled the crisp scent of the campus's *bahir-zaff* trees deep into my lungs. There wasn't a tense muscle or nerve anywhere in my whole body — I had nothing left inside me to make tension with.

Second, there was the joy of distinction — of being *seen*. An adult had singled me out, invited me to join a group of older boys, and I had held my own. I'd avoided Magellan's and Kenny's quizzical looks when we started out, but after they hadn't had to slow down for me even once, I now met their gaze directly as we sat on the wet grass by the gate, stretching our calves and quads. Their steady regard sent a thrill through my guts to my legs.

The third pleasure came as a surprise, because my body felt pummelled to such exhaustion that I didn't know it could register new sensations. Nonetheless, the hot shower after a long run on sloppy city streets wakened sensations I had never attended to before. I slipped out of my clammy T-shirt, shorts, and socks and stuffed them into the laundry bag. Once the temperature felt warm to my hand, I stepped under the stream of water. The mud slid down my hairless thighs and shins and into the drain. The musky perfume of Lux bath soap rinsed away the harsh street smells of diesel and sewage. The hot water drilled down on my head and tingled my neck and back. My muscles seemed to take on new energy from the water itself.

Why, I wondered, had I never taken a shower during the middle of the week before? For some reason, I had always taken baths, and tradition held that baths occurred only on Saturdays. When I was a preschooler in Obi and then when I came to Bingham, we had baths on Saturday nights so we'd be fresh and clean for Sunday. It had never occurred to me to take a bath or shower on just any old day.

Over the next few months, cross-country gave me a new identity. I'd always been an average kid. Timmy Maret and Kenny Veer were quicker readers than I; Philip Jackson and Ruth Lahadeho got higher grades; David Iwan and Beverly Radach were faster sprinters. I was always third- or fourth-best. However, as Mr. Porter gathered together a cross-country team of grades nine and ten boys over the next weeks, and our numbers grew from ten to twelve and then fifteen, I kept Kenny Cole's calves always in sight, and, despite being the only kid from grades seven and eight on the team, I managed consistently to finish in the top three.

"Do you think I'm proud?" I asked Beverly Radach, after she had agreed to be my girlfriend four or five weeks into the cross-country season.

"But you should be," she said. "Nobody else in our grade gets to be on the varsity cross-country team."

She should know, because she always got all the first-place ribbons on Field Day. She was talking about the feat I had accomplished in the first cross-country race of the season, which had been held at Bingham's main rival, Good Shepherd School.

After a month of training, Mr. Porter told us about the Saturday meet. He wanted us to wear ties throughout our Friday classes, so we'd concentrate on the race the next day. We were also to come fifteen minutes early for breakfast on Saturday, so we could sit together and talk.

When we arrived at the breakfast table that morning, we found he'd asked Ato Girma, the head cook, to make a special breakfast of porridge, fruit, and muffins. Something substantial but not too heavy or sweet, he said. He didn't want us running out of energy because we hadn't eaten well.

With sunshine slanting across the wood grain of the table and the smells of tea and oatmeal rising from our cups and bowls, he told us that, even though we'd be running against guys from GSS and ACS who were in grades eleven and twelve, we'd stack up just fine.

He looked around the table at each of us to see if we were listening. "Each one of them has to put on his pants every morning one leg at a time," he said. "So you don't need to be scared of them. We've been training hard over the past weeks, and that training is becoming second nature to you. You're building everything you need in your bodies — endurance, wind, muscle power. You guys are in good shape, and I know you'll do well."

During the half-hour ride in the Taunus van to GSS and then while we stretched on the soccer field, Mr. Porter told us it's normal to feel butterflies in your stomach before a race, and we should take the chance now to go to the bathroom if we needed to — in a few minutes we'd be shown the route.

The race was to be 5,000 metres, and the Good Shep officials led us to a high spot on campus where we could see most of the course. We would run on gravel at first, pavement for a few hundred metres, then dirt paths that circled the perimeter fence, and back up to the pavement. The final stretch of gravel led back to the soccer pitch, where we'd do one lap to finish. The killer was that the course went mostly downhill at the beginning, and then took a long uphill for most of the second half, until it climbed back to the pavement. The last bit of gravel and the lap of the soccer field would be a sprint — if we had any energy left.

I glanced anxiously at our huge opponents. Some of them were five years older than me. I was just taller than one young man's belt buckle. Another wore three-striped Adidas track shoes. In comparison, my high-top, rubber-and-canvas Alligators looked about as sprightly as hip waders. One of the ACS guys smelled strongly of a menthol-based rubbing compound, like Bengay or Tiger Brand.

We went back to our team huddle, and Mr. Porter led us through our last stretches. "Put your head down and chug on that long hill," he told us, while we pushed through our heels to stretch our calves. "And remember not to let your head tilt back. Don't worry about how big

they are. Big fellows suffer the most on the hills. That's where you can pass them. Remember: in-two-three-four; out-two-three-four."

Bingham's day of glory turned out just as Mr. Porter had said. At first the tall Good Shep and ACS runners took off way ahead, and I wondered how I would ever catch up. I sought out Kenny Cole's calves and measured my three metres. In-two-three-four-five-six; out-two-three-four. Off the pavement and on the dirt paths, we caught up to and passed three sagging competitors. Then came the long hill. I put down my head and chugged. I passed two, three, four pairs of big feet before I dared to raise my head enough to look for Kenny's legs. Good — four metres ahead. In front of him, one GSS runner, and ahead of him, the orange T-shirt of Magellan, in the lead, turning onto the paved road.

Rainy season was now over, but the grass alongside the red dirt of the path was still lush and green. The sky arched high and blue overhead, and the sun raised the smell of warm earth from the hillside. Good Shepherd School was on the very edge of the city, and, compared to the asphalt streets around Bingham, this rural back half of the Good Shep course reminded me of tractor rides through farm fields at Sheshemane and the steady breeze through the pasture grass at Obi.

I glanced uphill and saw Kenny's legs farther away than usual, so I increased my speed. Kenny heard me coming and increased his. We were on the pavement now, our runners slapping the hard surface. I couldn't hear any slaps behind me. We were gaining on the Good Shep guy. Then we were crunching gravel underfoot. The GSS runner heard us coming and turned on the gas. Magellan crossed the tape just as our rival, Kenny, and I started the lap on the soccer pitch. We were in a full-out sprint. My legs were numb and my throat burned. My lungs demanded a bigger ribcage. Kenny and the Good Shep runner were neck and neck when they crossed the finish line. I was three metres behind. The next runners were just starting the final 400 metres of the track when we stumbled to a stop, placed our hands on our knees, and waited for our breath and heartbeats to slow down.

"Who's that little kid?" I heard one GSS girl say to another. "He beat everybody on our team except Larry!" She had long honey-coloured hair, and she wore a black leather choker around her tanned neck.

Mr. Porter's hand rested on my shoulder. "Way to go, Dan Coleman!

You really stuck it to them on the hill, just like we said. I saw you make your move about a third of the way up. Got Kenny going too. You made me proud!"

My head spun with lack of oxygen and abundance of high praise. I glanced at the GSS girl and hoped she had heard.

"Hey, Coleman," Magellan shouted above the ruckus of excited voices in the Taunus on the way back to Bingham. "Way to go. You did good for a grade-seven punk."

"I'll buy you a Pepsi," said David Neville. He was the most popular senior boy at Bingham. "You top three — Magellan, Cole, and Coleman — you made us look real good today."

I wished I could sit on that bench in that van with those boys for the rest of my life. Right there.

Cross-country started me off. Over the next year, it was consistently Magellan, Kenny Cole, and me — the top three on the team. And with this new expertise in long distance, I didn't worry as much about other areas. I wasn't bothered that I was a slower sprinter than Lawrence Bergson or Beverley Radach, or got lower grades than Philip Jackson and Ruth Lahadeho. I had my thing. Even when the cross-country season ended, and we started track and field, nobody in Junior High could touch me in the 1,500 metres. The security of knowing I was good at this one thing made me willing to try others. Though I was the shortest boy in grade seven, I still tried out for and made it onto the basketball and volleyball teams. I knew if I couldn't rebound or spike, I could at least chase down the ball right through the whole game and not get tired. Same thing in soccer.

My being the youngster on the cross-country team also freed me from the competitive pressure that hampered older members. If a grade ten boy like Gary Veer or David Neville came in ahead of me in a practice race, I could always tell myself that he was two years older, with legs almost half again as long as mine. Any way I looked at it, I was doing fine.

This pressure-release served me well the day we went to a cross-country meet at ACS and were soundly whipped by runners from General Wingate and St. Joseph's, Addis Ababa's two schools for the children of the Ethiopian elite. Whereas we had easily dominated our previous meets with Good Shep and ACS, not even Magellan placed in the top ten against the students from Wingate and St. Joseph's.

Our running route at ACS took us through a much busier section of town than we'd run at GSS or Bingham. Like the Good Shep route, this one started and finished on the track around the soccer pitch. However, it looped out of the "Little America" suburb around ACS, took a tough uphill at the two-kilometre mark on the main road leading out of Addis towards Jimma, and then swerved back on a residential side street to the ACS campus. The Jimma road was crowded. Diesel fumes belched from city buses and confused my breathing count. I could hardly see Kenny Cole's calves through the choking oil in the air. A couple of times, I was brought up short when a donkey piled high with *chidd* or a woman lugging a square kerosene tin stepped suddenly in front of me. So I was shocked when I looked up and saw Magellan's orange T-shirt only a pace or two ahead of Kenny. When I swerved into the road to avoid a boy pulling an unwilling sheep by a rope around its neck, I saw what had put the grey lead in Magellan's legs — an apparently endless line of St. Joseph's and Wingate T-shirts shimmered mockingly all the way up the hill ahead of us.

A young pedestrian made me break my stride when he thrust a furled umbrella at me. "*Ay! Ferenjie!*" he crowed. "You are number twenty-two! Run hard, you are losing!"

I cursed under my breath, "*T'abat,*" and pressed on Kenny's heels. He in turn pressed on Magellan's. We did pass one or two of the Wingate runners, but the race was long over before anybody from Bingham, Good Shep, or ACS crossed the finish line.

"It's not fair," Magellan said. We hung our heads, panting, over our wobbly knees. "Some of those Ethies from St. Joseph's aren't even in their teens anymore. I'll bet some of them are pros."

David Neville took up the complaint: "And they've lived their whole lives in Addis, so they're used to running on crowded streets."

Mr. Porter spoke into the brooding silence in the Taunus on the way home. "Suck it up, guys. Nobody likes to get soundly thrashed. But it's actually good for us. We got cocky racing only against the white kids from GSS and ACS. Now we've got something to work towards."

I looked around the faces in the van. Everyone rubbed blistered feet, slumped over their knees, or stared at the floor.

I shared the team's general disappointment, but I wasn't personally embarrassed. If some of those St. Joseph's guys were in their twenties,

and I was only thirteen, then I had done just fine. I caught Mr. Porter's eye in the Taunus's rear-view mirror. He gave me a wink. I smiled back.

What did disappoint me, though, was something I'd known was coming all year. Mr. Porter had told us from the very beginning that he had come to Bingham for one year only, but something about the inner confidence he had given me generated the illusion that he would always be with us. In just one year he had become like that second nature he was always talking about. I was therefore caught off guard when he reminded us that he'd be leaving as soon as the school year ended in June. He needed to finish college, and to pay for college, he needed to go back to the States and find a summer job.

Would this new me survive Mr. Porter's absence? Would I still feel my inward surety without him? Would we even have cross-country at Bingham anymore?

Mr. Porter had been such a great success among the students at Bingham that the staff eagerly welcomed another young alumni from Kent Academy the following September. Mr. Flint was also in his early twenties. Like Mr. Porter, he wore wire-rimmed glasses, and he also wanted to take a year off from college to help out at Bingham. He, too, would teach science and phys. ed., as well as coach our sports teams. Although these similarities enabled him to step straight into the gap left by Mr. Porter, he was nothing like his predecessor.

Whereas Mr. Porter had been tall and lanky, Mr. Flint was short and wiry. The former had straight, ginger-blonde hair, while the latter's hair was curly and black. The biggest difference, however, was in character. Mr. Porter used sports to draw potential out of kids, whereas sports drew fury out of Mr. Flint. In the heat of competition, he would flare into a dizzy rage.

Off the sports field, he was fine — quirky but friendly Mr. Flint, our grade eight science teacher. But on the basketball court or soccer pitch, he could turn into a fiend — like the Incredible Hulk in the comics, except that he stayed the same size and didn't turn green. Mr. Flint didn't pace the sidelines during practices. Instead, he threw on a T-shirt

and put himself at the centre of the scrimmage. If he got an accidental elbow under the backboard, even from someone on his own team, in seconds that person would be nursing a bruised rib from Mr. Flint's sharp rejoinder. We came to fear his temper, and with good reason. Tim Maret got a bloody nose once when Mr. Flint thought Tim had crashed into him on purpose.

It was Mr. Flint's temper that ended cross-country workouts on the streets of Kwolfe district, and all because of a few watches. When Mr. Flint arrived, I'd graduated to second, and then first, place on the team. Magellan had completed grade ten, the top grade offered at Bingham, and gone back to Australia to finish school. That left Kenny Cole and me. However, Kenny got kicked off all sports teams when he and a friend slipped over the school fence one evening for a night on the town. When they returned, the principal assigned Kenny and his friend to the woodpile after school every day. There they could meditate on the wisdom of their adventure. I now held first place.

But my glory was short-lived. Mr. Flint had seen the sign to the stone quarry just beyond the brick factory on our earlier runs, and so one day he led us down this road to check out a possible new route. The road soon proved useless for our purpose — the gravel was composed of five- to eight-centimetre stones from the quarry, perfect for keeping trucks out of the red mud during rainy season, but perfect, also, for twisting runners' ankles. A wide dirt path led off from the road through a hectare of chest-high *bahir-zaff* shoots growing from the stumps of last year's harvested trees. Beyond these we could see the gravel piles of the quarry.

"Let's try the path," said Mr. Flint. His shoes raised puffs of red dust as he led the way off the stony road and through the thicket of menthol-scented shoots. Clearly, the path had been made by quarry workers to avoid the ankle-breaking road, for it led directly to the quarry gates, where Mr. Flint waited for everyone to catch up and take a breather before we headed back to Bingham.

"Hey, Coleman," he said, "Can you see where the path crosses that dry ditch, and then goes through some more of that young eucalyptus towards the pole market? Why don't you lead the way up there so we can keep off that killer road? I'm going to do a quick loop around this quarry. I'll catch up with you guys in a sec."

In-two-three-four-five-six-seven-eight; out-two-three-four; in-two-

three-four-five-six-seven-eight. Here came the ditch. I was thinking about how Mr. Porter would have been telling me to think of my foot as if it were a wheel — to roll smoothly from heel to toe and not let my toes slap the ground.

"Mammo Woldé!" I looked up to see an Ethiopian man who stood in a ragged shirt and short pants beside the path. He thrust out his left hand and said, "*Comostaré*!"

"*Tenastilene,*" I greeted him in Amharic and brushed his palm as I ran by. It struck me odd that he shook with the left.

I returned to my train of thought. Mr. Flint sometimes gave us running advice, too, but somehow it didn't sink in as much, maybe because he gave it to everybody when we were gathered on the soccer field, and not individually, like Mr. Porter, who had dropped back, watched a runner's stride for a minute, and then given a pointer or two.

Just then I heard Mr. Flint's voice shout behind me, "Oh no you don't!" Next, the thump of a fist.

I looked back and saw Mr. Flint, on the verge of the ditch we'd crossed, grappling with the ragged man in shorts. Down in the ditch itself, Eddie McClenny was trying to twist the arm of another Ethiopian man, while Steven Maret had blood running from a cut above his eye where a third man had hit him with the stone that he was swinging back for another blow.

I ran back to the ditch.

What to do?

I kicked at the buttocks of the man who now had Mr. Flint on the ground. My foot landed unconvincingly on the back of his thigh.

I'm useless here, I thought. I don't know how to make it hurt.

I should get help.

I took off down the path at top speed. Head down and chug, I told myself, as the path led up through the sharp-smelling *bahir-zaff* stumps to the pole market. Once I reached the pavement, it was downhill past the market, the forest latrine, and the tea shops to the school. I banged on the gate and crowded past the startled guard the instant he'd drawn the bolt. I ran straight to the workshop in search of an adult. Nobody in sight. Upstairs through the kitchen into the dining room, where they'd be setting up for supper. I almost ran straight into Mr. Ricker, who was coming around the corner of the hallway.

In minutes, we were speeding in the Taunus past the stacks of *bahir-zaff* poles in the market. We soon came upon Mr. Flint and the rest of the boys walking together down the street, a crowd of curious Ethiopians following along behind. Steven Maret's eye was starting to swell shut, and Eddie McClenny's nose ran blood. Mr. Flint was limping and had cuts on his forehead, cheekbones, and chin. He carried his broken glasses in one hand. Mr. Ricker pulled over, and the guys piled into the back of the van.

The man in the short pants and his two friends had got three watches, besides Mr. Flint's. They'd shaken each runner's left hand, looking for wristwatches, and simply intimidated the kids into giving them over. It wasn't until Mr. Flint reached the ditch and was attacked himself that the ruckus started.

I could see Mr. Ricker's irritation at how things had gone. All this over a few watches. He didn't say a word to Mr. Flint, though, in front of the team. At least nobody had been too badly hurt. We drove back to school, and everybody went to the showers to clean up.

After that day, we didn't go running on the city streets anymore. Mr. Flint laid out a route on the two hectares of our school grounds that started on the soccer field, followed the fence past the front gate, and dropped down between the new dorm and the chapel before it looped around the gym and descended into the woods below. Then it circled the Rickers' house and the tennis courts before it climbed the hill by the bag swing back to the soccer field. This route totalled 5,000 metres if we circled it three times. We still had cross-country meets against Good Shep and ACS, and when they were held at Bingham, we ran this route. I even came in first place a couple of times on it.

Nonetheless, the pleasure of cross-country running dissipated for me. Running on campus made cross-country feel artificial. Distance became unreal. We weren't really going anywhere, but just pacing out circles like lions in a cage. Granted, we didn't have to swerve around beggars or straw-laden donkeys, and we didn't have to worry about Ethiopians thrusting umbrellas at us or stealing our watches. In fact, we didn't encounter any people at all, except Bingham kids like us. But with the loss of danger, we also lost the thrill of adventure. Whereas cross-country with Mr. Porter had made me one of the big guys, I now felt as if I'd been put back in nursery school. I complained

of soreness in my knees, and the school nurse suggested that I take a few weeks off. That pretty much finished off the season, and we were into basketball by the time I got back in to sports. I didn't feel that I'd missed much.

I had written Mr. Porter a letter while I'd been resting my knees, telling him about the on-campus route and the ache in my joints. He wrote back with a detailed description of exercises I should do to keep the knees supple. I should also set up a schedule of workouts for myself. A person who had a little self-discipline, he said, could keep in good shape with or without a good sports program. I should alternate long runs for endurance with days when I ran hills and a series of short sprints to increase muscle power and speed. I should time my heartbeats before and after exercise to make sure that my heart was working more and more efficiently. I looked sadly at Mr. Porter's letter. I loved the care he'd put into his instructions, but I knew I would never actually carry them out. I needed him there to feel the joy of it.

Nonetheless, even as I mourned his absence, I couldn't deny the signs of his remaining influence within me. He had introduced me to cross-country, and it had got into my bones and blood, just as he said. Even though he was from another country and knew very little about Ethiopia, he had immersed me and the other team members in the very sport at which Ethiopians excelled. Foreign himself, he had given us a new way to make our lives out of the circumstances at hand. Our lungs and legs gained strength from the very thinness of the air and hilliness of the city. He had given us something that endured, even when the team felt less like a team and the coach felt less like a coach. Long after Mr. Porter had gone away, and Mr. Flint after him, and even after I myself had moved to faraway Calgary, where Viscount Bennett didn't even have a track team, let alone cross-country, I still had Ethiopia's gifts inside me.

I didn't have to think about rolling from heel to toe or pumping through the shoulders. I didn't have to tell myself to lower my head and chug. These habits had become second nature, and I could count on them, just as I could count on muscle strength and lung capacity. I realized that, even if a person moved great distances, from one side of the world to the other, there were some things that came along. Of

course, you had to be willing to change to fit the demands of the new country, but certain skills or habits were transportable. They could turn into advantages even in a far country.

I haven't lived in Ethiopia now for over twenty years, but I still feel my heart surge at the mention of my birthplace. In summer 2000, for example, I punched the air in triumph when CBC television showed Haile Gebre Selassie win the 10,000 metres at the Sydney Olympics. It was Gebre Selassie's hat trick, to borrow Canadian hockey parlance — his third gold medal at three consecutive Olympic games. With this win, he superseded the accomplishments even of his world-famous countrymen, Abebe Bekele and Mammo Waldé. I watched his lithe form sprint the last lap of the race and admired the even length of his stride, the discipline of his breathing, the way his shoulders pumped smoothly back and forth. His nappy head floated steadily, free of effort-wasting rise and fall. I rejoiced at how Sydney's low, ocean-side elevation gave his Ethiopian lungs, born and bred at 3,000 metres above sea level, the maximum benefit of their strength. I thought of what I knew about Gebre Selassie's life, how he was the child of a highland peasant farmer and how his mother had died when he was a small boy. How he had run the ten kilometres to school every day through his primary years. How his father had beaten him for sneaking away from his chores to try to catch some news about Mammo Waldé, Abebe Bekele, and the other Ethiopian marathoners on the radio. Although I had never heard his name until five years after I left Ethiopia, when he won his first Olympic gold in Los Angeles, I knew that we were close enough in age to have been learning our first paces during the same period of Ethiopian history. He would have been herding his father's cattle on the high bare plains of his northern home region while I was pushing Mulugeta in the red-wheeled wagon at Obi. He would have run barefoot to school while I conducted crusades in the boys' dorm at Bingham. He would have trained with a feeling of desperate urgency for a berth on the national team so he, like my friend Yared, could be

exempted from the twin jeopardies of *zemecha* and military service. By the time of the *Kai Shebbir*, he would have been living in Addis, too, praying that none of his teammates had connections with the EPRP and listening to the bursts of gunfire at night. When I was running Mr. Flint's on-campus route at Bingham, he would have been taking his first flights to Kenya and Nigeria to compete in all-Africa competitions. Not being from a wealthy family, however, he would not have been among the secondary school students from Wingate and St. Joseph's who cleaned our clocks at ACS. Against all odds, against poverty and lack of money for running shoes and coaches; against political chaos and military dictatorship — indeed, perhaps *because* of these adversities — he had more style and endurance than any runner in the world.

I watched Haile Gebre Selassie sail his nation's green, yellow, and red flag above his head on the victory lap at Sydney, and I saw the Australian wind ripple the muscles of the lion in the central amber band. The Lion of Judah had been dropped from the Ethiopian flag during the years of the Mengistu regime. Like Haile Selassie and his sixty cabinet ministers, and like the Orthodox and Kalleh Hiwot churches, the kingly lion had been suppressed during the Communist years. But the body's memory cannot be so easily buried. It is not composed of the will, which can be suppressed upon command, but rather of the unchosen elements of earth, air, fire, and water, which determine the substance of our every act and function. Even the shape and capacity of a person's lungs — Gebre Selassie's, mine, everyone's — manifest the imprint of a specific place and time. From the freckles on my face to the cast of my mind, I have been formed by the geography — physical, social, spiritual — of my childhood. Obi, Addis, Sheshemane, Saskatchewan. *Garar, zigaba, bahir-zaff.* Ato Angassu, Miss Willey, Negussie, Mr. Porter. HQ, SIM, R&R. Owl-bowel, Tota, Pupsi/Pepsi. Lux bath soap, DDT, gasoline. These are the coordinates of the cartography I was given, the elements that make up my compounded self.

There is no denying that cross-country hurts. My own thighs ached and a familiar faintness spun in my head while Gebre Selassie grasped his knees and waited for his breath to return at the end of his race. I was keenly aware of a sadness that accompanied my joy at his victory. For I was an Ethiopian *ferenjie*, an interloper in this moment of national triumph, a perpetual foreigner to the place of my birth. At the same time,

as I watched the Ethiopian lion flex its muscles in the Australian breeze during the champion's lap, I also knew that there is a strength or a value that can be translated, though it is deeper than words and ideas, more fundamental than the losses of displacement and foreignness. It is a hidden thing, merely gestured toward in the brokenness of words. At times it is a faith, an inner confidence in the face of the unfamiliar, while at others it is a humbling awareness of the limits of the local. At still other times, it constitutes a comparative perception that opens a door beyond the heavy truisms of a single convention. Whatever its specific combination of sadness and gratitude, it remains a quality that extends cross-country.

The Babies *in the* Colonial Washtub

I'm now a university professor. It has been ten years since I made the return trip with Wendy in 1993. Whereas the physical reality of the scenes I saw during that trip made me doubt my Canadian life, they've now faded enough for me to sometimes doubt the Ethiopian one. If childhood is the time when we set our life's stage, as Kristjana Gunnars says, and we spend the remainder of our lives rearranging those early props, then I sometimes wonder how my Ethiopian-made props are scraped across the boards of my daily life in Canada. What does being an English professor in Ontario have to do with being a missionary child in Africa?

One answer came to me by way of a round, galvanized washtub that brought controversy into the heart of my family stories. Although I've never seen this tub in real life, I've seen it in a photograph so notorious that it sparked outrage in newspaper headlines, letters to the editor, and editorials in publications ranging from *The Globe and Mail* and *The Toronto Star* to *This Magazine* and *The Christian Week*. I first saw the infamous washtub's grainy image in Vancouver at an academic conference, but I didn't realize until several months later that I'd been told stories about this tub by my parents when I was a boy.

It's March 1992, and five graduate students from the University of Alberta squash into a little Toyota and motor through the snowy mountains to Vancouver for a conference on Postcolonial Theory and Literature. All of us grew up with colonial histories of one sort or another: one comes from Bengal via Delhi, the family of another moved from the British Midlands to Ontario when she was a girl, the third hails from Ghana, the fourth descends from Scots who settled in B.C.'s lower mainland, and I am a Canadian born in the Ethiopian empire now living

in Edmonton. We're primed, each in our own way, for this conference. We're eager to hear the presentations on literature from Africa, the Caribbean, New Zealand, and South Asia. We've driven thirteen hundred kilometres to imbibe the latest thinking on how Europe's colonial ventures have shaped and defined so much of contemporary life around the world.

Saturday afternoon, we step into a raked theatre with plush seats, subdued track lighting, and the chemical smell of new carpet glue. There's standing room only. The session features Professor Linda Hutcheon on the problem of irony in postcolonial contexts — and she's showing slides. She's talking about the fiasco at the Royal Ontario Museum's 1990 *Into the Heart of Africa* exhibition of artifacts and photographs.

By composing the show of African items originally brought to Canada by turn-of-the-century soldiers and missionaries, the ROM curator had intended to expose the smug imperialism of these travelers by ironically juxtaposing images of colonial grandeur with reminders of the violence — military and cultural — that kept the Empire going. In the entry area, for example, one of those crisp, white pith helmets, bedecked with ribbons and plumes, radiated the romance and dignity of the Empire from a glass case that made it seem a relic, a jewel of great value. Nearby hung a wall-sized enlargement of an image from the *Illustrated London News* of 1879, captioned "Lord Beresford's Encounter with a Zulu": a mounted cavalry officer in a helmet identical to the one in the glass case plunges a sword into the chest of a loinclothed African warrior.

The curator intended, not only these colonial images, but also the African artifacts themselves — the carved masks, pottery, household utensils, drums — to be considered skeptically. After all, were they not the loot plundered from unsuspecting Africans by self-styled philan-thropists who went to Africa proclaiming peace and good will for all? She wanted viewers to remember that our understanding of historical artifacts changes with time and context. One interpretive plaque, for example, said, "What was once an African spear or shield became a trophy when collected by a Canadian soldier campaigning in Africa. It then appeared as a piece of decorative art when displayed in that soldier's home. Later, in a museum collection, it was catalogued as an ethnogra-phic object. Now, when viewed by you, it takes on another meaning as a museum exhibit."

Many members of Toronto's African and West Indian communities did not appreciate the museum's attempt to rehearse the shifting meanings of the various artifacts, even if the rehearsal did attempt to stand at a critical distance from the nineteenth-century collectors' mindset. They organized a group called the Coalition for the Truth about Africa, picketed the exhibition, and protested that the show too easily repeated the white adventurers' version of African colonial history with no counterbalance from African points of view. The museum may have wanted to satirize the attitudes of the English Canadians who had gone to Africa as part of the imperial enterprise, but by calling attention to those attitudes, it perhaps unwittingly required contemporary Africans to bear yet another recitation of stereotypes that have done enough damage already.

And what about the visitors who attended the exhibition and didn't get the irony? What about the many raised on TV, movie, and book versions of *Tarzan, Gunga Din*, and *King Solomon's Mines,* who saw only high derring-do in "Lord Beresford's Encounter with a Zulu"? What about those who'd never heard of Joseph Conrad's *Heart of Darkness* and didn't recognize the troubling joke in the exhibition's title, *Into the Heart of Africa*? What about those who'd never heard of Nigerian author Chinua Achebe's denunciation of Conrad as a "thoroughgoing racist"?

The striking thing, says Professor Hutcheon through the theatre's crystal-clear sound system, is that, although the museum tried to emphasize the fact that multiple meanings had been assigned to the African artifacts over time, it failed to anticipate the multiple responses that various audiences might have to these different meanings. It aimed a barb at smug nineteenth-century British Canadian artifact collectors, but it didn't consider how that arrow might strike twentieth-century African Canadians. There were more targets out there than the Royal Ontario Museum had foreseen.

Then, with a squeeze of the forward button, Professor Hutcheon flashes a new slide on the screen. There, for the first time, I see the two looping handles and the soldered seams of the embattled washtub. Four African women in wrap-dresses and headscarves crouch nonchalantly around the troubling item. They have paused for a moment to gaze at the photographer before returning their attention to the lumps of soapy cloth in their hands. In the foreground and to the right, a white

Mrs. Thomas Titcombe offering 'a lesson in how to wash clothes' to Yagba women in northern Nigeria about 1915. (Photo: Courtesy of the Titcombe family)

*The controversial photo from the Royal Ontario Museum
exhibition, with its caption.*

woman stands in an ankle-length checked dress collared with white lace. It's a black and white photograph: the white woman gazes down at the black women around the tub with a countenance we might call bemused. The fringed, wide leaves of a banana tree and several thatch-roofed houses in the background tell us we are in tropical Africa; the standing lady's full skirts and her hair pinned up in a bun tell us these are Victorian times. The museum's caption reads: "Mrs. Thomas Titcombe offering 'a lesson in how to wash clothes' to Yagba women in northern Nigeria about 1915. (Photo: Courtesy of the Titcombe family)." The African women's names do not seem to have been recorded.

Knowing laughter ripples around the semi-dark theatre after the slide hits the screen. As if African women had never thought of washing clothes before starched white Victorian women came along to teach them

how! Silly white people. Silly white missionaries. Silly white Victorian missionary colonialists.

Professor Hutcheon points out that this photo and its caption received mention in almost every public response to the exhibition. The Coalition's handout at the picket line on the museum's steps asked the question we now asked in the conference room: "Did Africans not know how to wash clothes before the arrival of Europeans?" "Tell me," challenged Susan Crean in *This Magazine*, "how you would explain the cultural bias and racial arrogance of that image to schoolchildren." Christopher Hume, a reviewer for the *Toronto Star,* defended the ROM. "An observant reader will note that the words 'a lesson in how to wash clothes' are in quotation marks. The description is offered as evidence, not of the actual activity, but of Mrs. Titcombe's intentions and sense of superiority," he argued. I'm an English professor, so I feel compelled to ask for more detail about those quotation marks. Are they the kind that signal irony, the kind that marks a word as suspect? Or are they quotation marks in the stricter sense, the kind that indicate that the words are quoted? Whose are those superiority-assuming words? Mrs. Titcombe's, as Christopher Hume suggests? Or did the museum's curators, confident they knew what Mrs. Titcombe's enigmatic smile meant, put those words in her caption?

But I'm also a missionary's child, and at the sight of the Titcombe name, my spine prickles up to my neck and my mind cuts down a different track. The slide show and the smell of carpet glue recede, and I'm back in boyhood, listening to my parents' stories.

Mrs. Thomas Titcombe! It's a famous name in the family lore. My father traces his youthful decision to become a missionary in Africa to a charismatic missionary preacher who was often billetted in Grandma Coleman's home — Tommy Titcombe, an early pioneer with the Sudan Interior Mission. Dad recalls sitting in the living room as a teenager, awestruck at the tales brought back by this energetic Ontarian from his missionary adventures in what was then the British colony of Nigeria. When Dad grew up, he joined Titcombe's SIM.

My mind then leaps to a segment of the Titcombe story, told to me by Dad but deliberately left out of the Royal Ontario Museum's ironic display. It's about why Mrs. Titcombe was decorated by King George V in 1935.

The Yagba people Tommy Titcombe encounters in the 1910s believe that twins are avatars of a malignant spirit. The doubling is considered unnatural, monstrous. As a result, when a woman gives birth to twins, she's driven from the village, and one or both of the babies are killed. Two days after Tommy's new bride, Ethel, arrives in the village in 1915, an anxious villager asks the young woman to come immediately: there's an emergency. Ethel is led to one of the houses, where a woman is still being cleaned after the birth of twins. The mother begs Mrs. Titcombe to take the babies into her protection quickly, before her relatives return with the medicine maker. Her four previous infants were stillborn or died early, and she can't bear the thought of losing these babies as well. As a foreigner, Mrs. Titcombe has immunity from the local cultural codes, and she's a woman, too, so perhaps she will understand and find a way to shelter the babies from Yagba rules about twins.

Ethel Titcombe is in over her head; she has no time to think. The woman's family could return any minute. That Victorian lady, smiling so enigmatically above her lace collar in the photograph, takes the babies and their mother to live with her and Tommy. When they get to the house, Ethel has no crib or cradle to put the twins in. So — this is a detail I'd forgotten till Mom and Dad sent me their copy of the published version of the Titcombe story, *Tread Upon the Lion* — she improvises and puts them in nothing other than the washtub. The silly-white-Victorian-colonialist washtub.

Thus the metal tub makes its first appearance at the centre of a controversy. The whole village buzzes in debate over this departure from tradition when the twins' lives are spared. And, as is so often the case, one controversy leads to another. One of the reasons for high infant mortality in the village at the time is that the Yagba believe mother's milk is harmful to infants for the first nine days; during this time babies are fed water fortified with herbs from the medicine maker, but no milk. The Titcombes insist that their mother-in-residence nurse her babies from the first day. She reluctantly agrees, and the babies not only live but grow sleek and fat. Tommy and Ethel give them the Biblical names of Reuben and Ruth. The whole neighbourhood can see for themselves these apparently human and apparently healthy babies being nursed by their apparently unharmed mother in the Titcombes' yard. Over the next months, a number of mothers and infants in difficulty appear

quietly on the Titcombes' doorstep. In time, the young missionary couple build a thatch-roofed house beside their own. Untrained in medicine, they call it the maternity ward.

It's easy to see how this story suggests a very different caption for the offensive photograph of the women at the washtub. By taking their children to the Titcombes' maternity ward, the Yagba mothers put themselves beyond the pale of local tradition. They would have been shunned, ostracized from daily village life, including, I'm assuming, joining the other women in such mundane chores as washing clothes and collecting drinking water down at the river. Here's an irony, then, that the museum didn't consider: it's likely that these women were washing their own babies' clothes in that tub, and it's likely they were using the European washtub because they weren't welcome at the river. This reading of the photograph doesn't deny that the washtub is a cultural imposition. It's still an example of the displacement of Yagba traditions by European practices, and it's not insignificant that Mrs. Titcombe's interventions received Imperial approval from the King for her work with Nigerian twins. However, the story does cast the issue of cross-cultural displacement in a different light. And there's a little bit more to add to the twins' story.

Four years later, as if the survival of the mother and her twins were not a strong enough statement, "God gave Mrs. Titcombe twins of her own." These are the words Dad used when I asked him to retell the story after I'd heard Professor Hutcheon's talk in Vancouver. Every villager who saw the adopted and home-born children, brown and pink, playing together in front of Ethel Titcombe's maternity house, had a daily lesson in the humanity of twins.

If the ROM had chosen to, they could have allowed their viewers a lesson in the humanity of missionaries, too, for I later learned that the curator selected the washtub photograph from a whole set SIM had sent her on behalf of the Titcombe family. Among the rejected pictures was one of that same woman, Ethel Titcombe, but this time I'd say her smile is shy rather than enigmatic. In this photo, she's looking directly at the camera and wearing her lace-collared dress with a straw hat, whose dome is similar in shape to that of a pith helmet. She is seated. In the nest of her arms and lap sit two naked, perky Yagba babies. Naked, that is, but for armbands and necklaces of beads. I'd guess

Mrs. Titcombe with the first twins she saved.
Yagbaland, Egbe, 1916.

they're around eight or ten months old. One intently watches something just to the photographer's left, while the other looks down at the safety rail of Mrs. Titcombe's arm around his or her middle. Maybe if I knew something about Yagba bead armbands and necklaces I would know what sex or age or class the babies are. This, too, is a black and white photograph: the white sole of one black baby's foot is barely bigger than Ethel Titcombe's white thumb. The caption on this photograph as published in the *Christian Week*'s rebuttal of the ROM exhibition reads: "Ethel Titcombe with Nigerian twins she rescued from death. This photo showing missionary compassion was rejected by the ROM in favour of one which seemed to illustrate imperialism."

That's the problem with this whole business. You never get the whole story. Each group makes its representations and then moulds the world accordingly. The ROM captions a racist, and the *Christian Week* captions a philanthropist. It's a struggle over representations, but this is not to say that there are no real blood-and-guts effects. Members of the Coalition for the Truth about Africa were willing to be dragged off the museum's steps by riot police over these representations. The curator of the exhibition lost her job over them. The shock waves raised by the exhibition rolled all the way from central Canada to the west coast, where even I, who wasn't in Toronto and never saw the exhibition, have been made to try to understand my own relation to the life stories of the family I love.

Powerful stories like the one about the Titcombes and the twins convinced my dad in the early forties that he wanted to be a missionary. But there were other stories too.

Dad retells the one about Tommy Titcombe travelling into an area of Nigeria where the people are known to be hostile to pink-skinned foreigners. Titcombe has heard terrible rumours about these people. His worst fears are confirmed when he and his Nigerian companions approach a certain village. Over the path leading to the village hang three human skulls, laced like beads on a necklace with a rope strung through holes in their crania. Titcombe's friends refuse to take a step

farther. They beg him not to pass. This is a dangerous place, they say. He should heed their words. However, he is determined: these villagers must hear his gospel message. Because the bush is so dense he can't walk around the barrier, he gets down on his hands and knees, and he crawls under the swaying skulls while his horrified friends set down their loads and anxiously await his return.

In the village, Titcombe walks directly to the chief's compound. The enclosure soon fills with the enraged chief's shouts that some audacious son of a pink-skinned monkey has forced his way uninvited into the village. Titcombe begins to doubt his determination. Maybe he made a mistake by ignoring his companions' fears and crawling under the skull barricade. His fears double when he notices more skulls strung from the rafters of the chief's house. Are the skulls a sign of some dark ritual in the village that outsiders must not view? Has he broken a taboo he didn't know about? Is that why his companions refused to cross the barricade? A crowd begins to gather in response to the chief's yelling. In their agitation, Titcombe begins to smell the scent of his own death.

I'm used to the next statement in Dad's story. All those pioneer missionaries lived in daily danger, so they regularly "commended themselves into the hands of God." I'd have done the same. What else would you do at a time like this? You've gone, at a huge sacrifice to yourself and your family, to take the gospel to people you don't understand in a landscape that is totally alien. Everything is unknown to you, from the sunshine to the food to the mosquitoes. The few facts you do grasp are gained mostly through the guesswork of intercultural translation. The whole venture relies on immense courage and unshakeable faith. In the realm of the spirit at least, you need to be absolutely sure of yourself.

Tommy Titcombe sweats out the headman's rage and wonders whether his skull will soon join the others swaying overhead. He commends himself into God's care. Just then, the crowd parts for a young woman, bringing the chief's meal. The angry man and his lieutenant dip their fingers into the calabash while they decide what to do with their intruder. During the moment's pause, Titcombe gets an idea: he has heard that according to local custom the person who eats meat with the headman enters into his protection. He becomes the chief's guest, and no one can touch him. So he says, in his best Yagba dialect, "Hey, what's

going on? I thought you were a powerful chief, yet here I am a stranger at your door, and you treat me worse than the lowest slave. You're eating with your friend, but you haven't even offered me a morsel."

Shamed before his followers, the headman invites Titcombe to join him. The shared meal will assure Titcombe's life. It's a brilliant inspiration, even though his companions have passed on disturbing rumours about these people's diet, and there are all those human skulls everywhere. What kind of meat is in the dish? The gravy doesn't look like anything Titcombe has seen before. "He didn't ask what kind of meat," Dad says. "He just thanked God for His mercy and ate the stew put before him. He said it was very spicy."

What am I supposed to do with stories like this? During my childhood, I thought I was supposed to live up to them somehow. Become a Tommy Titcombe — hear the call of God, study in a Bible college, and then head out Somewhere Far Away where I would rescue twins or call the bluff of possible cannibals. Later, in my college years, I tried to ignore these stories. I tried to pretend I hadn't heard them, that they didn't touch me. I wanted to dismiss them as the missionary equivalent of fairy tales. But they were too powerful. They were powerful enough to cause my dad to dedicate himself to a life of service in Ethiopia, powerful enough to bring about my being born there, powerful enough to bring me in my thirties to a conference on the continuing effects of colonialism. Deny it as I might, stories like these shaped my life.

And, like so many life-shaping stories, they were more complex than clear. They entangled each other, contradicted each other, led my thoughts in different directions. The story about the twins, for example, made me want to defend Mrs. Titcombe from the superior laughter at the postcolonial conference. It's easy to snicker at the condescension in teaching Yagba women to wash European-style clothes in a European-style tub, but that's not all these European-style missionaries did. They worked themselves to the bone — setting up medical clinics, building schools, campaigning in Britain and America against the slave trade. They saved lives. It's pretty comfortable for us to lean back in plush seats

under subdued lighting in Vancouver in 1992 and ridicule the naive part nineteenth-century missionaries played in promoting Imperial superiority around the world. At least people like the Titcombes made real efforts to right global injustice by taking something back from the rich and giving it to the poor. Literally, they did this: they collected tithes and offerings from bourgeois Canadians and recirculated the cash in schools, clinics, hospitals, and orphanages in Africa.

I wanted to remind the conference-goers that hasty condemnation of people like the Titcombes too easily rationalizes a new kind of racist self-protection. Rejecting the nineteenth-century myth of the "dark continent," we create the counter-myth of a utopian pre-colonial Africa, when Africans lived in harmony with each other in a perfectly balanced ecology, and this lets us make missionaries into serpents who despoiled that imaginary Eden. In so doing, we rob Africans of history and reduce them, again, to Rousseau's noble savagery. Having made up the pre-history of cultural innocence, pink-skinned liberals can use legitimate concerns about cross-cultural imposition to simply bow out of our own history, too. "Sorry," we say. "Through their own ignorance, my forebearers perpetrated violence and oppression against those who were colonized. Therefore, in order not to repeat their errors, I'll enter a plea of no comment until the dust settles." So the world can go to hell in a handbasket as far as we're concerned — at least we ourselves aren't participating in its ruin. We move into the intellectual equivalent of one of those walled housing developments with an empty sentry box at the remote-controlled gate.

But what about Tommy Titcombe and the cannibals — that favourite bugaboo of pink travellers around the world? Doesn't this story do a cultural violence similar to the purported lesson in how to wash clothes? One of the most compelling discussions in postcolonial studies circles around the oft-repeated cannibal story. It's almost a standard motif of any tale about Europe's contact with the Rest of the World: the civilized man fears or suspects or is told by the cousin-of-the-aunt-of-his-now-absconded-but-most-trusted-guide that the savages he is

about to meet are man-eaters. In a fascinating section of *Colonial Encounters: Europe and the Native Caribbean, 1492-1797*, Peter Hulme traces the history of the term "cannibal" back to its origins. The word comes to English from the sixteenth-century Spanish, *Canibales*, "originally one of the forms of the ethnic *Carib* or *Caribes*, a fierce nation of the West Indies, who are recorded to have been anthropophagi" (from *anthropos*, man; *phagos*, to eat). Hulme focuses on the passive phrase "who are recorded to have been," because, like all passive phrases, it avoids naming names. Who did this recording? What fifteenth- or sixteenth-century European sat in the shade of a palm tree calmly noting down the details while human arms and legs disappeared down Carib throats? As it turns out, the first recorder was none other than the mistaken discoverer of "India," Christopher Columbus. His record, however, isn't as solid a piece of evidence as the etymology implies. His journal reports that when his ships approached an island his native guides called *Bohio*, his new companions claimed that it was inhabited by some people with one eye in the forehead and others whom they called *canibales*, a people they greatly feared because they ate human flesh.

Hulme is not as interested in whether or not the one-eyed people or the *canibales* really existed as he is in how we got the word and its story in the first place. He goes on to point out that Columbus's journal has not survived intact. The only original disappeared in the middle of the sixteenth century, and the statement about the cannibals, therefore, comes to us from the only surviving version, a handwritten abstract made by Bartolome de Las Casas around 1552. Thus, the "record" consists of Las Casas's précis of Columbus's recollection of a statement he heard from people whose language he'd been introduced to only six weeks earlier. The confusion increases when Las Casas records Columbus as saying "that he well believes there is something in this [report], but that since [the *canibales*] were well armed, they must be an intelligent people, and he believed that they may have captured some men and that, because [these men] did not return to their own land, [his guides] would say that they were eaten." In short, Columbus didn't fully believe his own record. Nonetheless, the word and the horrifying story of cannibalism readily entered the European description of the Rest of the World. As Hulme puts it, the word and its fearsome energy "was adopted into the bosom of the

European family of languages with a speed and readiness which suggests that there had always been an empty place kept warm for it." The civilized European explorer's horror at such an unthinkable act proves to himself and to his readers that he is not like the people he meets.

I learned Columbus's lesson in the library at Bingham, when I sat in the sun that streamed in the windows and turned the pages of *Robinson Crusoe*, that staple of classic fiction commonly abridged for young readers. Crusoe lives on the island for some twenty years before the famous scene in which he finds the terrifying human footprint in the sand. In all that time, he never sees evidence of human habitation on the island. Yet from the first night after his shipwreck, he lives in terror of being attacked by savages and disappearing down their gullets. So he gets right to work. At the risk of his life, he returns repeatedly to the wrecked ship to arm himself with swords, muskets, and gunpowder. He works for years to build himself a double-walled stockade of thick logs behind which he can sleep secure. He bends his ingenuity to fashion cannon for himself out of carved tree trunks. He runs himself ragged securing a supply of food and water within his fort so he can withstand a siege from the savages he has never seen. His fear makes him thrifty, hard-working, inventive. It supplies the place of human company and keeps him busy. Anyone familiar with Winnie the Pooh's terror when he circles onto his own tracks might have been prepared to wonder if the horrifying footprint in the sand might not have been Crusoe's own. "Put your foot in the track, Robinson," we might have whispered at the page. "Does it fit?"

When humans do finally show up on the island, they turn out to fit his footprint exactly. In fact, unlike Columbus, the fictional Crusoe catches them in the anthropophagous act itself. Down the sights of his gun barrel and with his own eyes, he sees them at it beside their roasting fires. His years of preparation have made him more than ready. He's got the military strategy and the necessary hardware to intervene in the barbaric act and deliver the good man Friday from a fate worse than simple death. Thus the natives' cannibalism justifies the adventurer's civilizing mission.

This is the logic of the cannibal story. Like Friday, the savages fear the ever-present danger that they might get eaten themselves, and so

they submit eagerly to the pink man's gun and his Bible, which together ensure that they need never fear the great clay cooking pot again. They gladly enslave themselves to the civilized man's liberating technology and enlightened government. In this way, the horror of cannibalism justifies the slavery of Friday. He *wants* to be Crusoe's slave. We're made to understand that it's natural he should.

The Titcombe story, as I inherited it, repeats the formula almost exactly: I heard from my dad who had heard from Titcombe that he had heard from still others the disturbing reports about these people. We all knew before Titcombe arrived in the village what to expect. When he saw the skulls, he found the telltale foot track. Unlike Crusoe, however, he didn't immediately open fire. Instead, he played out his hand and ate the flesh. And unlike either Columbus or Crusoe, he didn't take captives or build a fort. Instead, he went on to live for more than twenty years among the people and ministered to their spiritual and physical needs, while his wife nurtured young mothers and twins.

I struggle with my inheritance of stories such as this, which number among the props on the stage of my childhood. They sometimes make me wonder why I couldn't have descended from mercenaries instead of missionaries. The mercenary inheritance would be much easier to deal with because the judgments are easy: guilty of imperialism as charged, on all counts. When Susan Crean went to see *Into the Heart of Africa* she had an experience parallel to but completely different from mine. That white pith helmet in the glass case belonged to her great-uncle, Captain John F. Crean of the Queen's Own Rifles. He had been on the oppressive side of imperialist battles all around the world: he had fought against Riel in Saskatchewan in 1885 and against the Asante in Ghana over control of the gold mines at the turn of the century. "To be blunt about it," Crean writes, "Great-Uncle John spent his entire adult life in one part or another of the globe killing native people on behalf of God, Queen, and Empire. His job was to provide the brute force necessary to keep 'Pax' Britannica operating in the interests of the British merchant class." It seems easy to pass sentence on an obviously

reprehensible figure like that. Crean goes on to say, "The truth is . . . that none of us gets to choose our ancestors, and none of us can claim any singular moral authority for condemning their exploits. Even if they can individually be a source of eternal shame, it's a shame that ultimately has to be shared; in Great-Uncle's case, by the white community as a whole."

Crean is pretty quick to move from individual shame to group shame, especially in an article entitled, not "Exorcising My Mercenary Forebearer," but "Taking the Missionary Position." Without false naïveté, I must ask, what exactly *is* the missionary position? Is it what I find in the story about the twins, or is it what I find in the one about the cannibals? Is it in the ROM's version of the washtub? It seems to me that any of these answers sidesteps the big question about cross-cultural missionary involvements: the question about proselytizing. With their determinedly secular world view, many anthropologists and post-colonial theorists rightly insist that you can't go to other cultures with the intention of convincing them to accept your religion without communicating, deliberately or not, a belief in the superiority of your religious culture to that of the people you're converting. To them, the missionary position assumes a rampant colonizer and a recumbent colonized. By contrast, the determinedly religious world view of missionaries and their converts insists that keeping spiritual insights away from people is a kind of spiritual bigotry — a chauvinism that refuses to share with others. To them the missionary position assumes a mutually interested face-to-face relationship. The anti-missionary position points out that religious missions necessarily impose cultural changes on non-Western peoples in favour of Western values. The missionary position argues that cultural change is inevitable: Islam proselytized throughout Africa long before, and Marxism long after, Christianity, and the secular liberalism of modern scholars is busy making its fair share of converts, too.

Crean's article, though, does raise what I think is a key issue. Essentially, her point is that the ROM made its choice between two story-images, obviously in favour of the imperialist washtub. Neither photograph, however, names the Yagbas, whether women or twins. Crean writes, "There, I think, lies the error. By presenting the African collection

through the history of its donors, by giving pride of place to the personal stories of the white Canadians who happened to bring them to Canada, [the curator] creates a context in which that history is claimed rather than criticized and rejected, showcased even while she tut-tuts from between the lines." Neither the women gathered at the washtub nor the twins in Mrs. Titcombe's lap get to tell their own stories. The stories are always *about* them, told by a pink narrator or photographer or captionist or museum curator — many of them well intentioned — to paying pink audiences. When I tried to find out what happened to Reuben and Ruth after they grew up, I ran into very real obstacles in trying to break out of this Western circuit of knowledge. I phoned and faxed the Titcombes' only surviving child, as well as SIM missionaries who succeeded Tommy and Ethel Titcombe at Egbe in Nigeria, but I failed to turn up anything about the twins. Even the Nigerian historian Adeleye Ijagbemi, in his book, *Christian Missionary Activity in Colonial Nigeria*, is vague about what happened to the adopted children in Egbe. He reports that some of these children grew up to serve as cooks, table boys, or gardeners in the missionaries' households, but he seems to rely for his information, as I do, on missionary and church records. He reprints the photograph of Ethel Titcombe holding the set of Yagba twins, but he does not comment on their particular circumstances. I am sure Yagba people in the Egbe area would know something about the twins, but my only access to these people is through missionary contacts. Images of Africa in the West, I keep discovering, are images for consumption, whether by the church-going middle class at the beginning of the twentieth century, consumers of TV footage of starving Ethiopian children in the 1980s, or museum audiences in the 1990s. As African Caribbean Canadian writer and Coalition activist M. NourbeSe Philip wisely said, "To discover the life histories of the objects on display, it was imperative that one also understand the *life histories of Africans in the New World and Canada*."

Because I grew up not African in Africa, I need to press things just one step further. Obviously, my stories don't qualify as segments of the life history of an African in Canada. What do you do, then, when your family stories emerge from the tangle of pink stories about Africa? Do you remain silent, so afraid of misrepresenting someone else's culture that you retreat to your walled, architecturally controlled community?

Do you keep silent because your story might function like the captions that named Mrs. Titcombe but not the Yagba women or the twins? I hope not.

For one thing, many fine writers of the African diaspora are telling their stories, beginning to satisfy the need for "life histories of Africans in the New World and Canada." Ibo novelist Chinua Achebe wrote about the arrival of missionaries and the treatment of twins in his country in his 1960s classic, *Things Fall Apart*. Kikuyu writer Ngũgĩ wa Thiong'o addressed the influence of missionaries on the practice of female circumcision in *The River Between*. In addition, a host of Caribbean and African-born writers — including Dionne Brand, Jamaica Kincaid, Austin Clarke, George Lamming, Claire Harris, M.G. Vassanji, Paul Tiyambe Zeleza, and Nega Mezlekia — have described the displacements of Africans to the New World. More than one has written about the role played by missionaries in the midst of these displacements. These stories are being told — and not just by whites.

There are other reasons, too, to sift through my own missionary stories, besides self-therapy. First, I think the ROM's deliberate decision to display the washtub photo and repress the one of the twins is all too common. Someone decides what the right answer is in advance and then selects the data to prove it. This is called scientific logic: you make a hypothesis and then set out to prove it. Of course, the honest scientist should discredit the hypothesis when counter-evidence turns up, but the point is that none of us are pure scientists, especially when it comes to describing the way our lives rub against others' lives. We have our own investments. Some of us need to exorcise the pink man's burden, so we set up a museum exhibition to mock the ancestors who embarrass us. Some of us want to argue for the sophistication of African aesthetics and culture before the impositions of colonialism, so we create the myth of the utopian Time Before. Others among us want to justify our missionary forebears, so we introduce the story of the twins and keep the story of the cannibals to ourselves. The point is that in our times, you can't live outside implication. There is no innocent space where you can stand, detached, and make disinterested judgments.

That's what troubled me at the conference in Vancouver. We weren't just looking at women around a washtub about whom we could make smart judgments. That black-and-white slide represented a history of

relationships so complex that no museum exhibition or postcolonial conference could give them adequate explanation. The Coalition for the Truth About Africa was right: images such as these could not be safely packaged as relics from a misguided past, for they continue to shape our lives today. The image of Mrs. Titcombe, for instance, was part of a story that reached forward across the years and determined that I grew up cross-country, that even as I sat in that dark theatre, I was tied by memory, bone, and blood to Oromo laundry ladies who had washed my pants and shirts at Bingham Academy, to a retired tractor-driver named Ato Warhana who taught me to drive at Sheshemane, and to a hunchbacked teacher named Negussie. I looked as pink and suburban as any other white conference delegate, but I would say my skin was thick, rather than white. It had been chafed during a young life torn between feudalism and socialism, between the modern world and the spirit world, between the simultaneous calls of justice and luxury. The lively debate at the conference made my heart beat quickly in my throat, even though Vancouver lies at sea level, and I knew I had a heart and lungs inured to running great distances, even at elevations up to 3,000 metres. I had witnessed exorcisms and revolutions, and I had calculated the gaps between Julian, Gregorian, and Greenwich concepts of time. So I could not reduce this dizzying, complex world to simple divisions between colonizer and colonized, black savage and white saviour, European rapist and African virgin. I do not deny the racism and cultural arrogance of my missionary youth, some of it between *ferenjies* and Ethiopians, and some of it between Amharas and Oromos, but I have witnessed remarkable love and mutual respect, too. To reduce it all to a dichotomy vastly underestimates the people, missionary and Ethiopian, Amhara, Oromo, *ferenjie,* or Walaitta, whom I know.

It seems to me that to try to understand the complex relations of the real world, we need to hear as many stories as possible, even when they are broken and confusing, and we need to tell the fragments to which we each have access. A useful understanding doesn't develop by repressing the photos that don't fit our interpretation, nor does it develop when some of us back out of the conversation. Some of us need to put our foot into the track in the sand to see how it fits. Some of us need to speak the names of the women around the tub. Others could help by explaining what the armbands and necklaces say about the twins, while still others

could tell what it was like to grow up saved by a concerned white woman but distanced from the neighbour kids by that very salvation. Some of us need to tell about the mercenary great-uncle, while others should tell about the Yagba great-uncle. More stories make more complexities, but more stories also make a better composite. And that's exactly what we need, a better composite.

Selected References

General

Gunnars, Kristjana. *The Prowler.* Red Deer: Red Deer College Press, 1989.

Hancock, Graham, Richard Pankhurst, and Duncan Willetts. *Under Ethiopian Skies.* London: H&L Communications, 1983, 1987.

Huntingford, G.W.B. "Main Cultural Features." *The Galla of Ethiopia: The Kingdoms of Kafa and Janjero.* Ethnographic Survey of Africa Series. North-Eastern Africa, Part II. London: International African Institute, 1955.

Messing, Simon D. "Group Therapy and Social Status in the Zar Cult of Ethiopia." *American Anthropologist* 60 (1958): 1120-1126.

Pankhurst, Richard. *A Social History of Ethiopia: The Northern and Central Highlands from Early Medieval Times to the Rise of Emperor Téwodros II.* Trenton, NJ: Red Sea Press, 1990, 1992.

Parker, Ben. *Ethiopia: Breaking New Ground.* Oxford: Oxfam, 1995.

Prouty, Chris. *Empress Taytu and Menelik II: Ethiopia 1883-1910.* London: Ravens Educational and Development Services / Trenton, NJ: Red Sea Press, 1986.

Tareke, Gebru. *Ethiopia: Power and Protest.* Cambridge: Cambridge University Press, 1991.

Selassie, Bereket Habte. *Conflict and Revolution in the Horn of Africa.* Monthly Review Press, 1980.

On SIM in Ethiopia

Bascom, Kay. *Hidden Triumph in Ethiopia.* Pasadena, CA: William Carey Library, 2001 (on Negussie's life).

Cotterell, Peter. *Born at Midnight.* Chicago: Moody Bible Institute, 1973.

Cumbers, John. *Living With the Red Terror: Missionary Experiences in Communist Ethiopia.* Kearney, NE: Morris Publishing, 1996.

Davis, Raymond. *Fire on the Mountains: The Story of a Miracle — The Church in Ethiopia.* Grand Rapids, MI: Zondervan, 1966, 1975.

On the *Into the Heart of Africa* ROM exhibition:

Banfield, A.W. Frank. Letter to the Editor. *Toronto Star.* 26 May 1990. D3.

Cannizzo, Jean. *Into the Heart of Africa.* Toronto: Royal Ontario Museum, 1989 (exhibition catalogue).

Crean, Susan. "Taking the Missionary Position." *This Magazine* 24.6 (Feburary 1991): 23-28.

De la Haye, Sophie. *Tread Upon the Lion.* Scarborough: SIM Publications, 1974.

Hulme, Peter. *Colonial Encounters: Europe and the Native Caribbean, 1492-1797.* London & New York: Methuen, 1986.

Hutcheon, Linda. "The Post Always Rings Twice: The Postmodern and the Postcolonial." *Textual Practice* 8 (1994): 205-38.

Ijagbemi, Adeleye. *Christian Missionary Activity in Colonial Nigeria.* Lagos: Nigeria Magazine, 1986.

Koop, Doug. "Missionaries Unfairly Maligned by ROM Exhibit." *Christian Week.* January 8, 1991. 3.

Philip, M. NourbeSe. "Museum Could Have Avoided Cultural Clash." *Toronto Star.* January 14, 1991. A4. Reprinted in Philip's *Frontiers: Selected Essays on Racism and Culture, 1984-1992.* Stratford, ON: Mercury, 1992. 103-08.

Samarin, William J. "African Exhibit Indicts Canadian Missionaries for Arrogance." *Christian Week.* June 12, 1990. 14.

Acknowledgements

Writing looks like solitude. But that solitude is animated by the voices that make writing and memory possible in the first place. This book would not exist without the wonderful community of friends, family, advisers, and colleagues that helped me find my way to words. Wendy Coleman asked key questions, listened patiently to agonized self-doubts, and built an environment of love that made the exploration of memory possible. Ven Begamudré, Timothy Bascom, and Laurel Boone read the entire book in manuscript and offered wise advice from their long experiences as writers and editors. My family members, especially my parents, bravely allowed themselves to be implicated in stories that we remember from different angles, and they offered important corrections of fact and cultural milieu. Many good friends offered comments while I was in the process of composition. Lori Kerr read each chapter draft and kept me believing that another one would soon emerge. Deborah Bowen, Michael Bucknor, David Gray, George Onjima Nyikabe, Doug Stinson, Craig Vance, and Joan Yates gave me perceptive responses to various parts of the book. Established writers generously read and commented on parts of the manuscript; these include Sandra Birdsell, Daniel David Moses, and M.T. Kelly (all of whom, along with Ven Begamudré, served as Writers-in-Residence at McMaster University), as well as Hugh Cook and John Terpstra. I am grateful to have had the chance to workshop parts of the manuscript at the 1999 Glenn Workshop, sponsored by *Image: A Journal of the Arts and Religion* at St. John's College in Santa Fe, New Mexico. The workshop at the Glenn, under the guidance of Diane Glancy, involved lively and inspiring discussion with co-participants Timothy Bascom, Heather Connolly, Marcia Hunter, Glenn Mitchell, Kathryn Moore, Barbara Beasley Murphy, Carolyn Purcell, Carol Rose, and Brian Volck. I am grateful to Shelley Sopher, Director of the Saskatchewan Writers/Artists Colonies, for making an uninterrupted week of writing possible in February 2002. I am fortunate to have colleagues in the Department of English at McMaster University who

engage their work with the seriousness of play. I particularly wish to thank Donald Goellnicht, Grace Kehler, Susie O'Brien, Mary O'Connor, Antoinette Somo, Peter Walmsley, and Lorraine York for making the office something to look forward to each day. This rich community has made my hours at the computer a well-populated solitude.

An earlier version of chapter three appeared in *Going Some Place* (ed. Lynne Van Luven, Coteau Books, 2000), of chapter eight in *The Toronto Review* (Summer 2001), and of chapter eleven in *The New Quarterly* (Summer 1998). The Canada Research Chairs Program has generously supported my scholarly research, which in turn has stimulated many of the ideas for this book. Readers should note that some characters' names in this book have been invented.

Jeff Ellis

Daniel Coleman

The child of Canadian missionaries serving in Ethiopia, Daniel Coleman lived through the violent upheavals of Haile Selassie's fall from power in 1974, the Eritrean-Ethiopian war, the devastating famines of the mid-1970s and early 1980s, and Mengistu Haile Mariam's brutal military dictatorship. After finishing high school in Africa, he earned university degrees in Regina and Edmonton. He now holds a Canada Research Chair in the English department of McMaster University. Several essays on his missionary childhood have appeared in magazines. "The Babies in the Colonial Washtub," published in the *New Quarterly*, won a National Magazine Award Silver Medal.